IMAGES
of America

ROXBURY AND BRIDGEWATER

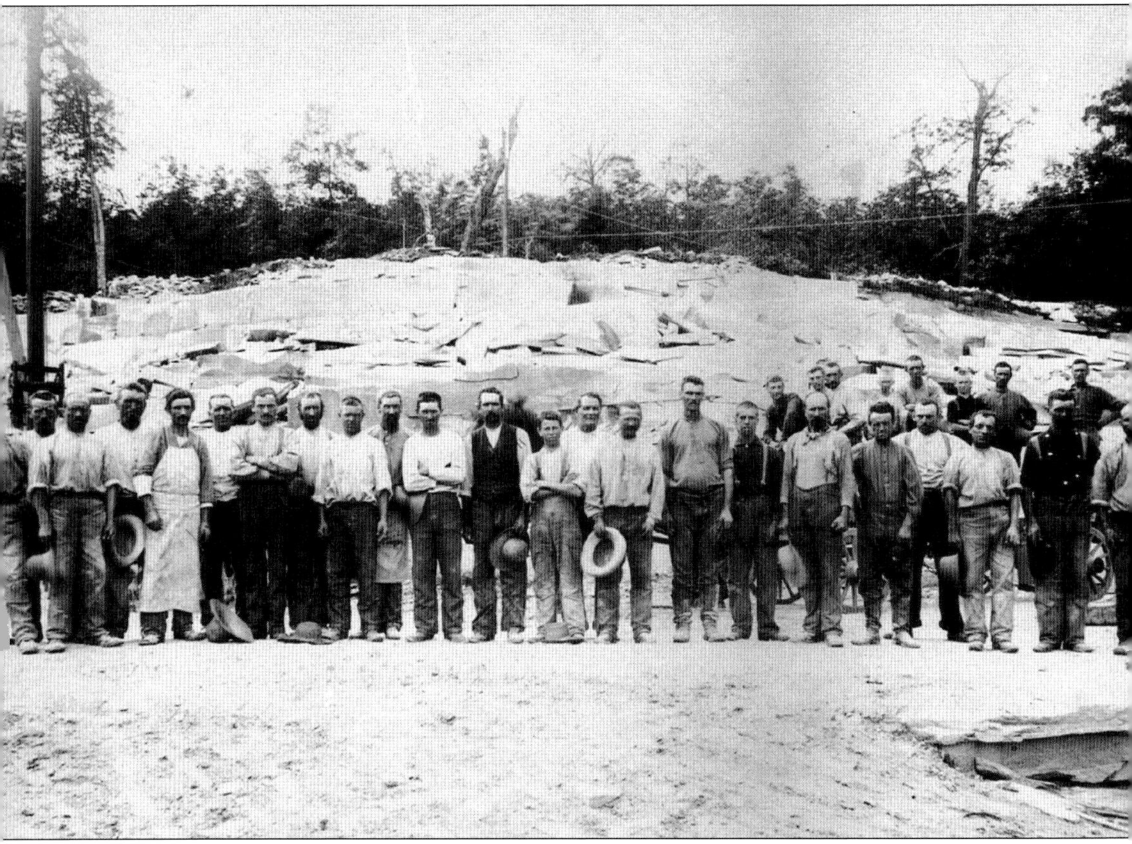

In the mid-1800s, skilled quarrymen, derrick tenders, stonecutters, and masons came from Ireland, Russia, Poland, and Italy to work in the quarries at Mine Hill. They settled in Roxbury and Bridgewater and created a population boom and a housing shortage. Nearly every household in or near the quarries took in boarders. For close to two centuries, Mine Hill's eight granite quarries brought a steady income for their owners. (Albert Pokrywka.)

On the Cover: The National Grange of the Order of Patrons of Husbandry was founded in 1867. It is the oldest agricultural organization in the United States. While they were active in nonpartisan political issues like railroad regulation, the banding together of farming families encouraged social gatherings such as this annual outing at Curtis Farm. The Roxbury Grange was credited with organizing that town's first volunteer fire department in the mid-1940s. (Bridgewater Grange.)

IMAGES
of America

ROXBURY AND BRIDGEWATER

Jeannine Green and
Eileen M. Buchheit

ARCADIA
PUBLISHING

ISBN 978-0-7385-7535-3

Published by Arcadia Publishing
Charleston, South Carolina

Printed in the United States of America

Library of Congress Control Number: 2010940872

For all general information, please contact Arcadia Publishing:
Telephone 843-853-2070
Fax 843-853-0044
E-mail sales@arcadiapublishing.com
For customer service and orders:
Toll-Free 1-888-313-2665

Visit us on the Internet at www.arcadiapublishing.com

CONTENTS

Acknowledgments

The authors are grateful for the enthusiastic support of Roxbury's First Selectman Barbara Henry and Bridgewater's First Selectman William T. Stuart. The support of many others in both communities made this book possible. We thank Joe Buchheit, who generously contributed his time and talent to scan and organize the hundreds of images needed to present the pictorial history of Bridgewater.

Others loaned photographs, helped scan images, and provided historical information. Some helped in their professional capacity; others loaned family photographs and opened up family scrapbooks. Among those we want to thank are Bob Burden and Audrey Wilkicki for access to the archives of the Bridgewater Historical Society; Marie Swanson and Kim Pokrywka, trustees of the Roxbury Museum; Dr. Paul Elwell of the Roxbury Volunteer Fire Department; and Susan Payne, executive director of the Roxbury Land Trust. Our thanks also to Jean Hopkins and Jean Kavanek, historians of the Roxbury/Bridgewater Garden Club; Laura Shail, president of the Bridgewater Ladies Auxiliary; director Valerie Annis of the Roxbury Minor Memorial Library and Hodge Library and Museum; and Betty Synnestvedt of the Roxbury Minor Memorial Library. We also thank director Elizabeth McCormick at the Institute for American Indian Studies, Michelle and Bill Bennett of the Bridgewater Grange, and the Rev. David Peters and Molly Wright of the Roxbury Congregational Church.

We reviewed hundreds of images and wish we could use them all. We hope our readers will enjoy those that made it into this book. Our thanks to all who loaned photographs and supported our project along the way: Raymond Livingston Booth, John Botsford Coleman, Cathleen Hurlbut Bronson, Dan Coppolo, Cameron Gardella, Joan Gardella, Elinor Hurlbut, Wayne Piskura, Albert Pokrywka, David Gaylord Ryerson, Julie Stuart Seger, Constance N. Sherman, and the Woolwich family. The authors especially want to thank our editor at Arcadia Publishing, Hilary Zussman, for her guidance every step of the way. All royalties received by Jeannine Green will be donated to the Roxbury Museum.

Key to Organizations

BG: Bridgewater Grange
BHS: Bridgewater Historical Society
BWA: Bridgewater Fire Department Women's Auxiliary
BVFD: Bridgewater Volunteer Fire Department
HMLM: Hodge Memorial Library and Museum
IAIS: Institute for American Indian Studies
MML: Minor Memorial Library
RBGC: Roxbury-Bridgewater Garden Club
RCC: Roxbury Congregational Church
RLT: Roxbury Land Trust
RM: Roxbury Museum
RVFD: Roxbury Volunteer Fire Department

INTRODUCTION

This book presents Bridgewater and Roxbury vintage photographs with annotations that represent aspects of life in these rural communities in Litchfield County, Connecticut. Chapter headings identify themes that recall the towns' settlements, notable families, agrarian roots, industries, merchants, and good times shared in schools, at church, and at festivals throughout their history. Like most of Connecticut's 169 towns, Bridgewater and Roxbury developed from settlement, to ecclesiastical society, to incorporated town. Both are the "children" of larger, adjoining towns. Bridgewater's parent town is New Milford; Roxbury's parent town is Woodbury.

Their histories and geography are intertwined—both parent towns were settled in the 1600s by farmers and tradesmen from Massachusetts and southern Connecticut. In their earliest days, Shepaug Neck was the name given to what is now Bridgewater; Roxbury was known as Shepaug Plantation. "Shepaug" is a Mohegan word meaning "rocky river," taken from the name of the Shepaug River that forms Roxbury's western border and is a branch of the Housatonic River that runs along Bridgewater's southern border. "Housatonic" is a Native American word meaning "great river."

Church attendance was mandatory for everyone in the 1700s, but to travel long distances by horse and buggy along rocky, dirty, muddy roads, especially in winter, was a hardship for settlers whose churches were as many as 10 miles away in their parent towns. Settlers in the Shepaug Valley petitioned the Connecticut Assembly to become ecclesiastical societies with the right to hire their own preachers and build their own churches. As each town's population grew and they could afford the taxes necessary to manage their own affairs, they petitioned to become incorporated towns. For Roxbury, that was in 1796; Bridgewater would need to wait until 1856. Education was highly valued, and the towns formed school districts, each with its own one-room schoolhouse. Mills, blacksmith shops, cobbler's shops, general merchandise stores, meat markets, and other small businesses began to dot the landscape. Cottage industries blossomed as craftsmen and tradesmen became dependent upon one another for goods and services. Throughout their history, both towns' populations rose or fell according to the success and extent of local industry.

By the mid-1800s, the United States was a mecca for immigrants from Europe. Agriculture was still central to these two towns, but immigrants had an influence on the growth of population and industry. While most settled in cities, many came to New England and worked as farm laborers, living in tenant houses, eventually buying their own farms. Irish and Eastern-European immigrants who arrived in Roxbury and Bridgewater worked in the mines and stone quarries at Mine Hill; others worked in Roxbury's garnet mines. The Shepaug Valley Railroad, completed in 1872, brought controversy and new hope to farmers who anticipated selling their dairy products to neighboring towns and to craftsmen who hoped to ship their wares to larger cities. The railroad was only moderately successful, but agriculture, dairy farms, hat factories, tobacco crops, mines, stone quarries, and the railroad helped support the economy of the small towns.

After World War I, farm prices fell. By 1930, the population of Roxbury reached an all-time low of 553. Only half of these residents were native born. Farmers were eventually driven off their land, and only a few farms remained in the hands of the original families. During the Great Depression, wealthy people escaped the cities and bought farms in rural Connecticut. After World War II, highways improved, and people with automobiles were on the move. Artists, sculptors, authors, playwrights, and actors from the stage and screen wanted second homes and privacy. Among the first to arrive in Roxbury was playwright Arthur Miller, followed by author William Styron, sculptor Alexander Calder, actress Sylvia Sydney, and mystery writer Ellery Queen. Literary critic Van Wyck Brooks, actress Mia Farrow, and wildlife artist and sculptor Lanford Monroe all took up residence in Bridgewater.

The 1950s brought major change to Bridgewater with the creation of a series of hydroelectric dams. In changing the depth and course of the Housatonic River, a manmade lake was created—Lake Lillinonah. This required the flooding of the southern end of Bridgewater, an area called Southville. The destruction of this portion of the town, an area already in decay, gave rise to a new shoreline. This part of town became most desirable, offering a boat launch and town beach for the citizens of Bridgewater. This is not to say that all residents approved the drastic change, but the government's power of eminent domain had greater clout than anyone's desire to keep things the way they were. Nonetheless, today, many in Bridgewater continue to strive to preserve this pristine and inarguably historic American community.

Today, Bridgewater's population remains under 2,000 residents; Roxbury's is just over 2,000. Bridgewater's area totals less than 18 square miles; Roxbury has a total area of 26.5 square miles. Even though the one-room schoolhouse is a thing of the past, education continues to be important. Each town has an elementary school, but their middle and high schools are combined into Washington's Shepaug Valley High School, which has been designated a Blue Ribbon School of Excellence.

Both towns are governed by a Board of Selectmen and, since Colonial times, residents have debated, discussed, and decided local issues at town meetings. Annual summer festivals like the Bridgewater Country Fair, celebrated on the third weekend in August and, for 36 years, Roxbury's Pickin' 'n Fiddlin' contest in July draw thousands from the tri-state area.

Like many towns in America, Roxbury and Bridgewater have people, events, and other reminders of their significance. Roxbury, for example, recognizes the Green Mountain Boys (Ethan Allen, Seth Warner, and Remember Baker), great leaders of the American Revolution, as her heroes; visitors to the town green will see the Seth Warner Monument. Bridgewater's men of distinction were outstanding entrepreneurs and merchants. One was Capt. William D. Burnham, founder of the American Hawaiian Steamship Company. His generous bequests made possible the library and the school on Main Street that bear his name. Mail-order pioneer Charles B. Thompson was born in Bridgewater and made the town his place of business.

In many respects, time has stood still in these primarily residential towns. Strict zoning laws, active land trusts, and a strong sense of community ensure that residents enjoy privacy and quiet. Roxbury resident and playwright A.R. Gurney described his town as having "rural beauty reminiscent of a 19th-century farm village."

One

The Towns

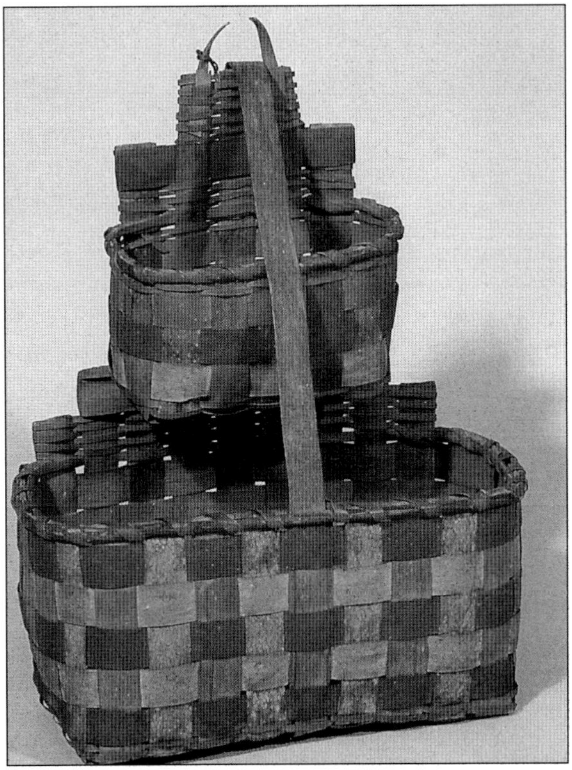

Sometimes called a "wall pocket," these baskets were made by Native Americans for sale to local settlers in the late 19th century. Chief Waramaug's people lived near the Great Falls on the Housatonic River and were among those who made this a cottage industry. The chief, who died in 1735, was the sachem of the Pootatucks, Mohegans, Weatinokes, and other small tribes that lived around Bridgewater and Roxbury. (IAIS.)

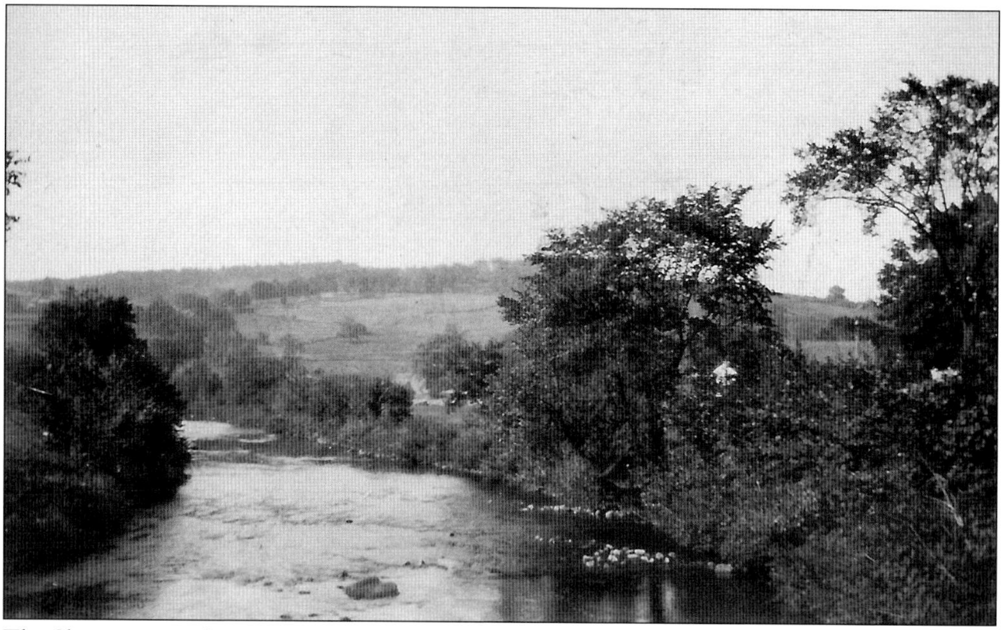

The Shepaug River bears a Native American name that honors a Bantam chief and means "rocky waters." A 1659 map identified an island in the river, called Paquabaug or Munnacommock. The river flows through 11 Connecticut towns and defines Roxbury's western border as it tumbles south into Lake Lillinonah, a dammed portion of the Housatonic River. This image was taken around 1903 by Andrew W. Gillette. (BHS.)

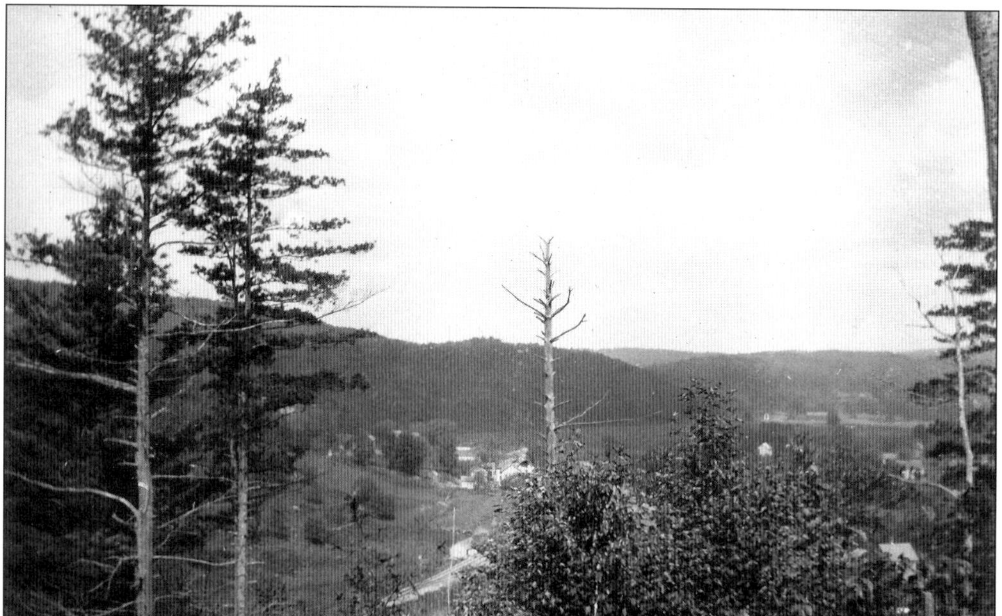

Three centuries ago, the Native Americans living among these hills and valleys of rolling land and unbroken woods were joined by European-born settlers. In 1901, photographer Andrew W. Gillette captured this scenic view of Roxbury Station from Pine Cobble, called a "queer little hill" by one local historian. The mound rose northeast of Mine Hill on the banks of the Shepaug River. (BHS.)

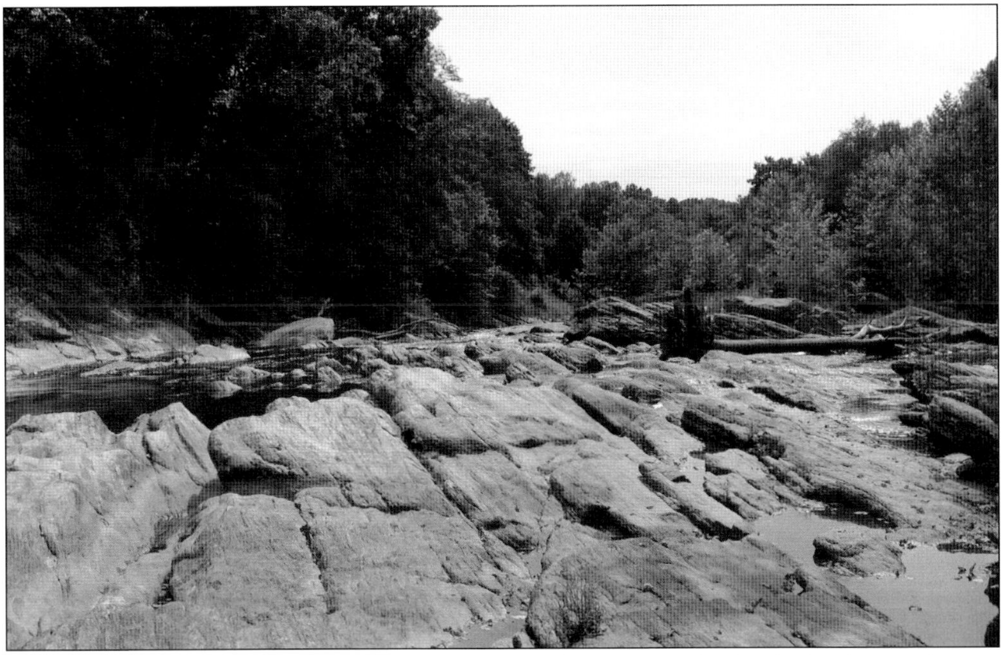

Shepaug River, "rocky waters," or "rocky river" are all apt names for this body of water. It is no wonder that, in 1743, the Connecticut General Assembly bestowed the name Roxbury on the town along the riverbank. Early records called the river and the original Woodbury plantation Shippauge, Shippaug, or Sheepaug. (Jeannine Green.)

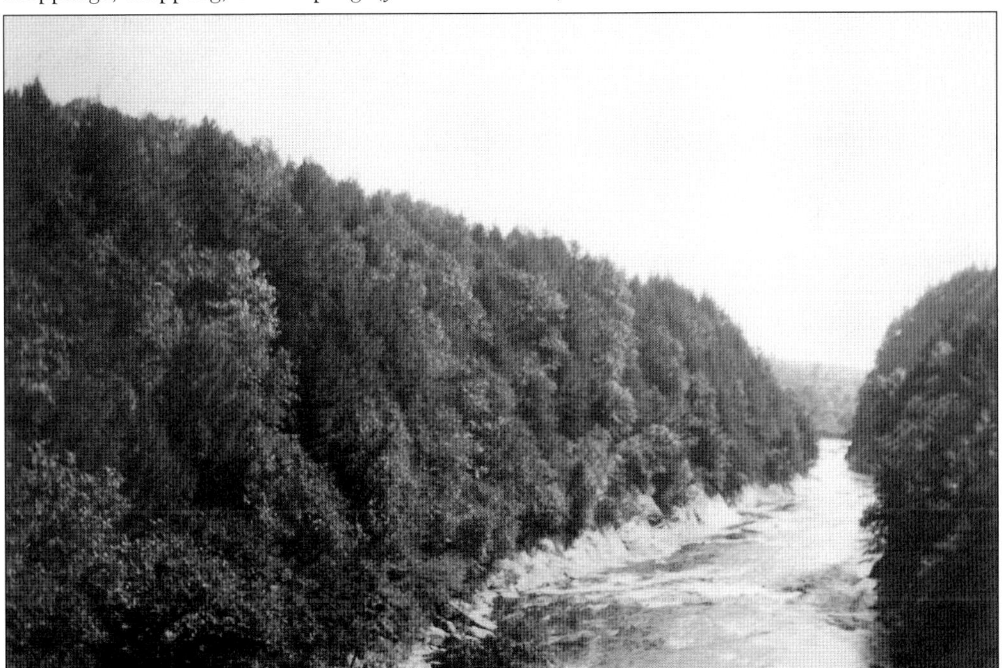

The Housatonic River passed through a gorge below the Great Falls. To the east was Lovers Leap; to the west was Metichewan, a Native American camp. Another spelling, "Metichawon," translates to "an obstruction or turning back of the fish." (BHS.)

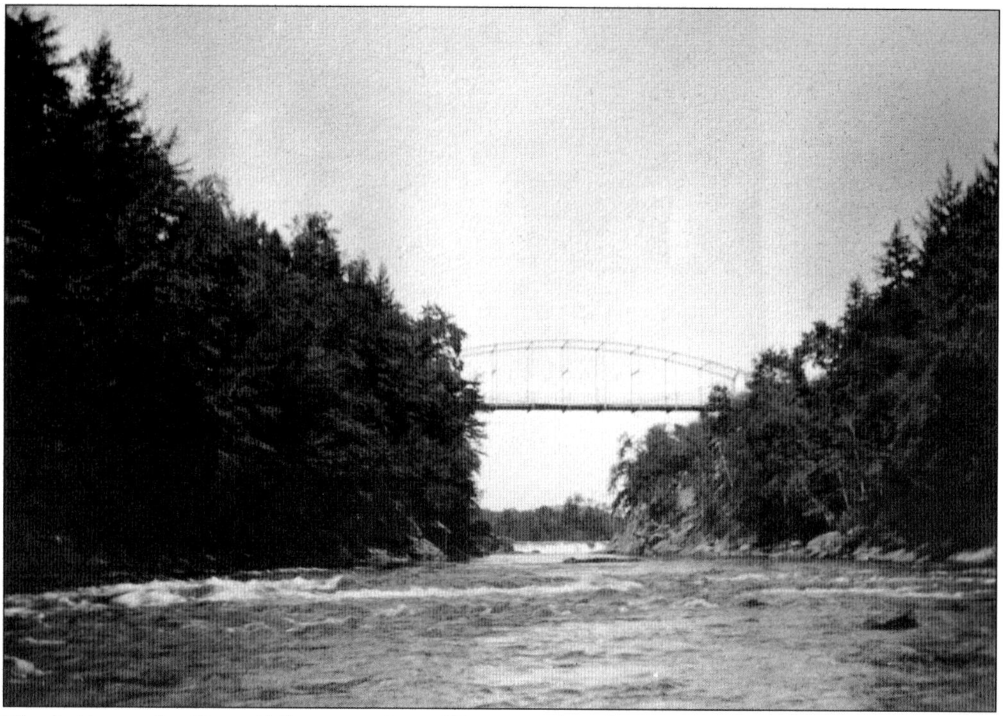

The bridge at the Great Falls is seen here. The river that flows under it has had the same name spelled in different ways. It was either "Housatonic," "Westenhuck," or "Ousatonick." (BHS.)

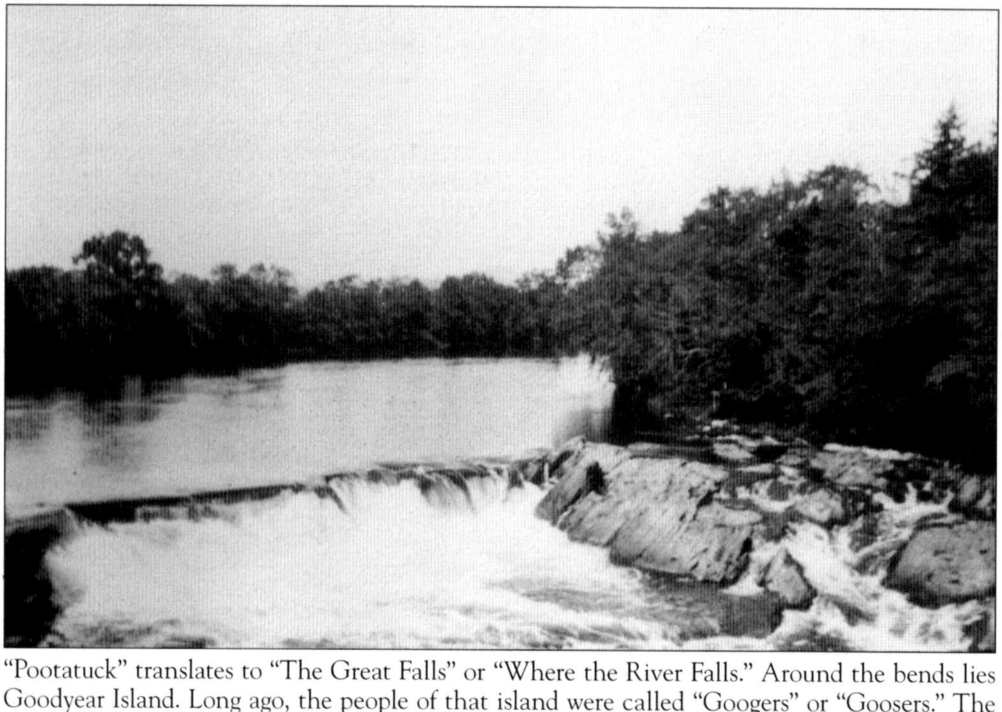

"Pootatuck" translates to "The Great Falls" or "Where the River Falls." Around the bends lies Goodyear Island. Long ago, the people of that island were called "Googers" or "Goosers." The island is under the waters of Lake Lillinonah now and the people have long moved to different locations. This is the area of Lovers Leap on the Bridgewater/New Milford border. (BHS.)

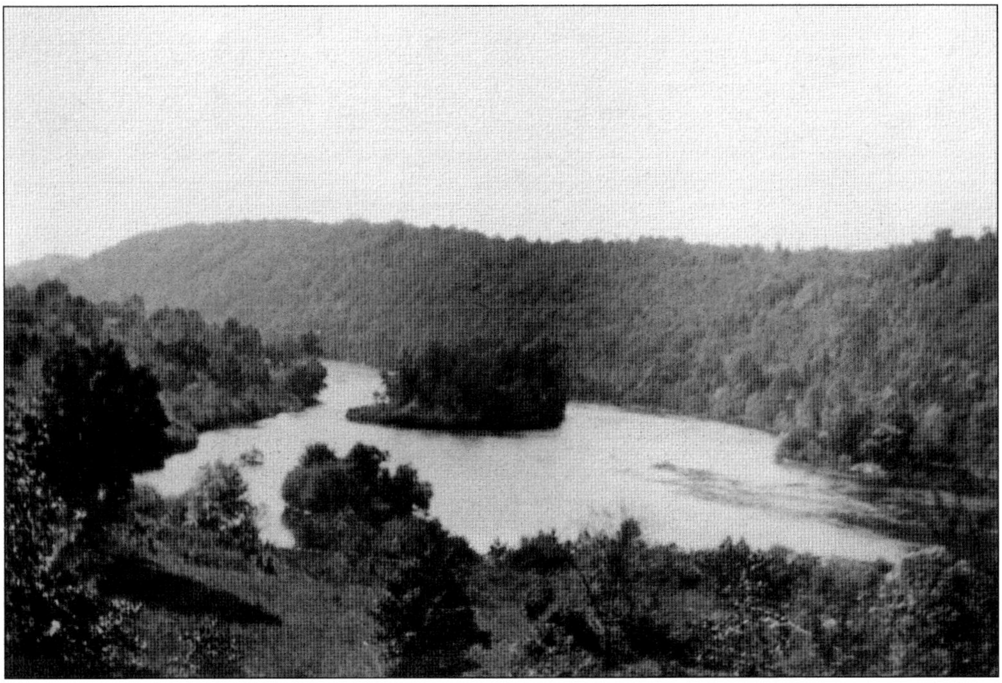

This vista was called "The Cove" by local residents. It was a popular site for artists, including W.H. Hilliard, of the Hudson Valley School, who painted this scene in 1875. Goodyear Island is visible in the background. (BHS.)

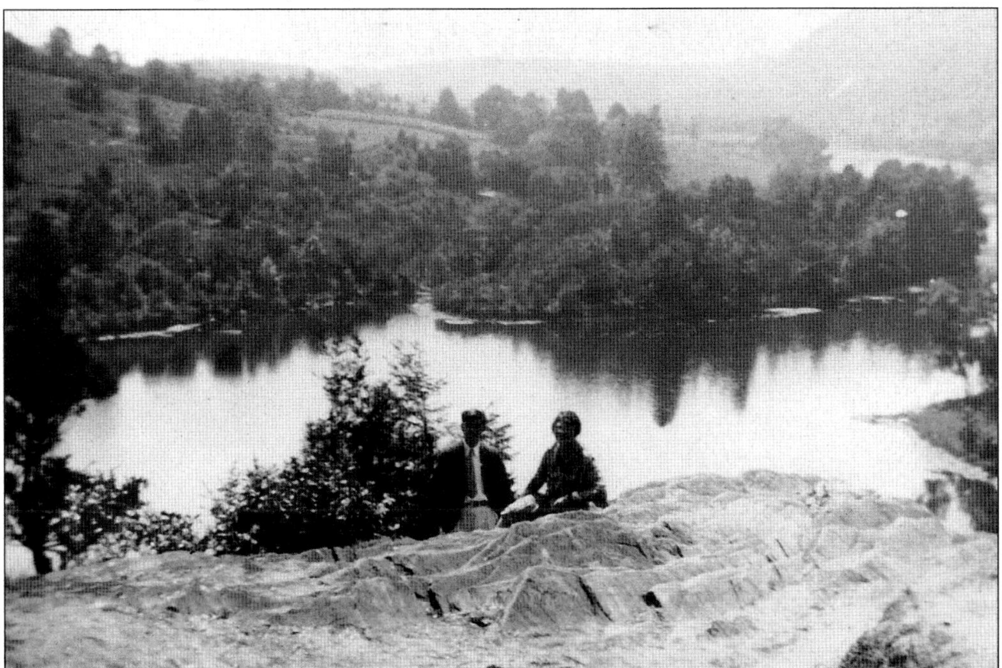

Here is a view of Goodyear Island and Lovers Leap. The legend of Princess Lillinonah, daughter of Chief Waramaug, states that she jumped to her death here when she believed that her lover, a white settler, would not return to her. He arrived as she jumped, and they both perished. (BHS.)

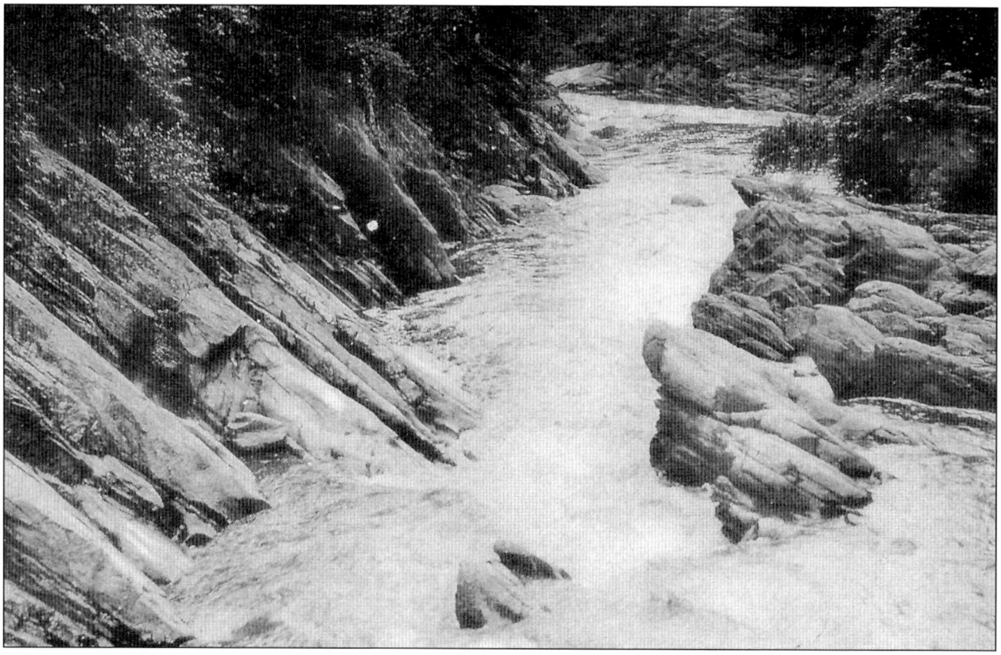

Water sloshed over mammoth grey boulders and rocks on the day a cameraman took this undated photograph of the Shepaug River in Roxbury. The dramatic image was later made into a postcard. (RM.)

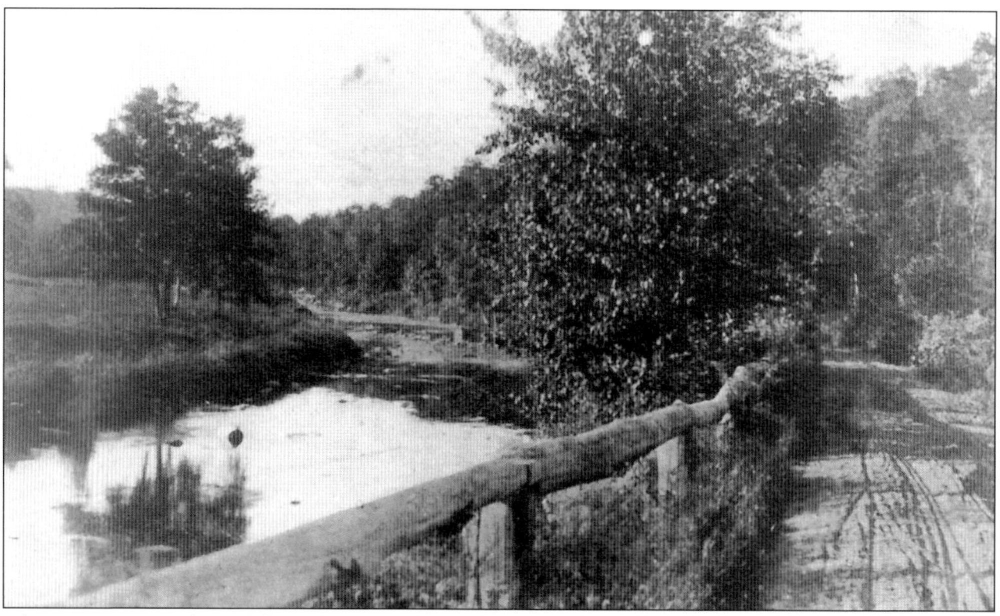

This picturesque drive follows the Shepaug River and is now called Baker Road. Baker was the name of a prominent local family whose descendants included John Baker (1681–1750), who settled in Woodbury and married Sarah Hurlbut—daughter of the man reputed to be Roxbury's first settler. Another descendant was Remember Baker Jr. (1737–1775), member of the Green Mountain Boys and grandson of John Baker. (HMLM.)

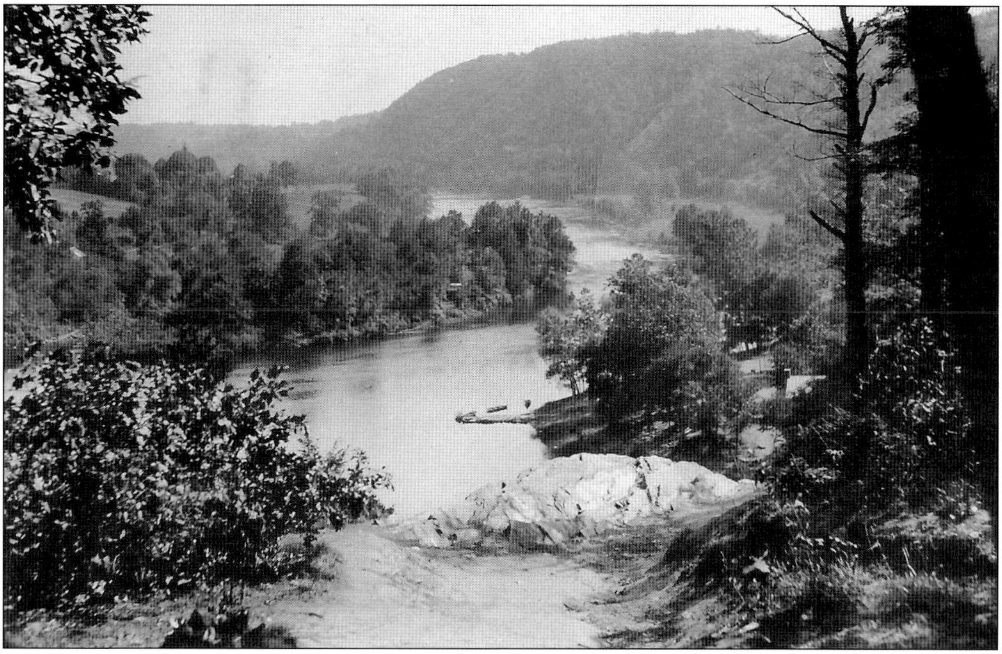

This vista of the Housatonic River predates the construction of bridges between Brookfield and Bridgewater. When John Noble was deeded the land that became New Milford, Bridgewater was a part of that town. His purchase of the land from the Weantinoke people in 1702 was signed in Clatter Valley, the present border between New Milford and Bridgewater. (BHS.)

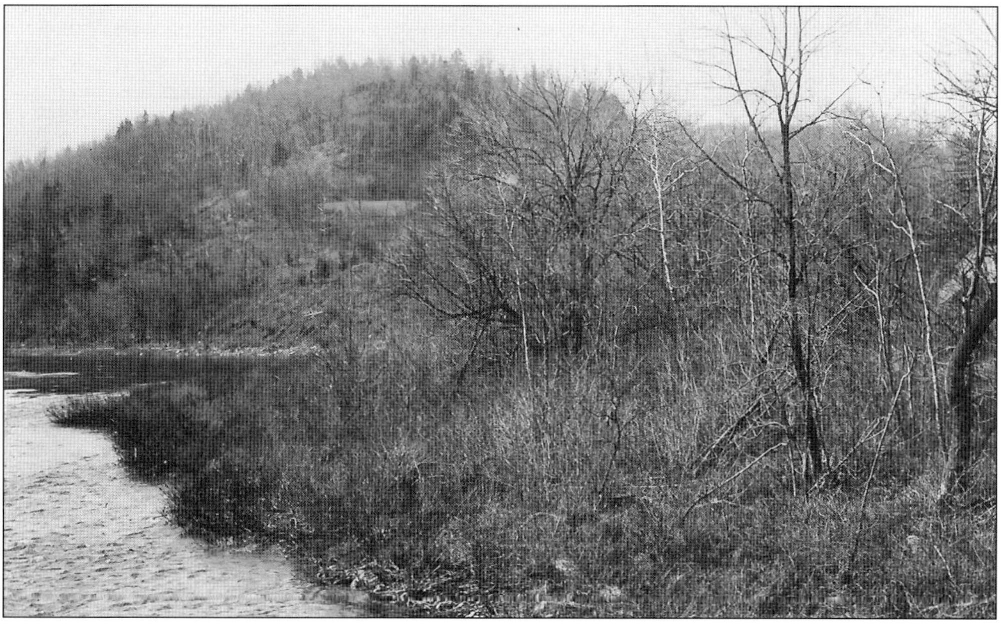

This is a view of Southville, the southern boundary of Bridgewater, showing the banks of the Housatonic River, named after an Algonquian word that means "Where the Waters Meet." The two rivers are the Housatonic and the Shepaug. The area was home to wolves, bear, and mountain lions—so many that during the Colonial period, a bounty of three pounds was offered for each head brought to the town hall. (BHS.)

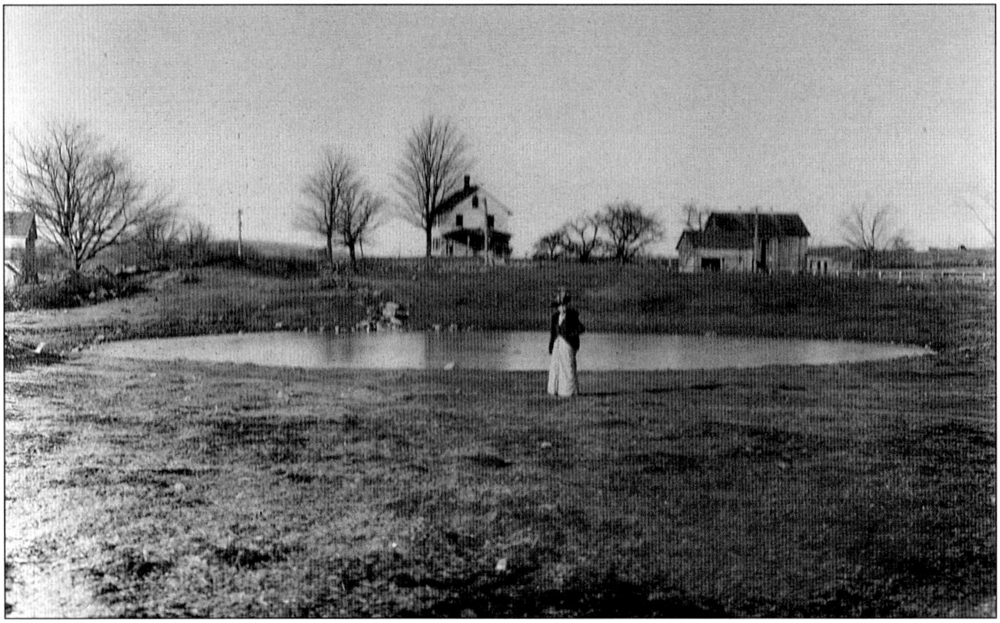

Tim Pond, or "Tim's Pond," still exists today on Clapboard Road. New homes have been built near the landmark. Many trees and shrubs surround the area, but the pond lives on. It was named for Revolutionary War hero Timothy Randall. Long ago, ice was cut from this pond, which was a favorite of children for skating. Local legend says that it has never run dry, even in extreme drought conditions. (BHS.)

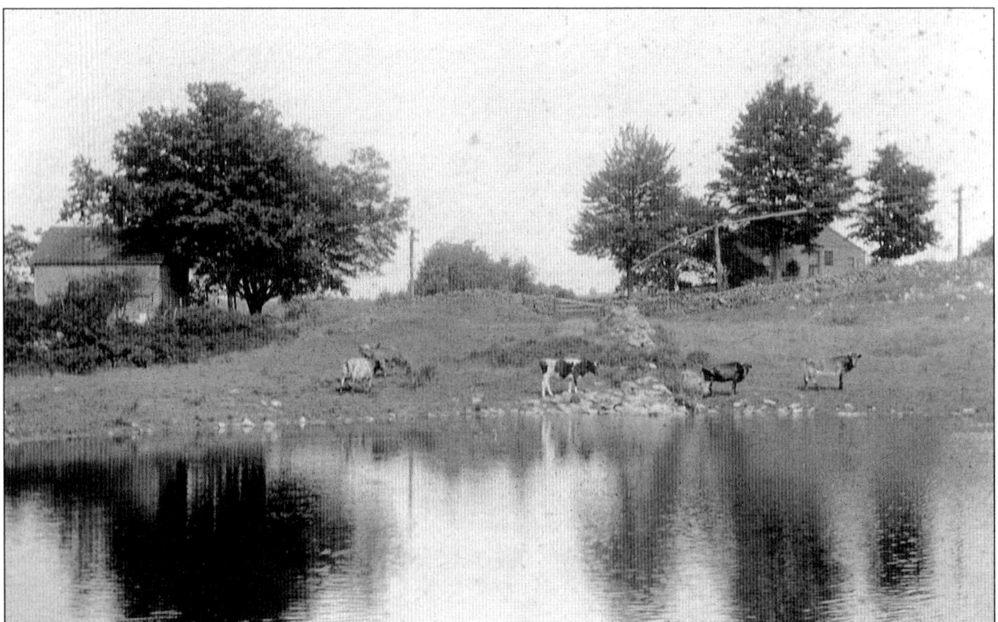

Here is another view of Tim's Pond. Timothy Randall, buried in the old South Cemetery, fought with the Connecticut Light Horse Militia. Taken prisoner on November 16, 1776, he was held on a British ship off the coast of Brooklyn. He nearly died of starvation, but was released in a prisoner-exchange program, recovered, and lived to the age of 88. (BHS.)

Two

THE PEOPLE

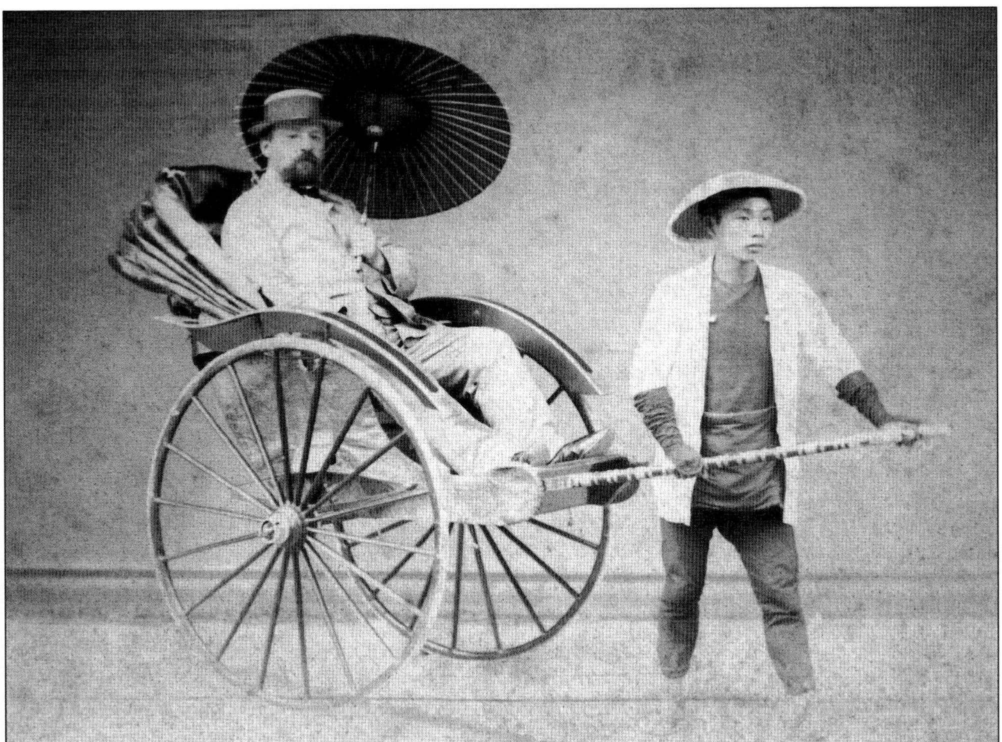

Capt. William D. Burnham is in a rickshaw while visiting Hidgo, Japan. As a boy, he lived in Bridgewater. His family moved to New York City. He went to sea at 14 and built up a fortune. He was very generous to the town, establishing the Burnham Library, donating to the school, creating a fund for the poor, and making a $5,000 donation to the Congregational Church. (BHS.)

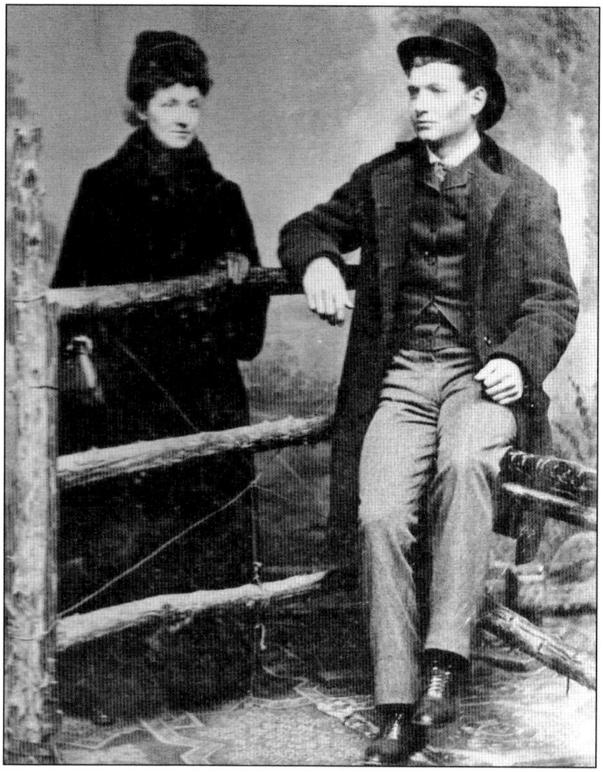

Isaac and Sarah Cole Babbitt were married on November 7, 1855. Both came from distinguished families, and were descendants of Plymouth colonists. After settling in Bridgewater, Isaac was a carpenter, joiner, and builder who served in the Connecticut House of Representatives. Sarah kept a journal of her daily life for many years; it serves as a time capsule of those long-ago days. (BHS.)

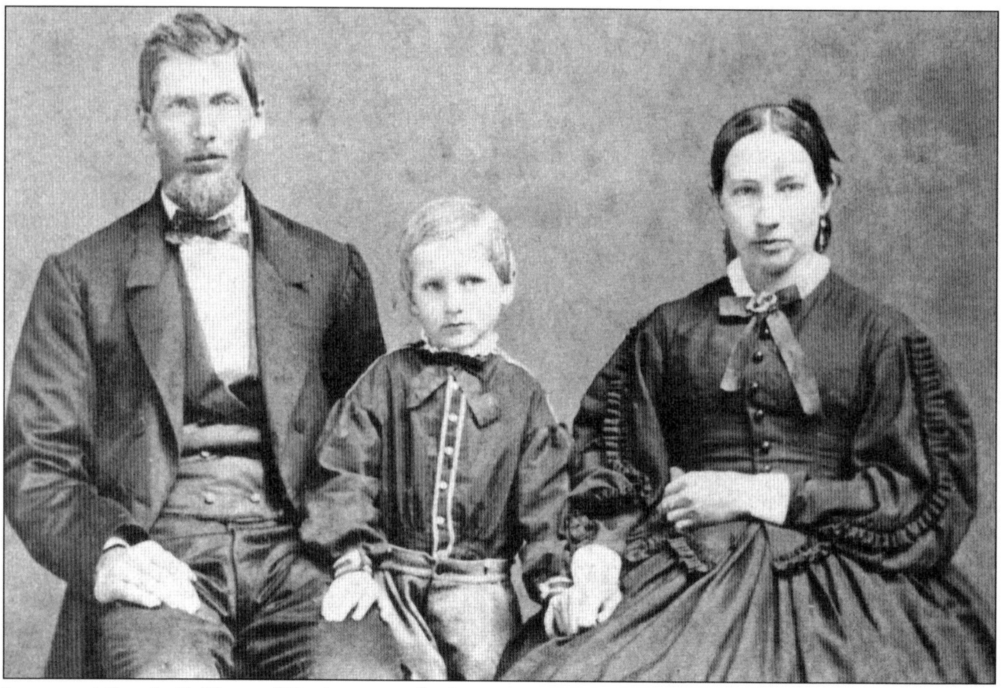

Isaac and Sarah Babbitt of Bridgewater had two sons: Eugene (shown here) and Frank. Sarah's love of learning spurred on both boys to pursue careers in academia. Both became linguists and taught in Ivy League universities. (BHS.)

David Bankhead, a hatter from Danbury, stands with his friend, Austin Gillette, on the green in Bridgewater in 1898. (BHS.)

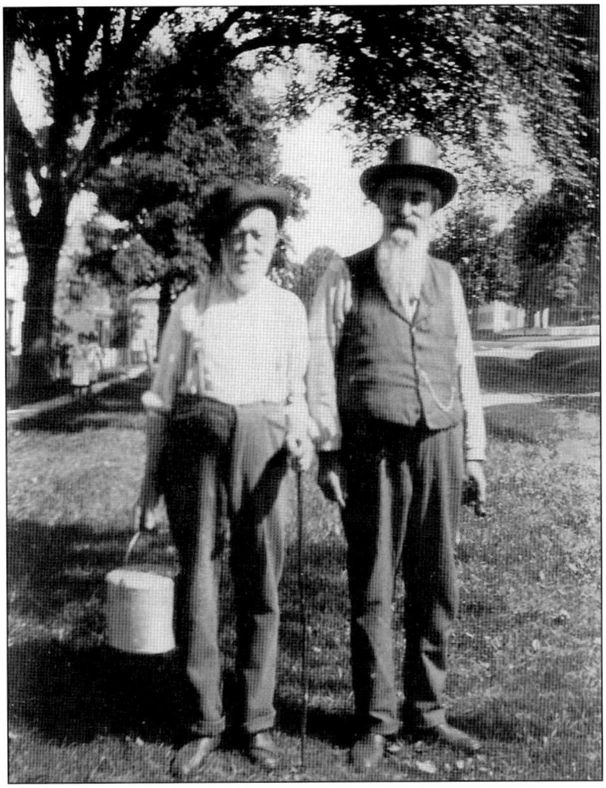

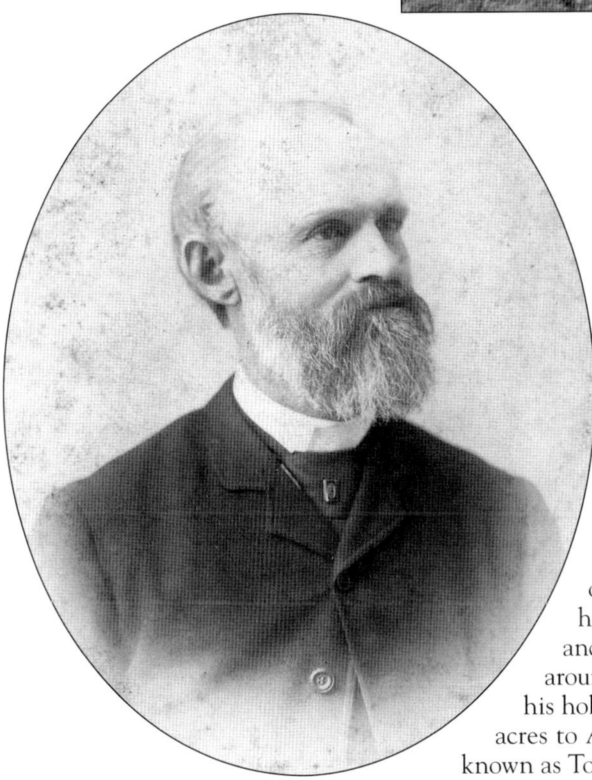

Born in 1836, Edwin G. Seeley was a dairyman, cattle breeder, and importer of purebred Dutch Holsteins. He owned hundreds of acres of land around Roxbury and most of the land in the area of town around Painter Hill. In 1919, he deeded all of his holdings to his son who, in 1943, sold 512 acres to A. Richard Diebold, whose property is known as Toplands Farm. (Elinor Hurlbut.)

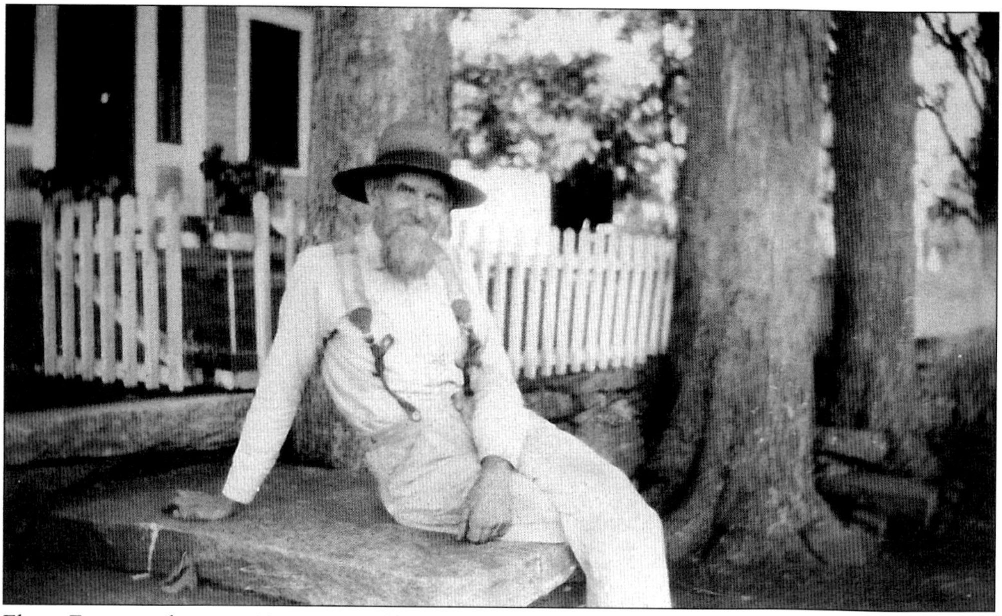

Elmer Frost was born in 1842. He and his wife, Emma, born in 1848, were married in 1868. They farmed in Bridgewater with their sons, Franklin, George, and Willis. Willis remained in Bridgewater, marrying Ruth Estelle Frost and raising three children, William, George, and Ethel. By the 1930 Census, William remained, taking care of his mother and family on Christian Street. (BHS.)

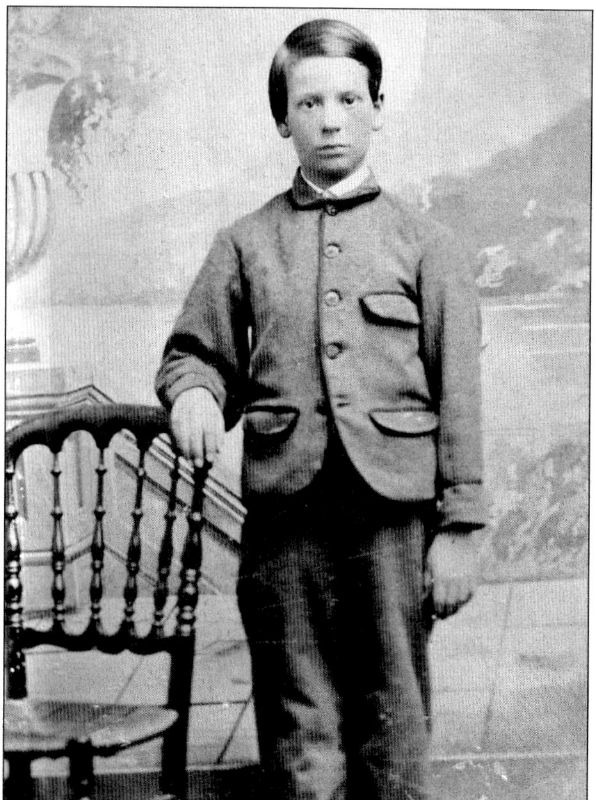

Henry Merwin Bronson (1858–1934) was the son of Daniel Gaylord Bronson, a carpenter and plow maker who had a mill and casting shop on Squire Road near Jacks Brook. His maternal grandparents were Alden and Clara Beers. This undated photograph is taken from a tintype. (John Botsford Coleman.)

After his father died, Henry Merwin Bronson (1858–1934) and his brother continued to operate the Bronson Plow Company built by their father. Henry followed in his father's footsteps and became a carpenter, as well as a plow maker. He bought land from Horace Squire in 1893 and, a year later, built his home on that land at 96 Squire Road. (John Botsford Coleman.)

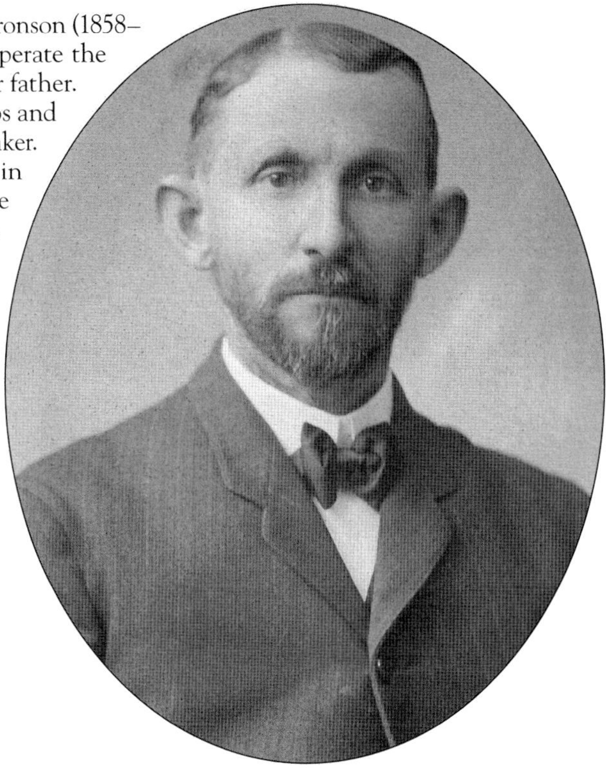

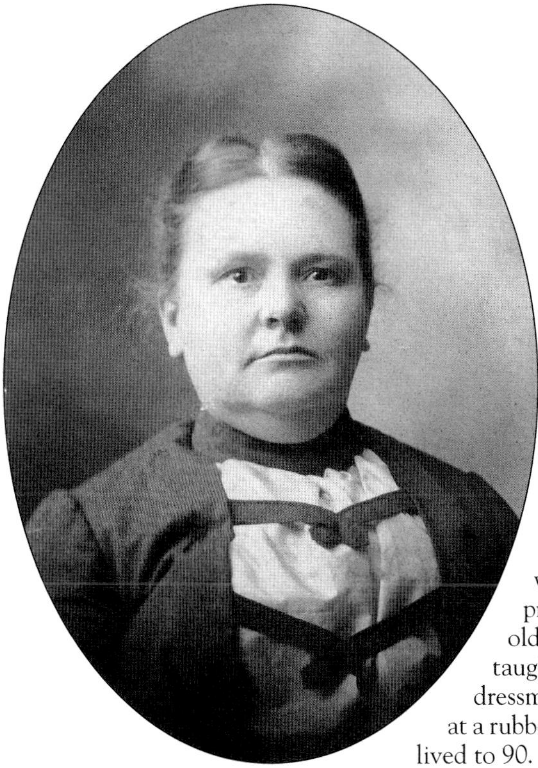

Carrie Estelle (Seymour) Bronson (1861–1951), wife of Henry M. Bronson, must have been proud of their five daughters and one son. Their oldest daughter, Alice, became a nurse, Bessie taught in a district school, and Flora became a dressmaker. Their son, Merwin S., spent his career at a rubber company where he rose to manager. Carrie lived to 90. (John Botsford Coleman.)

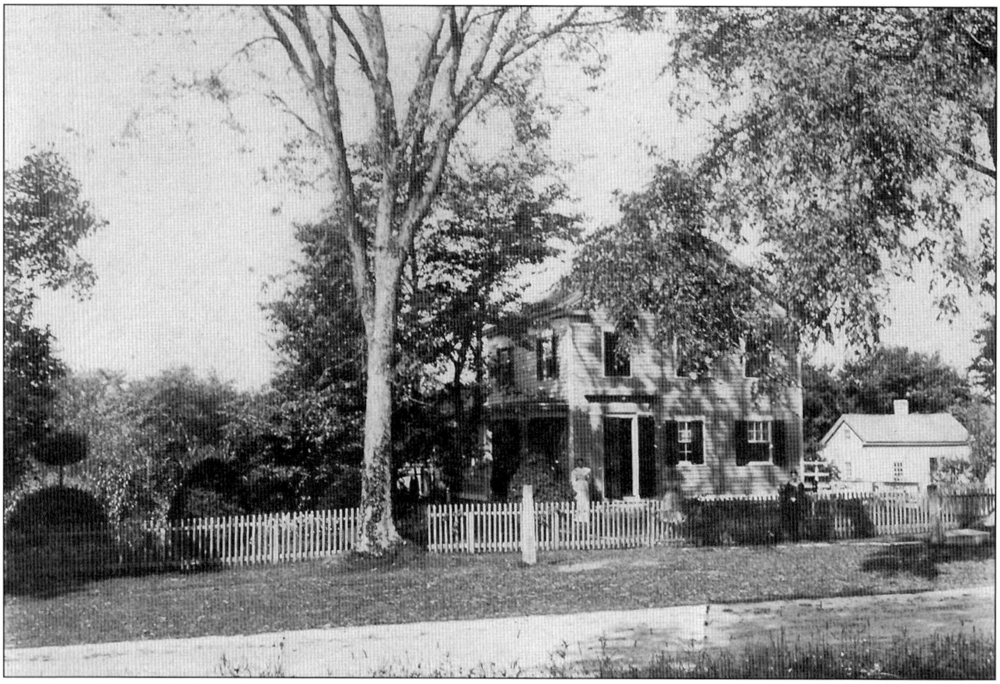

This fine home was the Bridgewater residence of Austin Gillette. Originally known as "The Burnham House," it was built in 1851 by William G. Burnham. It was sold in 1860 to Stephen B. Keeler, who passed it to Austin Gillette. (BHS.)

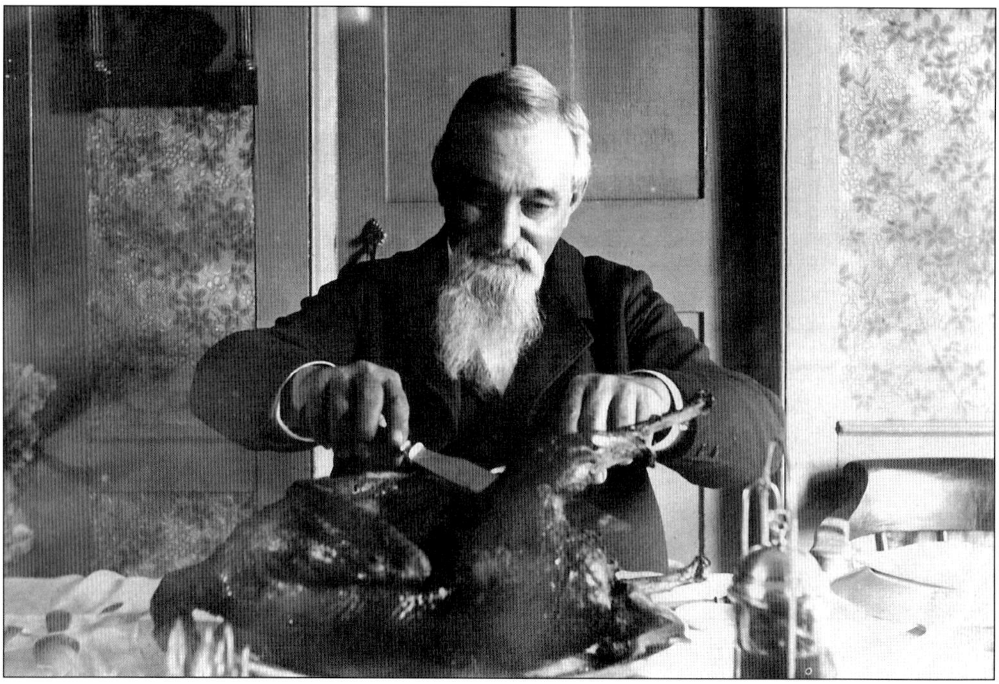

Austin H. Gillette carves the Thanksgiving turkey in this image. Thanksgiving became an official holiday in 1863. This picture dates to 1898. The Gillettes moved to Bridgewater from Roxbury following his marriage to Emily A. Weller. They had four sons. (BHS.)

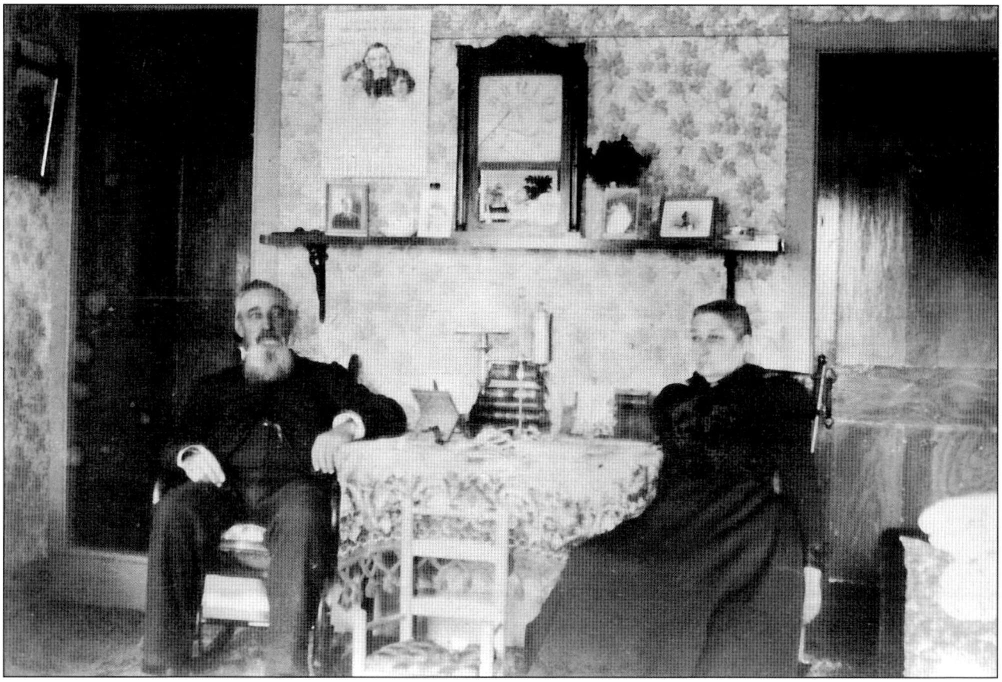

Austin and Emily Gillette relax in the sitting room of their Bridgewater home. Such rooms were the show places of the time. Wallpapered walls, brick-a-brack, and overstuffed furniture were highlighted. The Gillettes also had a large organ, which occupied the opposite wall. (BHS.)

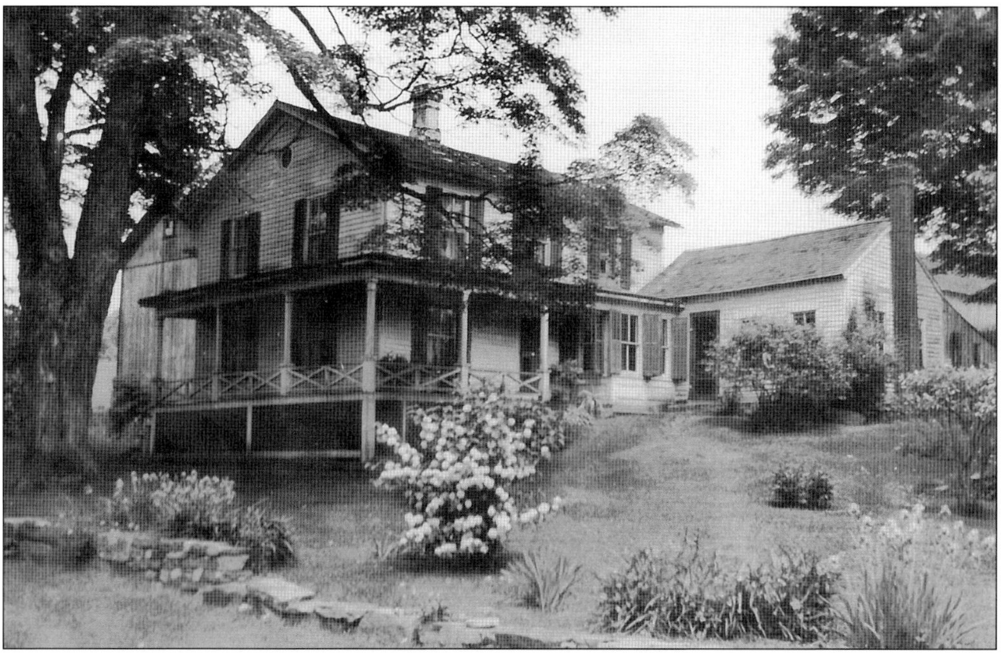

Lina Hartwell was called the "Grandma Moses of Bridgewater." This was her home. The daughter of Monroe and Sallie Hartwell, she was a self-taught primitive painter who depicted local scenes in her art. Born on April 8, 1894, she died in August 1968, leaving behind countless pieces she made for gifts to friends and neighbors. (BHS.)

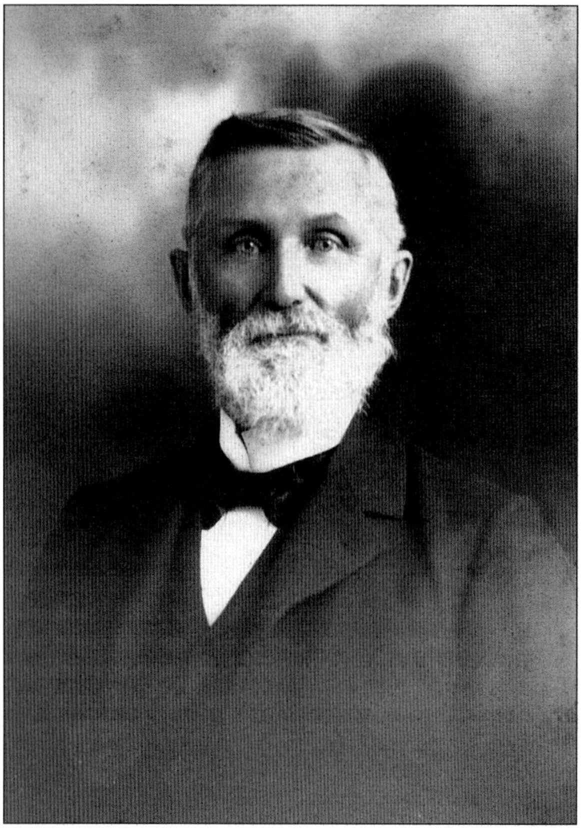

The Hurlbut family has farmed in Roxbury since the early 1700s and been town leaders throughout its history. Henry S. Hurlbut (1834–1910), son of Garry and Ann Hurlbut, inherited the family farm on Church Street and served as town clerk from 1872 until his death. His home and office passed to his son, Norman, who continued the family traditions of farming and public service. (Elinor Hurlbut.)

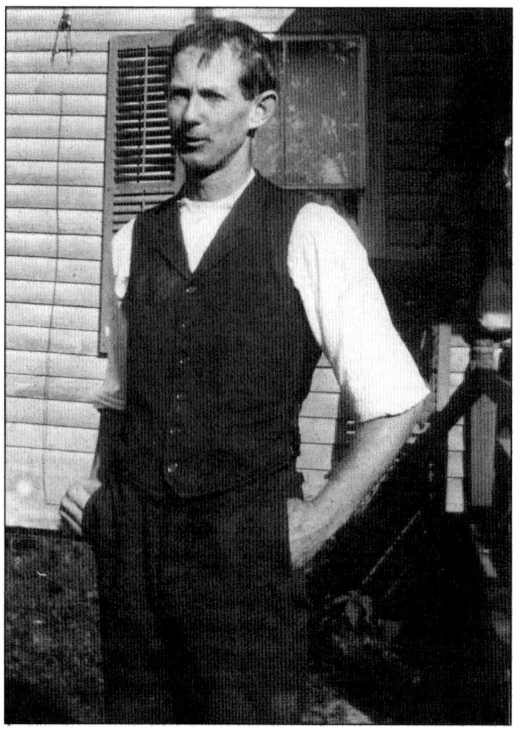

Norman Henry Hurlbut (1879–1957), son of Henry S. Hurlbut, farmer and town clerk for 45 years, posed in front of his house and farm on Church Street. The relaxed pose, rolled-up sleeves, and vest encouraged someone to pen on the back of the photograph, "ain't he handsome"—indeed he is! His sons, Alden and Lewis, operated their own farms, grew extensive apple orchards, and served as town officers. (Elinor Hurlbut.)

In 1927, these descendants of Roxbury's founding family—brothers Alden B. (1911–1998) (left) and Lewis Elmer (1909–1992) (right) Hurlbut—posed for a formal photograph. Their contiguous farms along Church Street became known as "Hurlbut Corners." Both men managed large general farms, grew extensive apple orchards, and served on town commissions. Alden served as town clerk for 20 years, and Lewis wrote a history of Roxbury. (Elinor Hurlbut.)

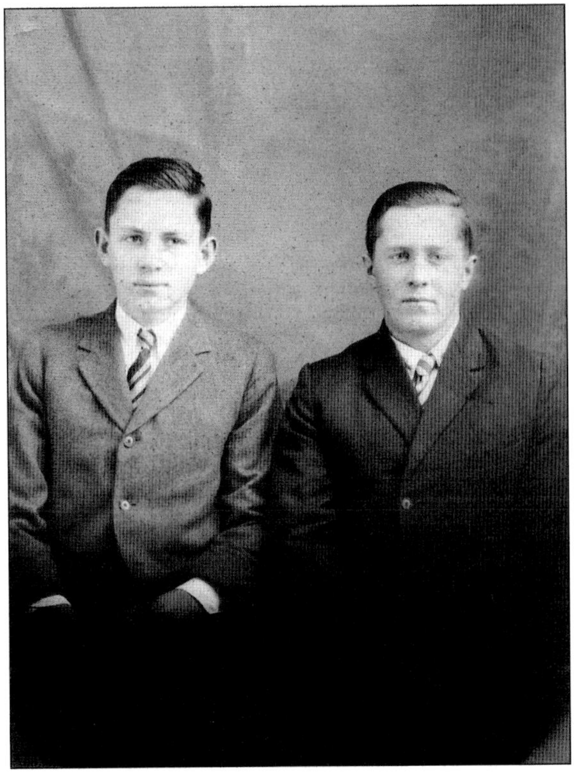

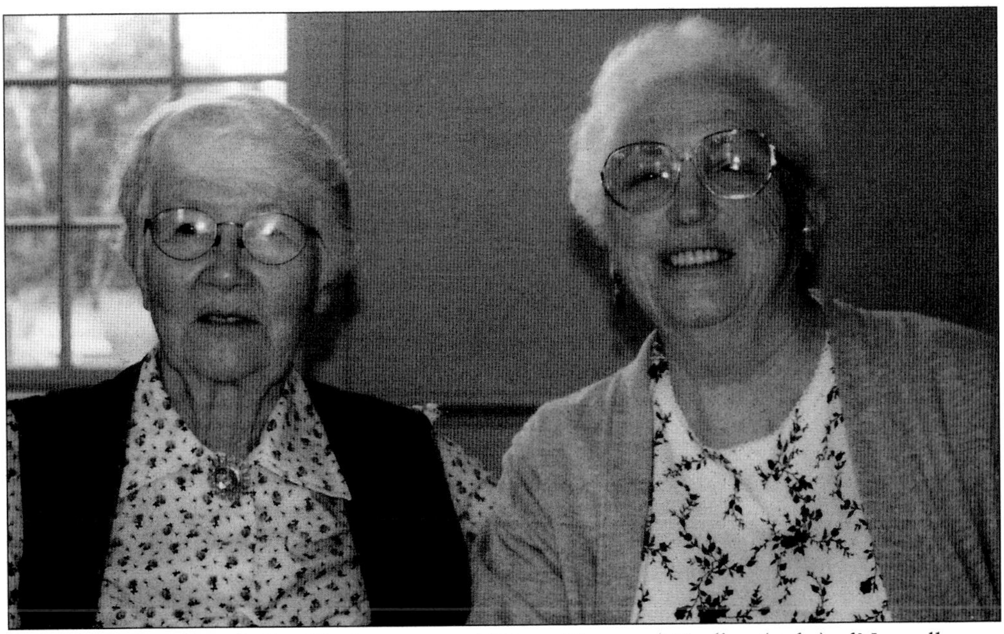

Ethel (Frost) Hurlbut (left) of Bridgewater and Elinor (Peterson) Hurlbut (right) of Norwalk were cousins who married Lewis and Alden Hurlbut, respectively. They were emergency first responders, active in the Grange, Shepaug Club, and PTA. Ethel's daughter Cathy operates the centuries-old family farm. Elinor served in the town clerk's office for 50 years. Her son Peter is town clerk and her grandson, James, is assistant town clerk. (Elinor Hurlbut.)

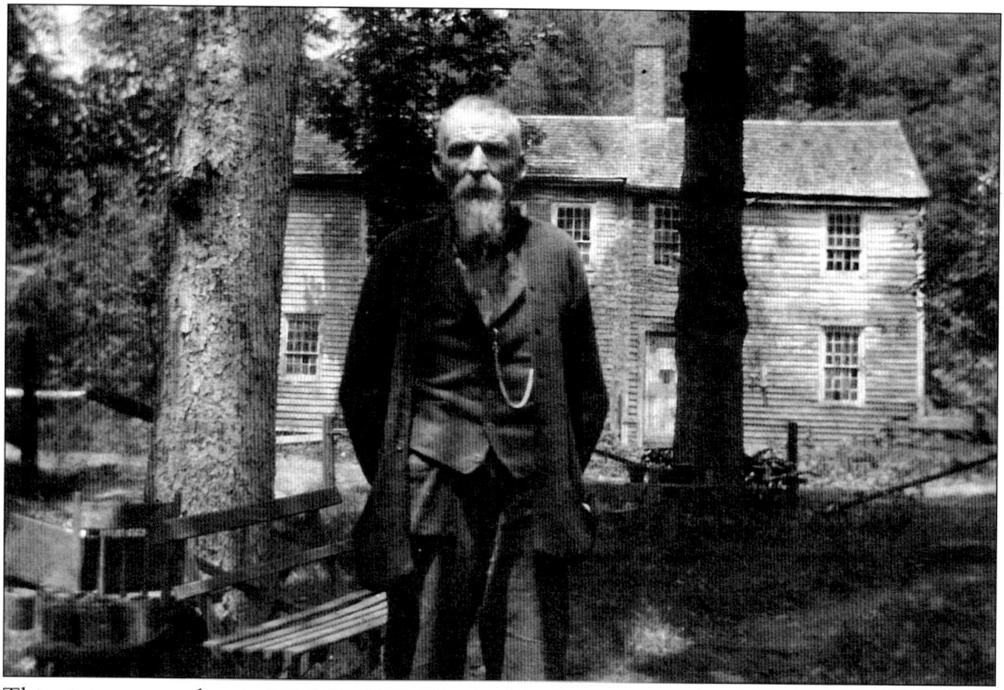

This picture was taken in 1898. By 1922, Charles Northrop was ready to dispose of his Southville holdings. Following the sale of his farm, he placed billboards throughout the town announcing an auction, selling all his livestock and household goods. (BHS.)

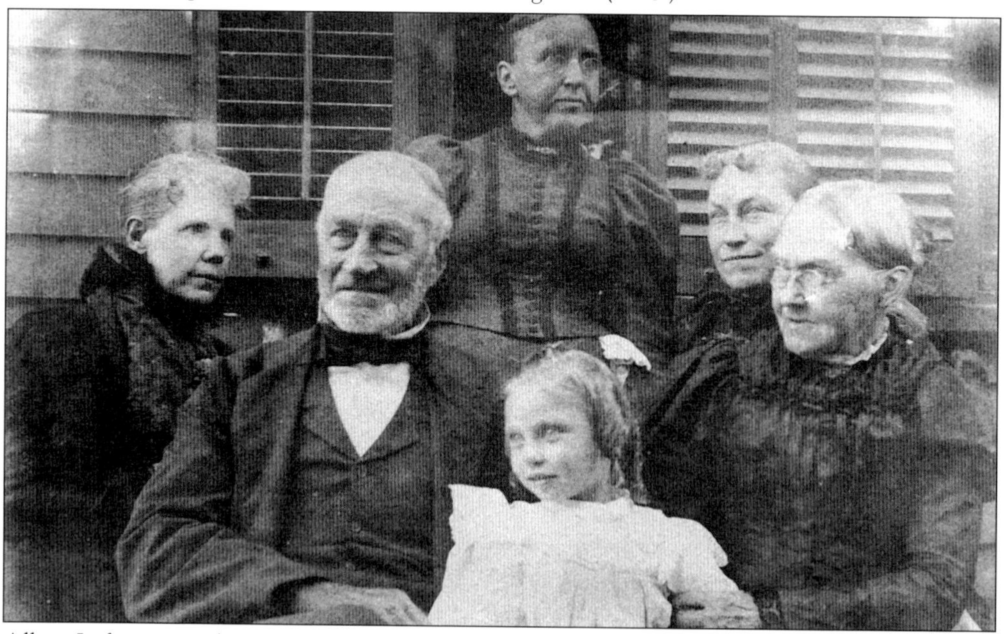

Albert Lafayette Hodge (1822–1920) and his family gathered for this undated photograph. Hodge was town selectman in Roxbury for 13 years, representative to the state legislature, and a manager and owner of Mine Hill. He also owned and operated a sawmill, lumberyard, and hardware store. At 84, this extraordinary man traveled to the west and joined a group to climb the Rocky Mountains. (RM.)

Henry Sanford and his wife, Dolly, pose on their porch in Bridgewater. Born on October 14, 1807, he was a farmer as well as a carpenter and joiner. Two branches of his family were prominent in Bridgewater. (BHS.)

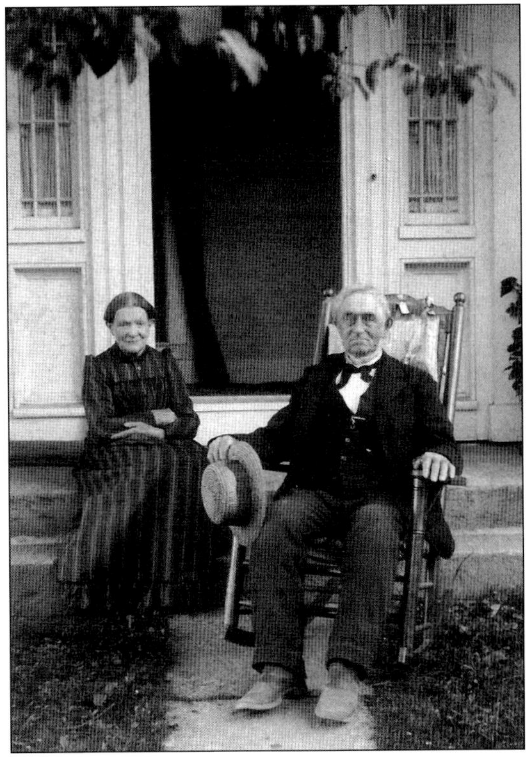

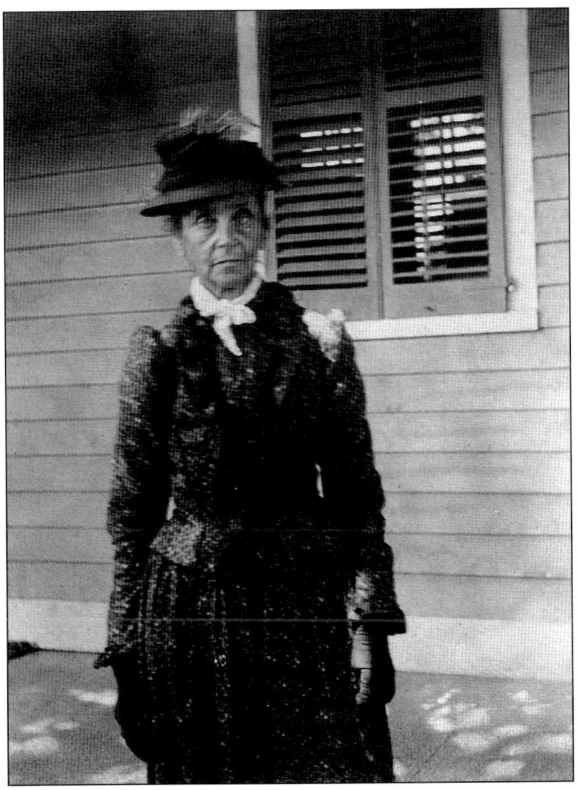

This 1900 image shows Sarah Sanford (1830–1917), the daughter of Harley and Alosia Sanford. Sarah became the head of the house upon her parents' death. In the 1900 Census, she is listed as a Bridgewater "farmer" who lived alone. Sarah Sanford Road is named in her honor. (BHS.)

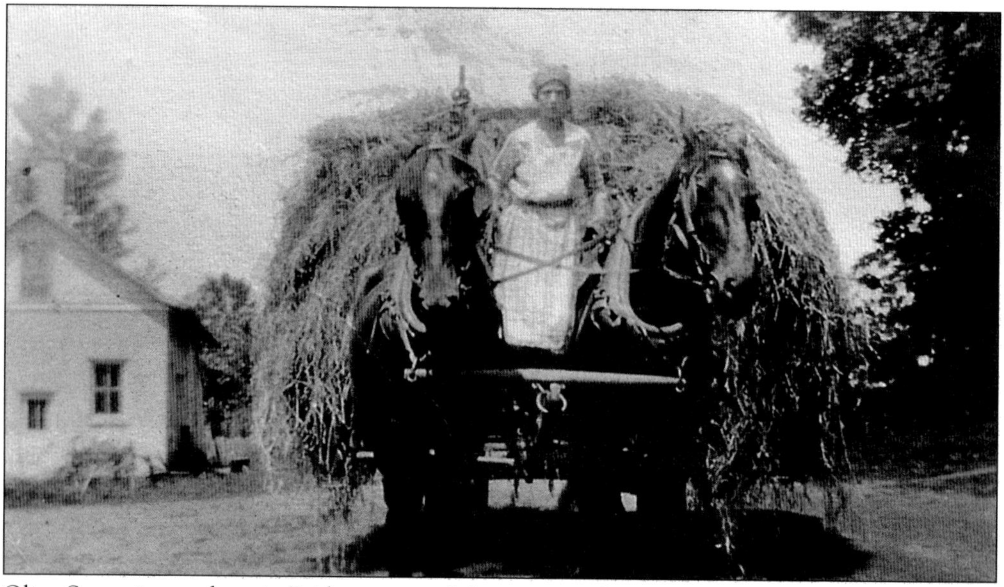

Olive Stuart is seen here in Bridgewater with her team and wagon. Born on August 21, 1905, she married C. Henry Stuart on July 1, 1924. Always a lady, she dressed the part—even when called upon to perform farm work. (Julie Stuart Seger.)

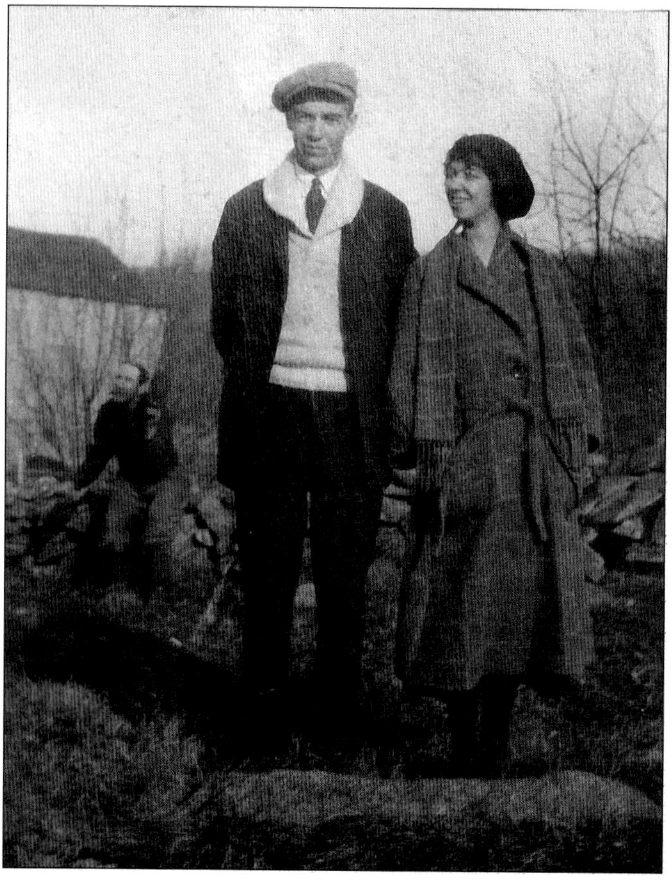

Olive and Charles Henry Stuart are pictured here at their Christian Street home. Charles was a horse trainer and breaker. Together, they had 12 children, 39 grandchildren, and 13 great-grandchildren. (Julie Stuart Seger.)

It may read like something from the Wild West, but this poster from pre-1888 Bridgewater shows how seriously horse theft and burglary were taken. The list of members reads like a who's-who of mid-to-late-19th-century Bridgewater. (BHS.)

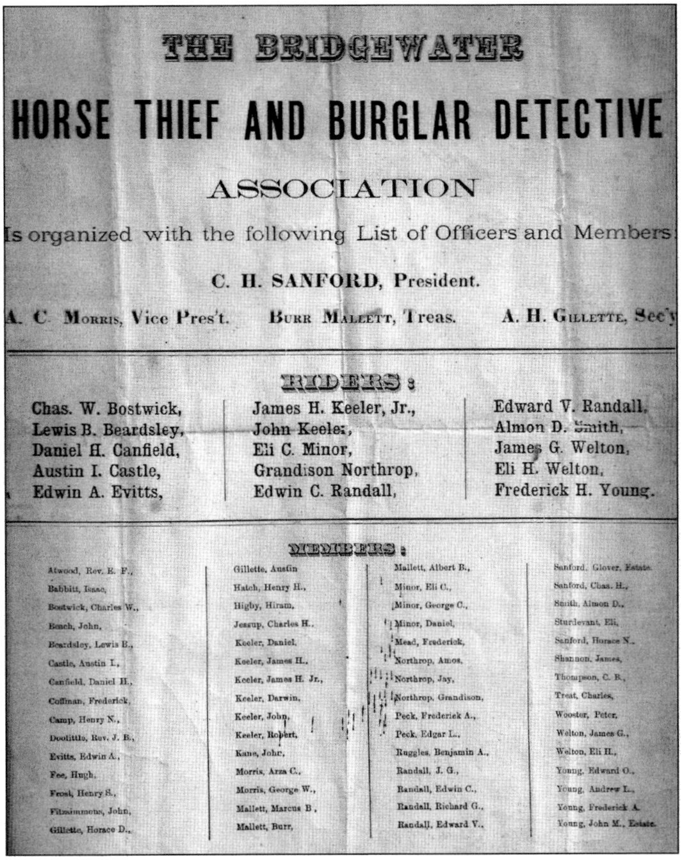

THE BRIDGEWATER

HORSE THIEF AND BURGLAR DETECTIVE

ASSOCIATION

Is organized with the following List of Officers and Members:

C. H. SANFORD, President.

A. C. Morris, Vice Pres't. Burr Mallett, Treas. A. H. Gillette, Sec'y

RIDERS:

Chas. W. Bostwick,
Lewis B. Beardsley,
Daniel H. Canfield,
Austin I. Castle,
Edwin A. Evitts,
James H. Keeler, Jr.,
John Keeler,
Eli C. Minor,
Grandison Northrop,
Edwin C. Randall,
Edward V. Randall,
Almon D. Smith,
James G. Welton,
Eli H. Welton,
Frederick H. Young.

MEMBERS:

Atwood, Rev. E. F.,
Babbitt, Isaac,
Bostwick, Charles W.,
Beach, John,
Beardsley, Lewis B.,
Castle, Austin I.,
Canfield, Daniel H.,
Coffman, Frederick,
Camp, Henry N.,
Doolittle, Rev. J. B.,
Evitts, Edwin A.,
Fee, Hugh,
Frost, Henry S.,
Fitzsimmons, John,
Gillette, Horace D.,
Gillette, Austin
Hatch, Henry H.,
Higby, Hiram,
Jessup, Charles H.,
Keeler, Daniel,
Keeler, James H.,
Keeler, James H. Jr.,
Keeler, Darwin,
Keeler, John,
Keeler, Robert,
Kane, John,
Morris, Arza C.,
Morris, George W.,
Mallett, Marcus B.,
Mallett, Burr,
Mallett, Albert B.,
Minor, Eli C.,
Minor, George C.,
Minor, Daniel,
Mead, Frederick,
Northrop, Amos,
Northrop, Jay,
Northrop, Grandison,
Peck, Frederick A.,
Peck, Edgar L.,
Ruggles, Benjamin A.,
Randall, J. G.,
Randall, Edwin C.,
Randall, Richard G.,
Randall, Edward V.,
Sanford, Glover, Estate.
Sanford, Chas. H.,
Smith, Almon D.,
Sturdevant, Eli,
Sanford, Horace N.,
Shannon, James,
Thompson, C. B.,
Treat, Charles,
Wooster, Peter,
Welton, James G.,
Welton, Eli H.,
Young, Edward O.,
Young, Andrew L.,
Young, Frederick A.
Young, John M., Estate.

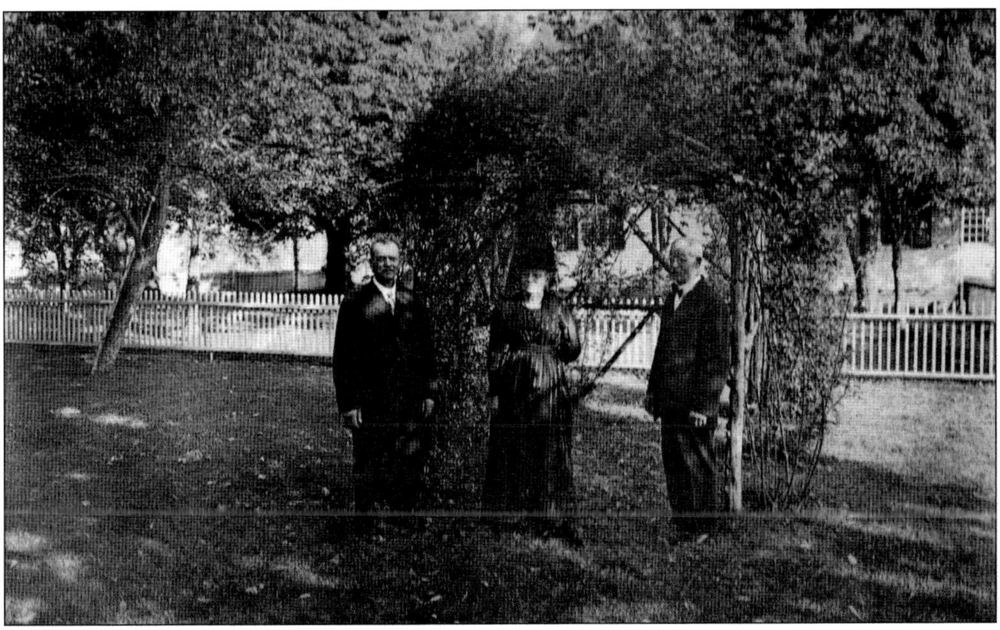

Reuben M. Warner and his wife, Alice, stand in their Bridgewater garden with their son Dan. (BHS.)

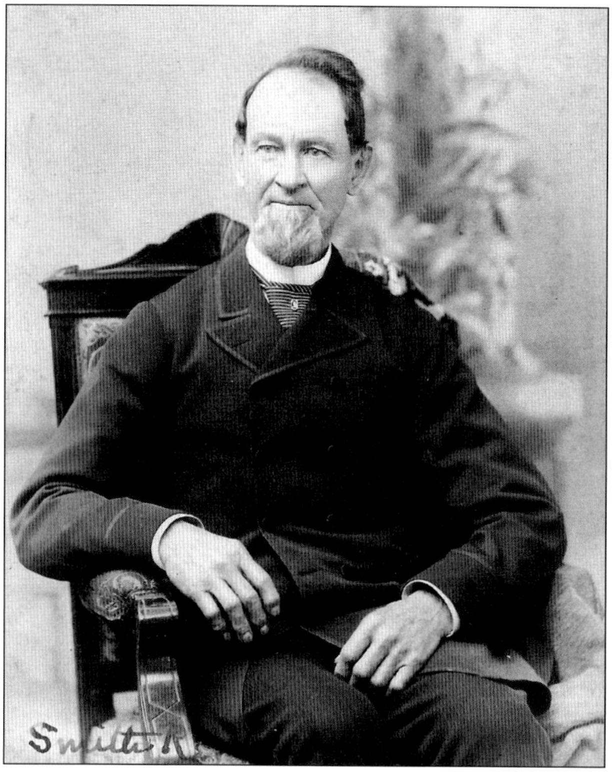

Smith Weeks had his portrait taken in New Milford by "Chipman" on Bank Street. Weeks served as the postmaster of Bridgewater. His sharp memory, even at an advanced age, made him a much-valued reference source regarding sales of property and businesses. He died at the age of 90. (BHS.)

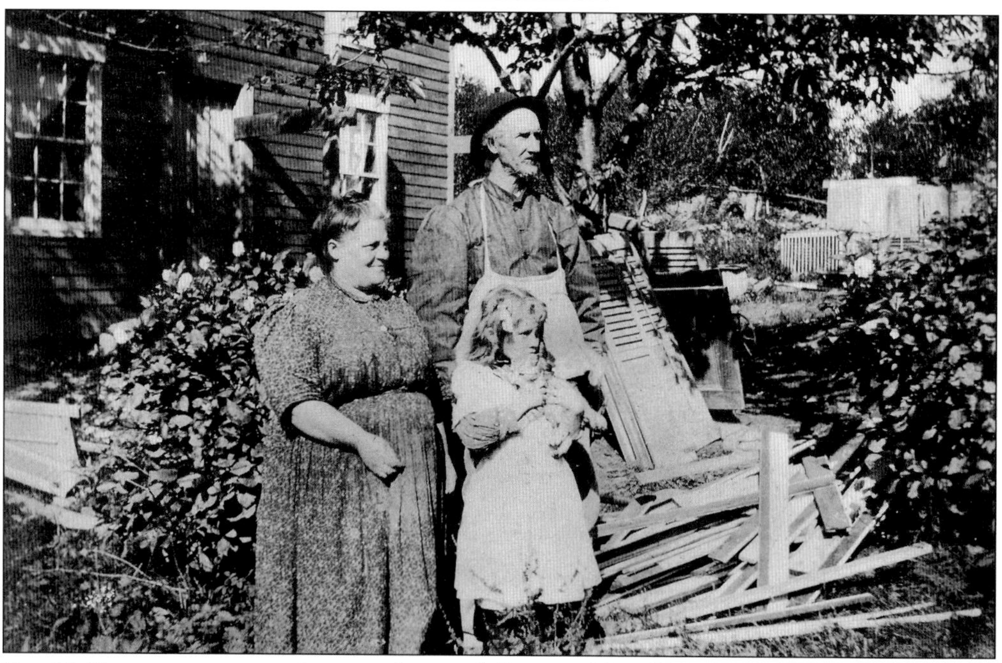

Ezra M. Young was a man who moved around. Born in May 1839 in New Jersey, he resided in three New Jersey towns before adulthood. In 1876, he married Frances C. Young. By 1880, they had two children, Burr M. and Clara F. They were living in Pawling, New York. Then came their move to Bridgewater, where they stayed until 1910, when they moved to Newtown. (BHS.)

Three

THE SETTLEMENTS

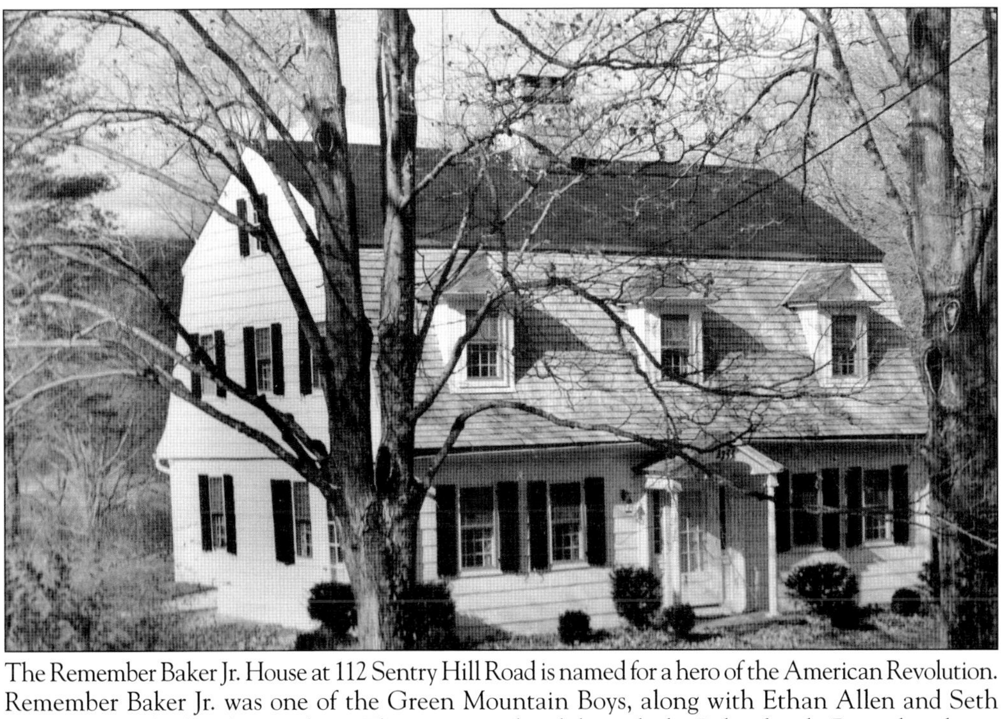

The Remember Baker Jr. House at 112 Sentry Hill Road is named for a hero of the American Revolution. Remember Baker Jr. was one of the Green Mountain Boys, along with Ethan Allen and Seth Warner, who also lived in Roxbury. The men are related through the Baker family. Records indicate the house may have been built as early as 1733, making it the oldest house in Roxbury. (RM.)

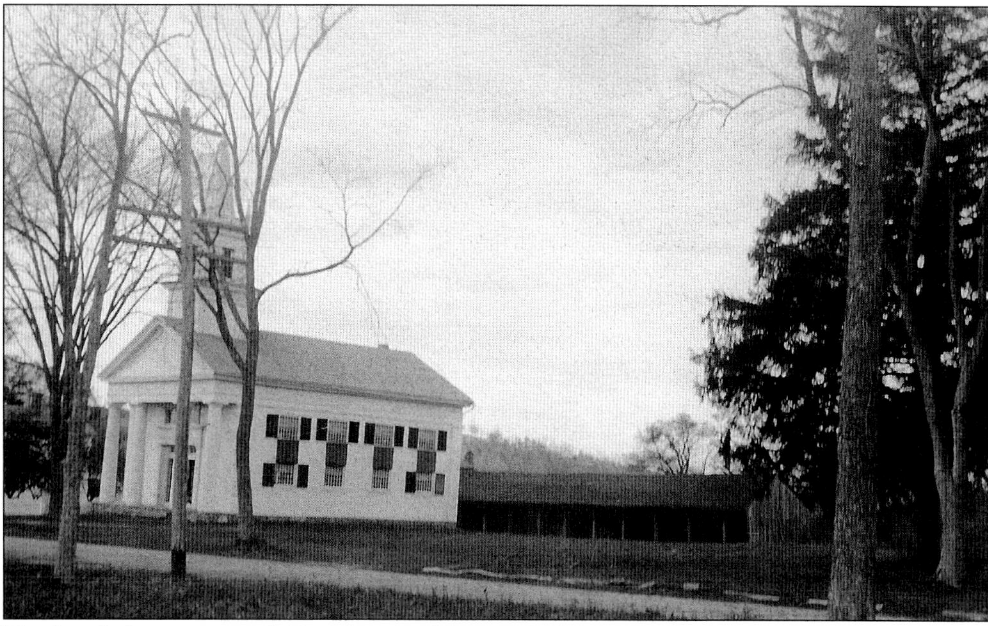

The fourth Congregational Church in Roxbury was built in 1838; four years later, the congregation built the sheds and stalls shown in this 1934 photograph. Later, with population shrinking, churches banded together to survive. In 1940, it became a yoked church with Bridgewater and, in the 1950s, the church merged with the Evangelical and Reform Churches to become the United Church of Christ. (RCC.)

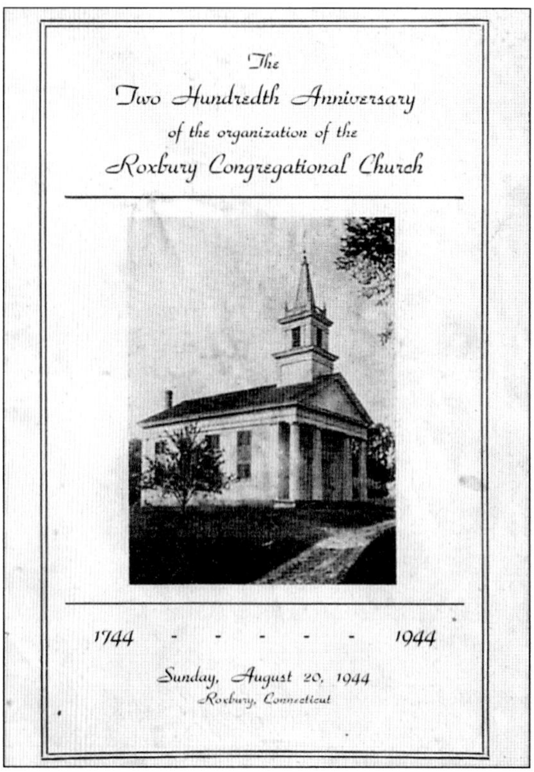

The

Two Hundredth Anniversary

of the organization of the

Roxbury Congregational Church

1744 - - - - - - 1944

Sunday, August 20, 1944

Roxbury, Connecticut

The Connecticut General Assembly, in 1743, established the ecclesiastical society known as Roxbury, after years of petitions from the citizens to have permission to have their own minister and build their own churches. This program announces the 200th anniversary of the organization of the Roxbury Congregational Church, held Sunday, August 20, 1944. In 1990, under the leadership of the Rev. David Peters, the church celebrated its 250th anniversary. (RCC.)

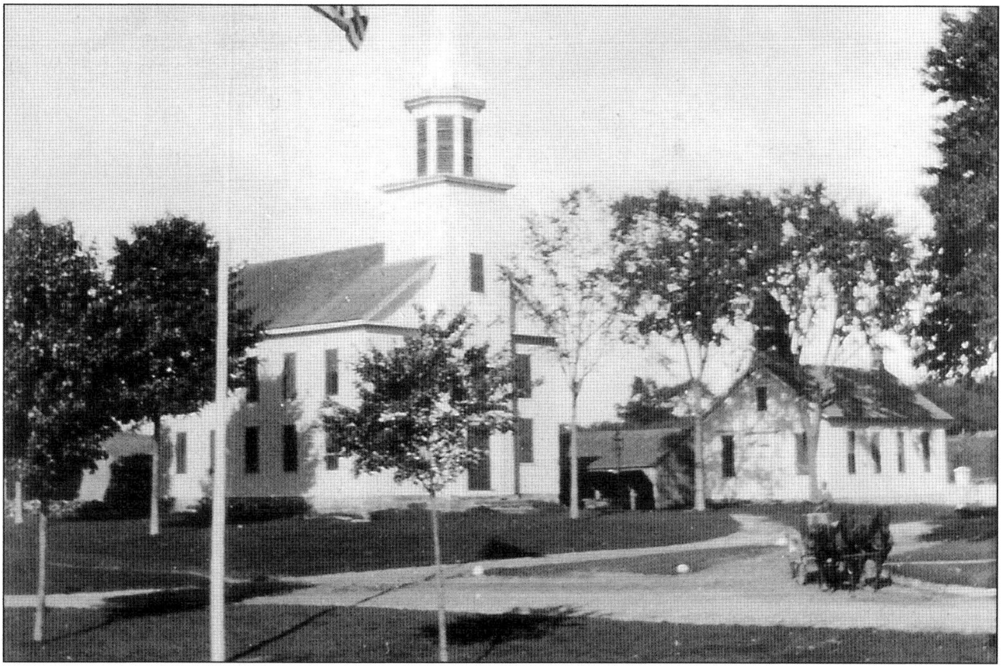

Founded in the late 1700s, the Bridgewater Congregational Church was established as a "meeting house" in 1807. This picture, dated 1898, shows the Congregational chapel and the horse stalls in the background. A horse and buggy passes the town green. (BHS.)

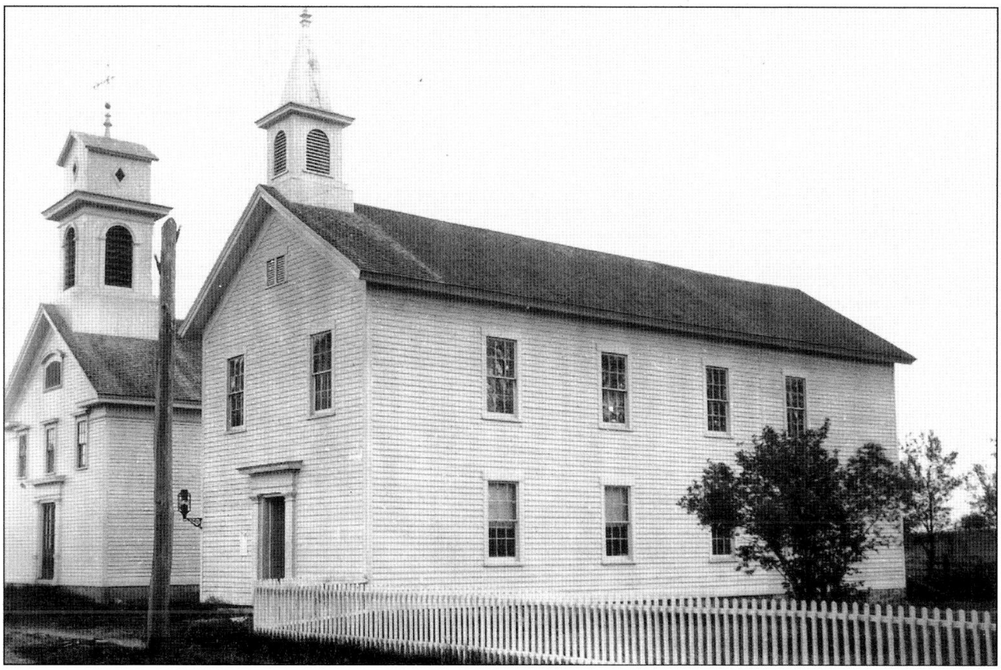

The Methodist Church (left) and Roxbury Town Hall (right) are shown in this undated photograph with a gaslight fixture on the front of the town hall. The church, built in 1867, fit snugly between the Hall of Records and the town hall until 1940, when membership dwindled. The church was demolished, and the steeple disappeared from the landscape. (Cameron Gardella.)

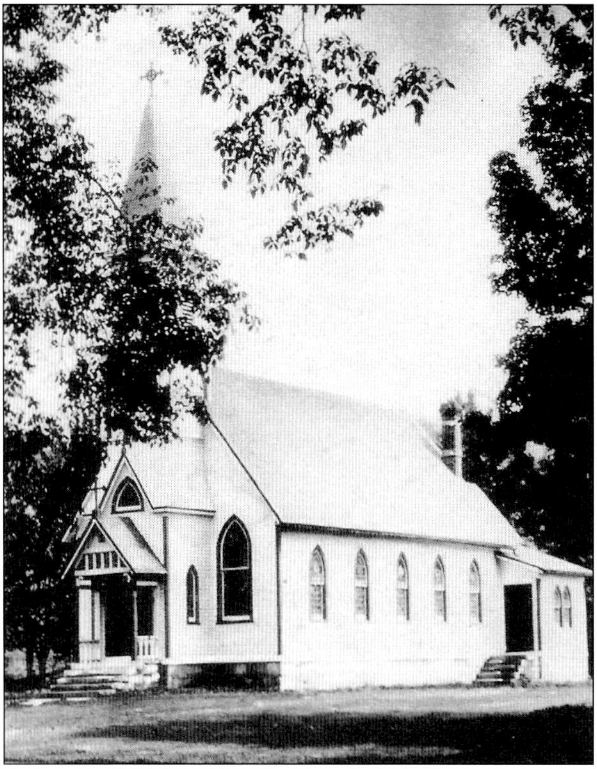

Church bells rang out on Sunday, July 4, 1886, when Roxbury's first Roman Catholic Church opened its doors to 125 worshippers. In this photograph, the entrance to St. Patrick's Catholic Church faces the road, but was later turned away from the highway. Stained-glass memorial windows bear the names of immigrants who came to work on the railroad, in the mines, and in the quarries. (RM.)

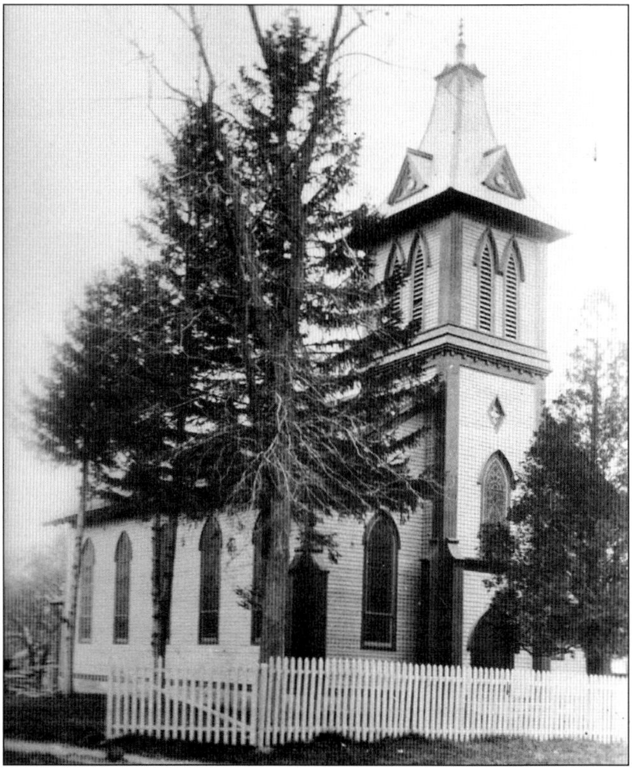

The Episcopal parish in Roxbury, established in 1740, was the oldest Episcopal parish in Litchfield County. Built in 1807, this church faced east and stood between a schoolhouse and a tavern. A picket fence surrounded the church. In 1841, this church took the name Christ Church. In 1861, it was turned to face south. Later, the schoolhouse became the parish house, and the tavern became the rectory. (RM.)

St. Mark's Church was founded in 1810, the first meetings taking place in the home of Jonas Sanford. For 25 years, services took place in parishioners' homes. This image shows the original St. Mark's Church, built in 1835. It was located on Main Street South on the land of G. Lester Randall. When new, it had a spire and peaked roof. The foundation was granite, the walls clapboard. (BHS.)

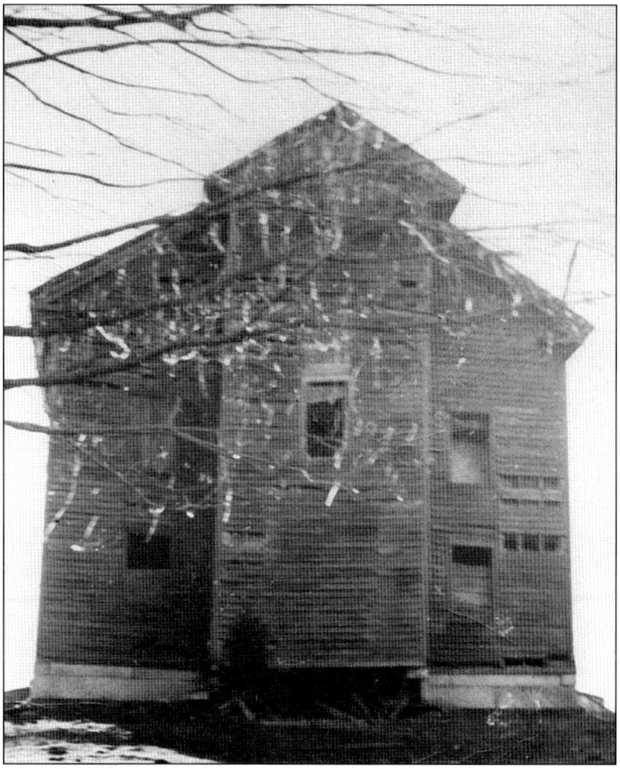

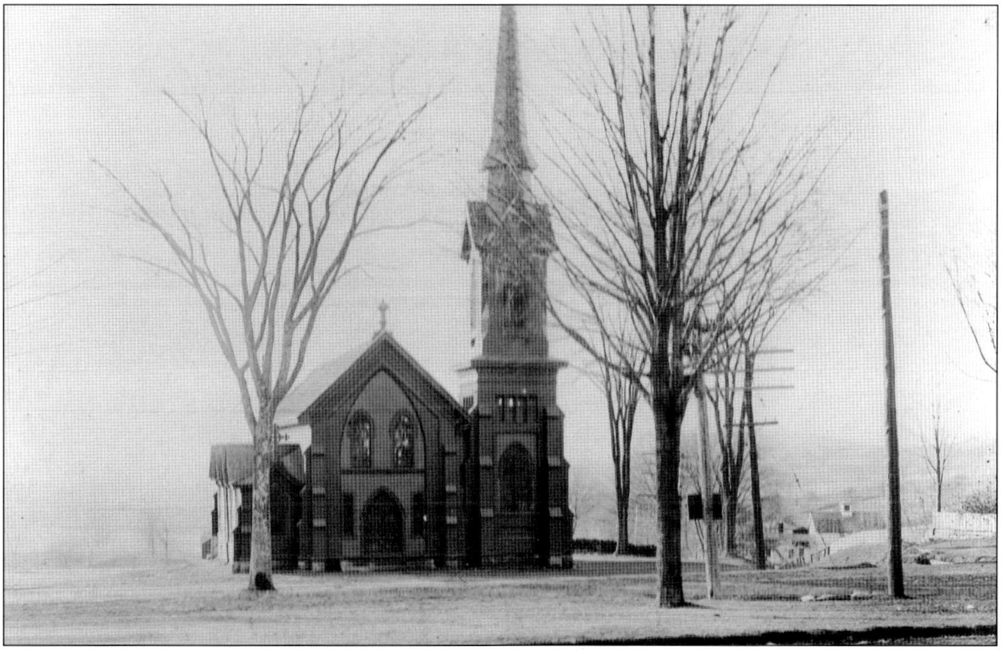

On March 14, 1860, this second St. Mark's Church was consecrated in Bridgewater Center. They began to search for a rector, temporarily sharing a priest with Christ Church in Roxbury. This church featured a 90-foot spire. This spire was declared unsound in 1929 and replaced with a Latin trefoil cross, which remains today. (BHS.)

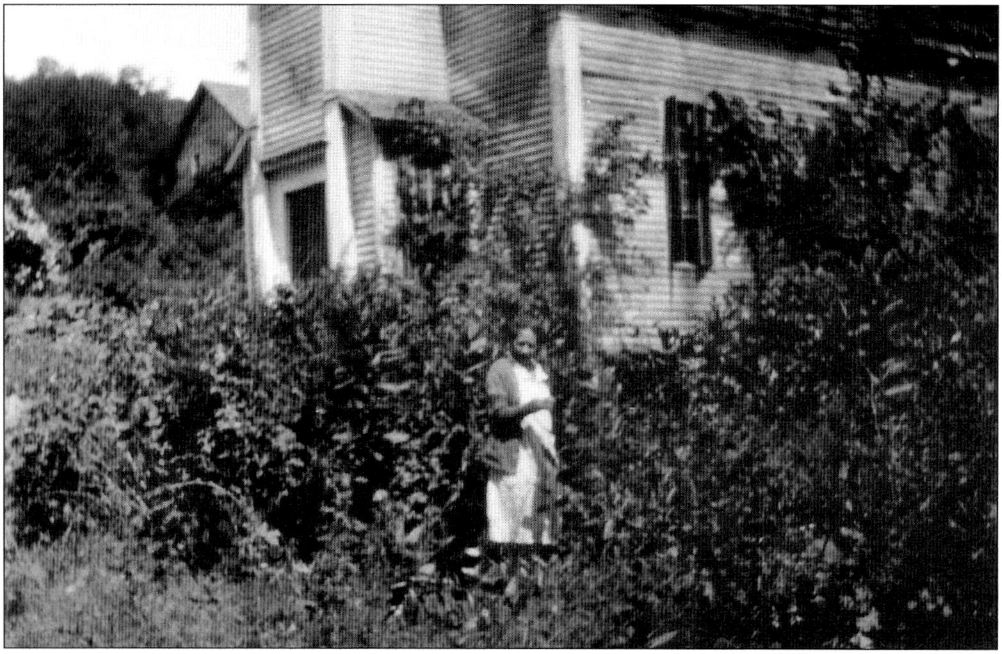

Harriet Randall stands beside the Union Church in Southville around 1930. This congregation had disbanded many years before the picture was taken. At this time, the Northrup family used the structure to store farm tools. Mrs. Randall was a fixture in Southville, her pies being so popular that people would travel for miles to buy them. (BHS.)

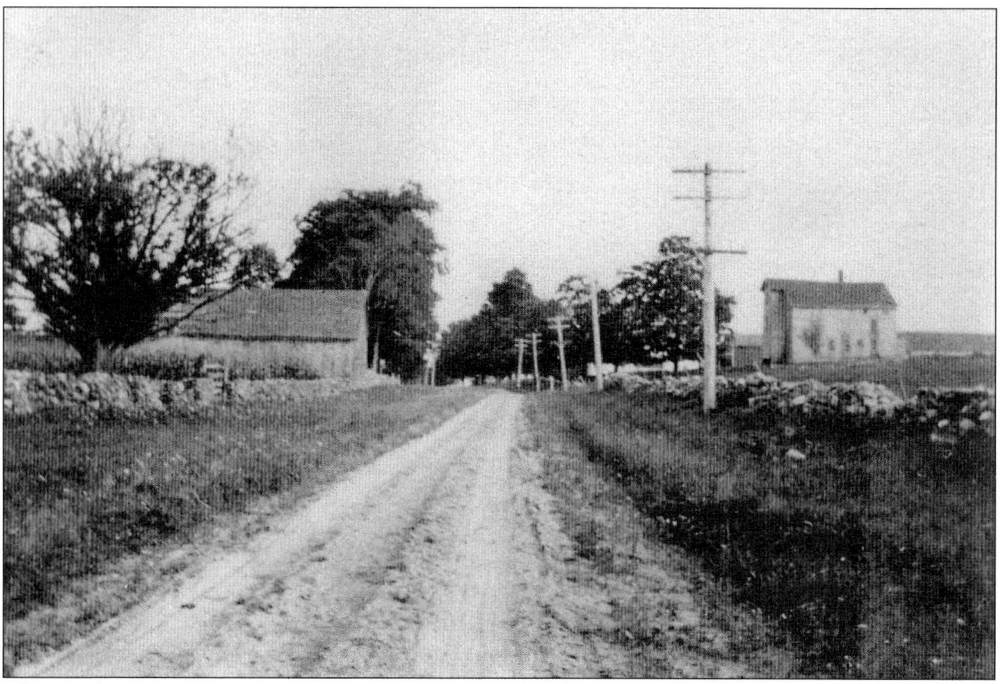

The building on the left served as a church from 1833 until 1859. It was located on Main Street South, south of Sarah Sanford Road in Bridgewater. By the time this picture was taken, it was long abandoned. It eventually burned. (BHS.)

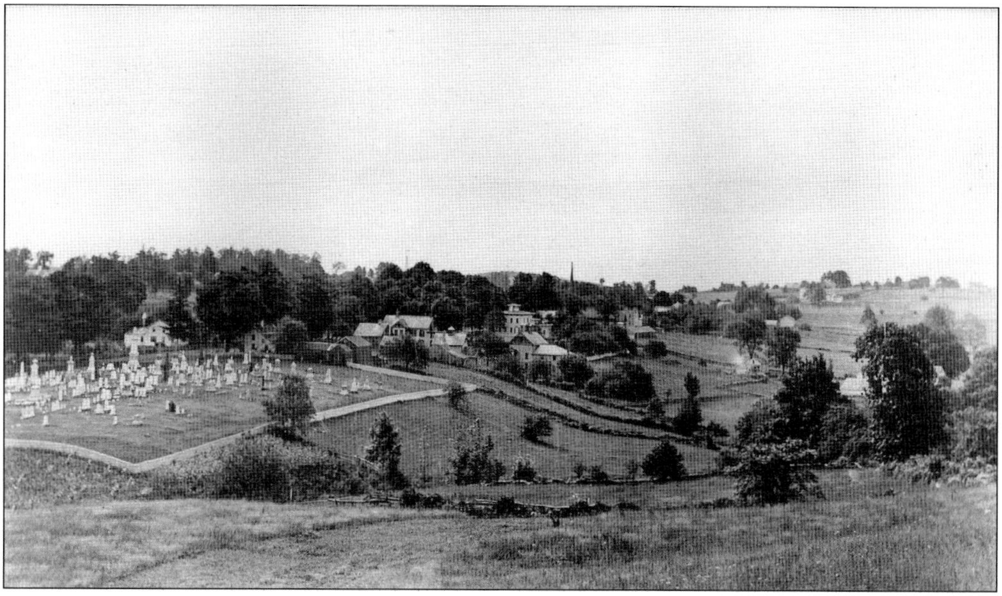

The Bridgewater Center Cemetery was established in 1824. The residents of the town requested this second burial ground because the Old South Cemetery was a distance away and, as town-owned property, it was free to all—making family plots impossible to reserve. The first burial was that of James Phippeney. Eli Sturdevant created the beautiful iron fence that surrounds the property. (BHS.)

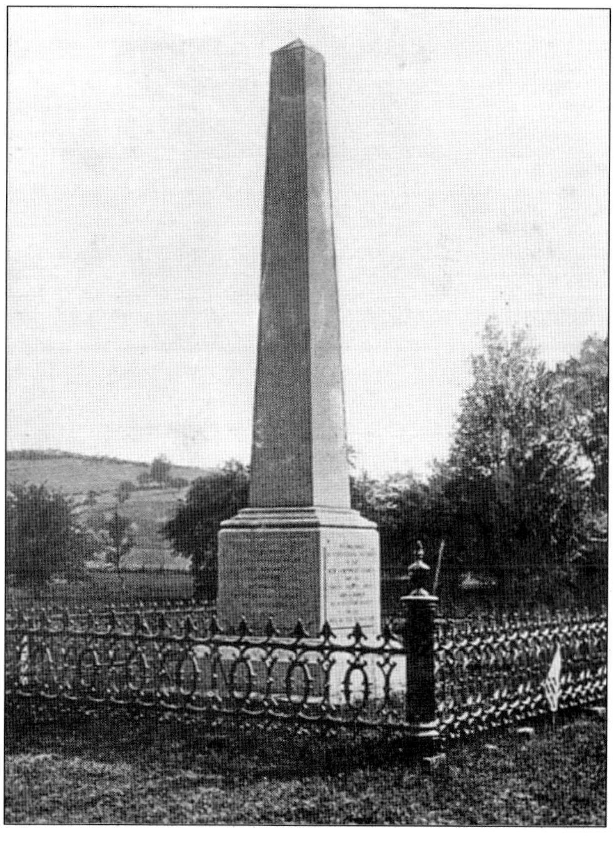

This monument honors Col. Seth Warner (1743–1784), hero of the American Revolution and leader of the Green Mountain Boys. Seventy-four years after he was buried near his home on Old Roxbury Road, his remains were moved to this monument on the town green. In 1976, Vermont promoted Warner to brigadier general to block his descendants from suing for back pay. (RM.)

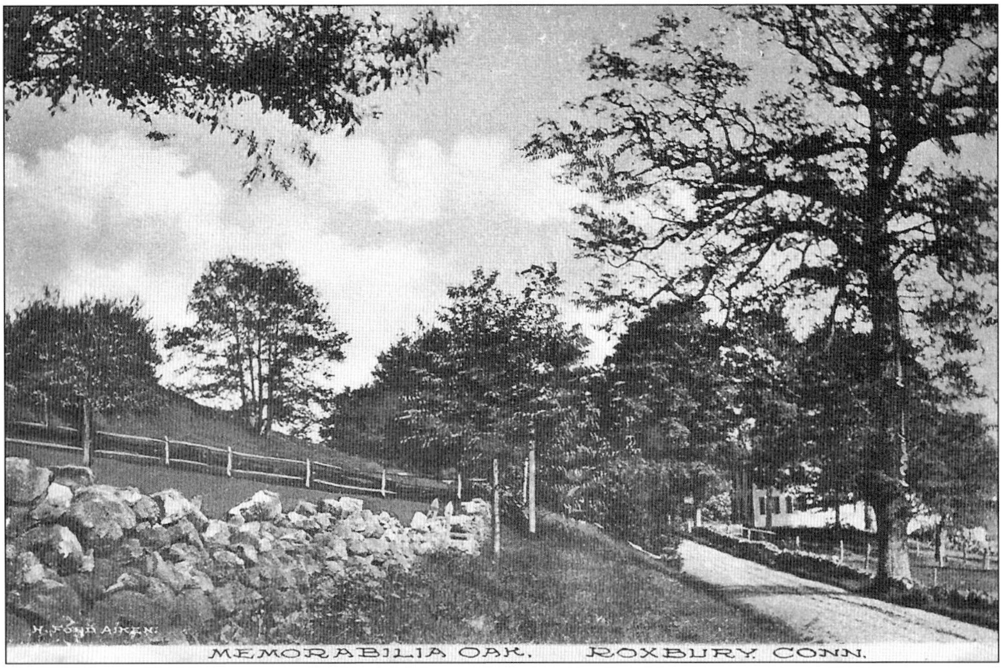

The majestic white oak, nicknamed the Memorabilia Tree, was photographed by H. Ford Aiken and made into a postcard. The gargantuan tree has stood for over 380 years and is treasured by Roxbury residents as if it were an ancestor. It can be found north of the Center Cemetery on North Street. (RM.)

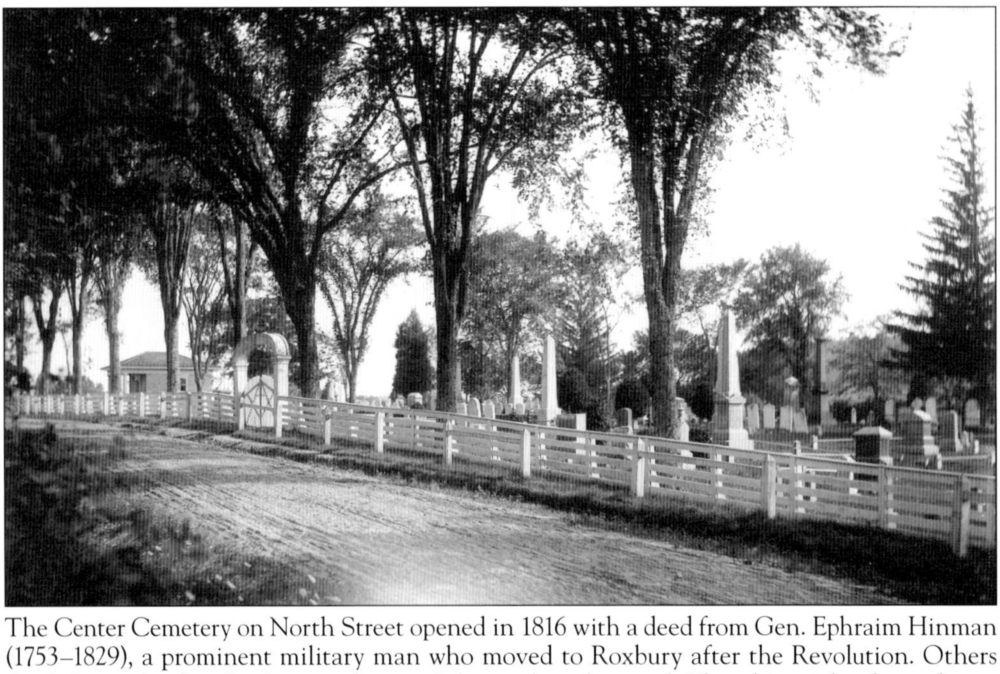

The Center Cemetery on North Street opened in 1816 with a deed from Gen. Ephraim Hinman (1753–1829), a prominent military man who moved to Roxbury after the Revolution. Others deeded more land and today it is the town's largest burial ground. The white picket fence shown in this 1905 photograph is gone now. A monument near the entrance commemorates soldiers buried here since the American Revolution. (RM.)

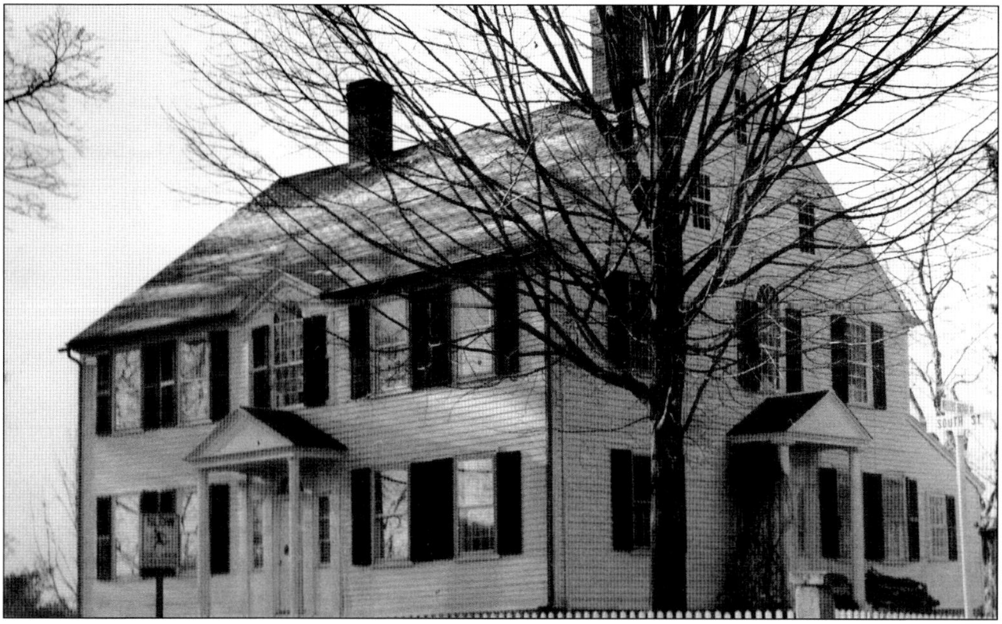

Only four families have owned the Asahel Bacon House since it was built in 1784 at 3 South Street near Roxbury center. Bacon (1764–1838) was a wealthy merchant, farmer, and landowner from Woodbury. In 1850, his grandson sold the property to George Hurlburt (1809–1904), a railroad promoter, hatter, merchant, postmaster, farmer, and soldier. The property passed through four generations of the Hurlburt family until it was sold to the current owners. (RM.)

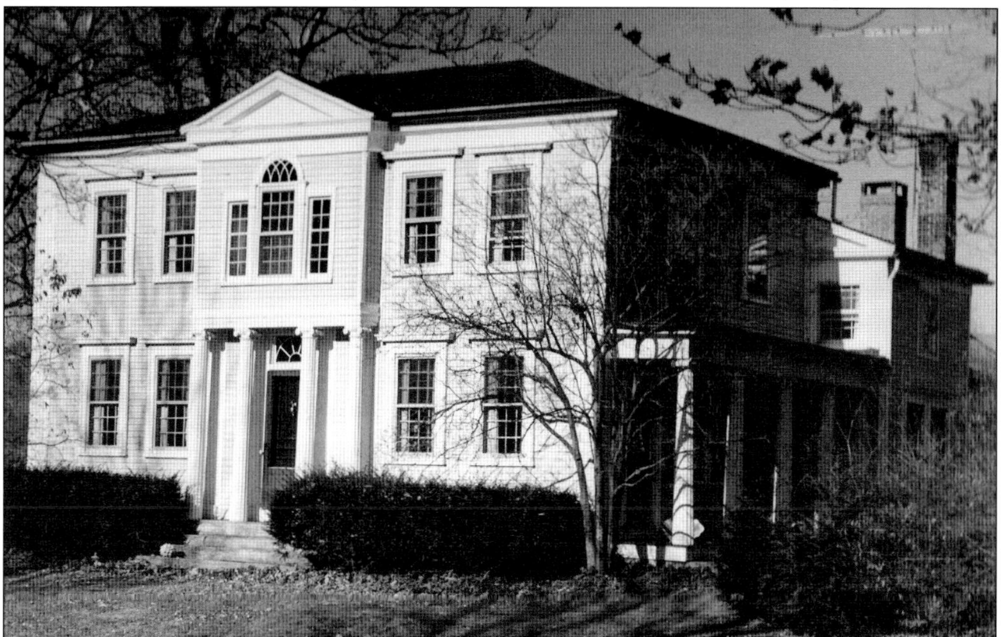

The Judge Nathan Smith House at 12 Church Street was built in 1790 by the Hon. Nathan Smith (1767–1835), a judge, senator, and member of a wealthy and prominent Connecticut family. He and his brother, Nathaniel, a superior court judge, both attended the Tapping Reeve Law School in Litchfield, Connecticut. (RM.)

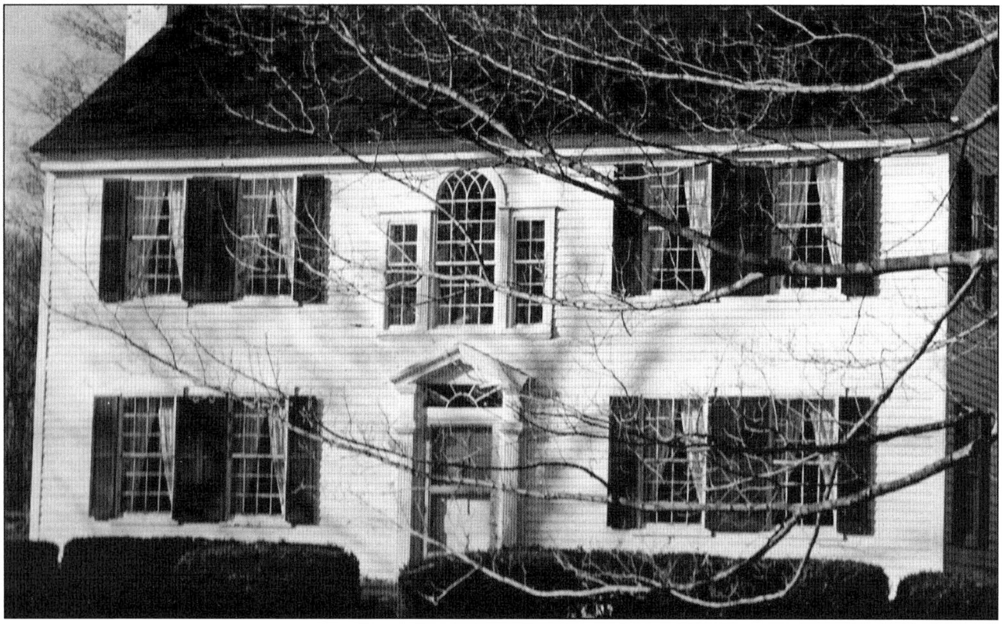

Built in 1795 by a minister of Roxbury's Congregational Church, the Rev. Zephaniah Swift House remains a fine example of Federal/Georgian-style architecture with its Palladian window over the main entrance. The well-preserved house on Chalybes Road has been home to a town clerk, state representative, a doctor, and a probate judge. In the early 1900s, it was a private boys' school; today it is a private home. (RM.)

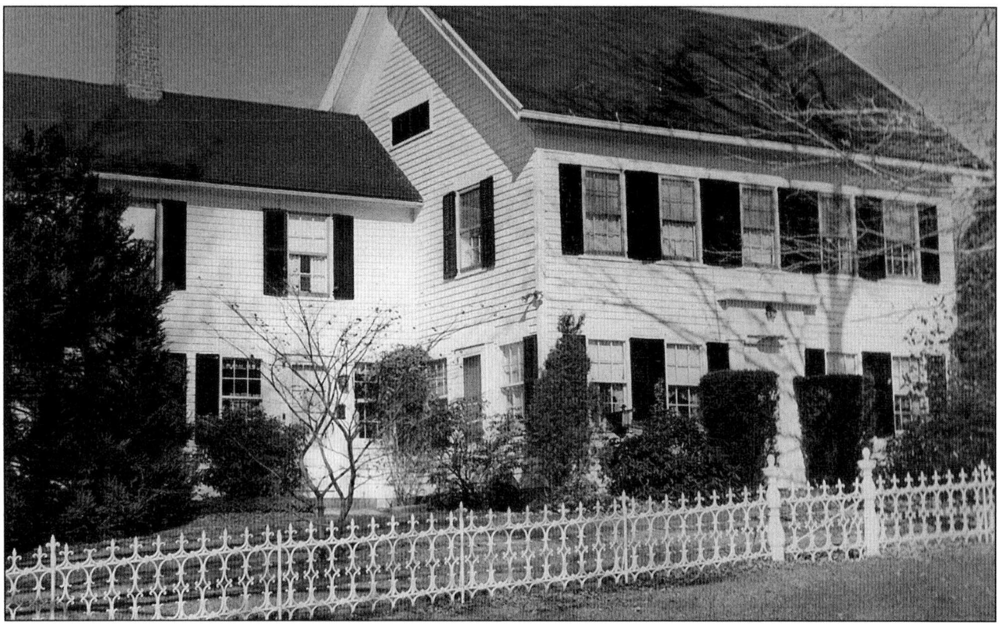

The Nathan T. Beardsley House, built around 1860, remained in the family for three generations. Nathan P. (1868–1943), a breeder of prize-winning Devon oxen, and his son, Percy P. (1891–1968), a World War I hero, were among the last of the family farmers. The two sociable men entertained such celebrities as Marilyn Monroe and Norma Talmadge, who came to taste from the Beardsley's well-known cider barrels. (RM.)

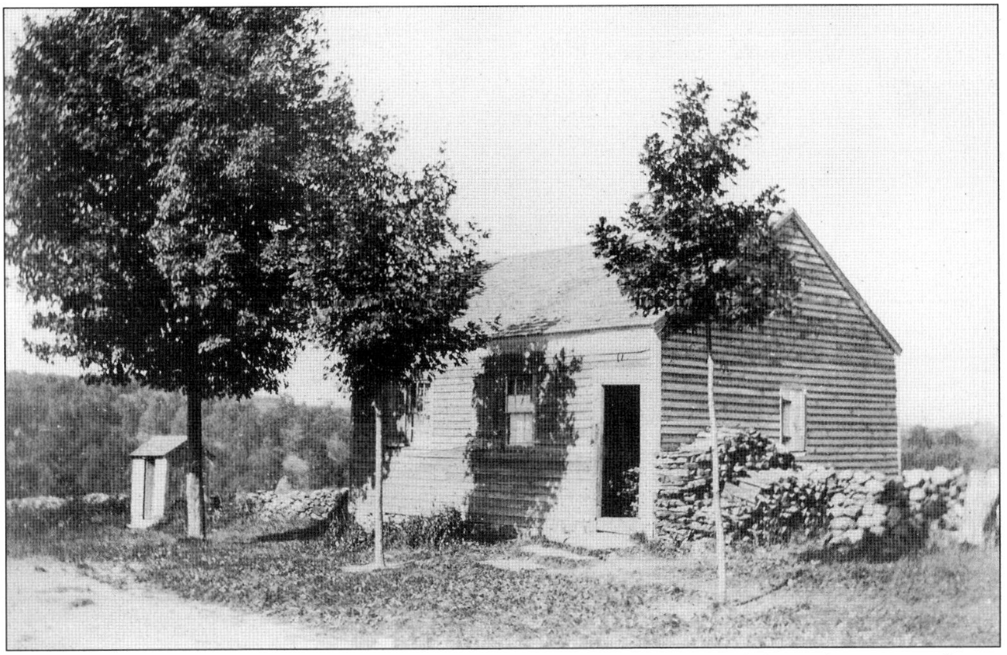

Andrew W. Gillette taught in this building, the Mallett District School, from the winter of 1879 until the summer of 1880. It was a one-room schoolhouse. At that time, seven school districts made up the town of Bridgewater. The Gillette family donated their father's, uncle's, and grandfather's photographs to the Bridgewater Historical Society in July 1931. (BHS.)

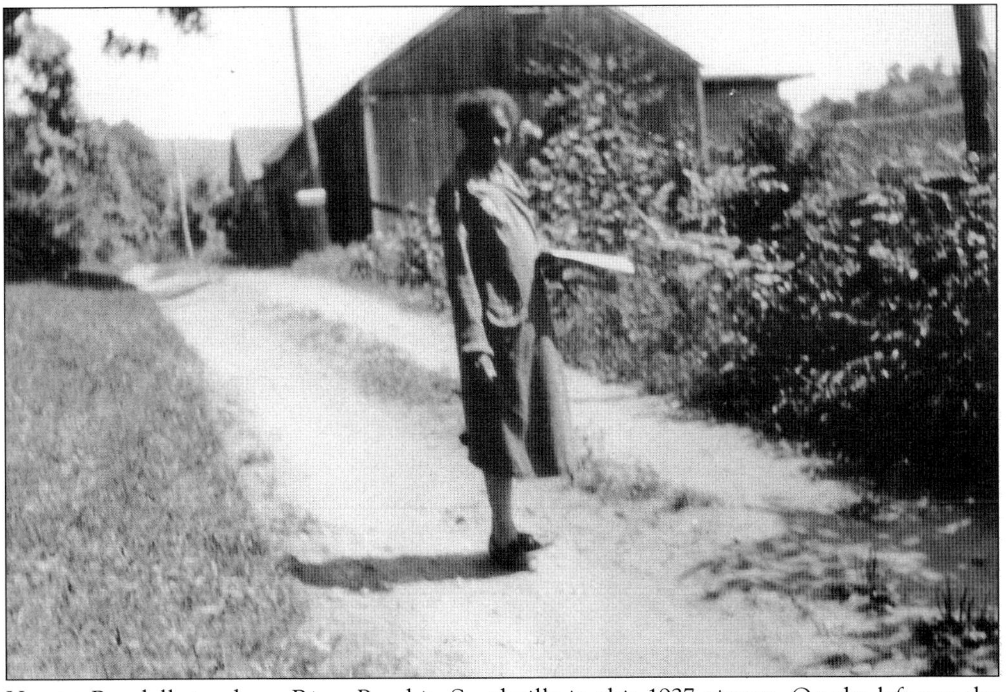

Harriet Randall stands on River Road in Southville in this 1927 picture. On the left was the abandoned Southville Schoolhouse. It was later used as an icehouse by the Northrup family. By 1923, only three families remained in Southville. (BHS.)

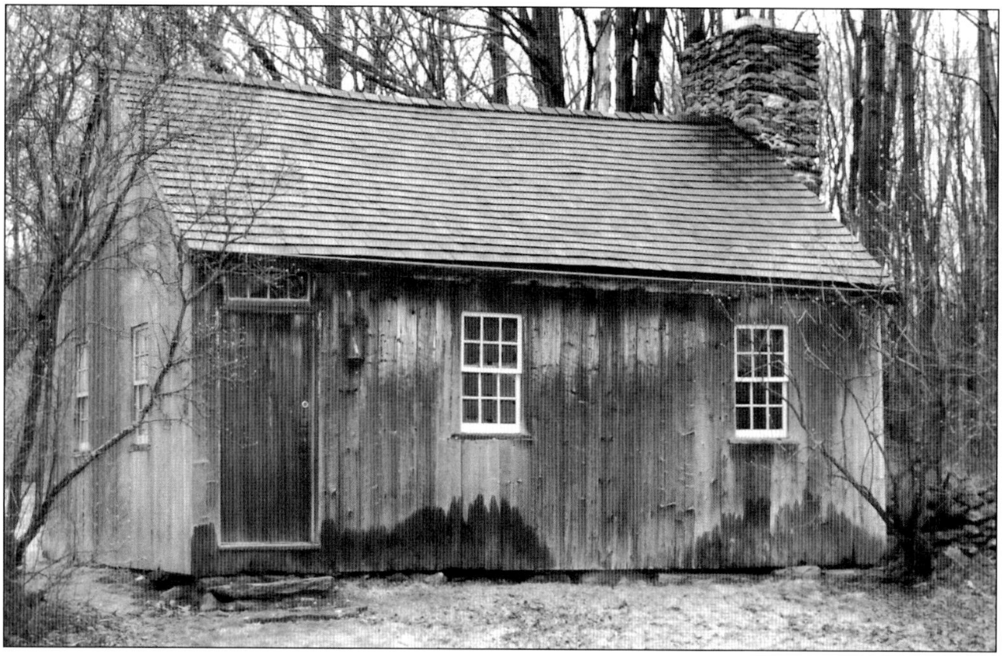

Good Hill District School No. 4 is the only remaining one-room schoolhouse in Roxbury. The sturdy-looking building was noted on an 1874 map. Today, it is part of the Widmark Preserve on Tophet Road near the corner of Schoolhouse Road. In 1977, resident actor Richard Widmark donated the building and five acres to the Roxbury Land Trust. (RLT.)

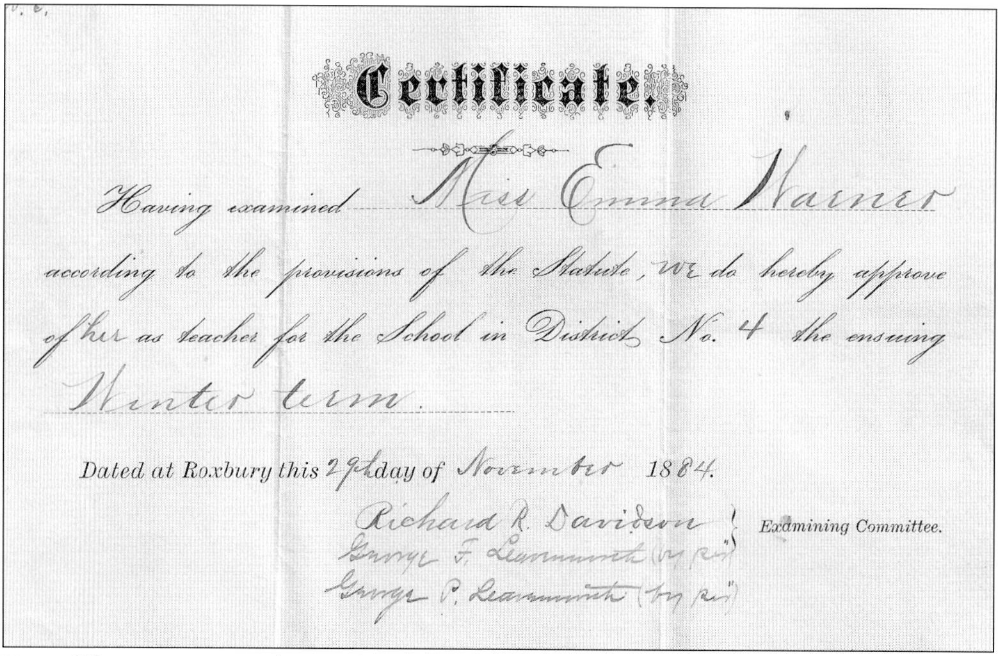

Certificate.

Having examined Miss Emma Warner according to the provisions of the Statute, we do hereby approve of her as teacher for the School in District No. 4 the ensuing Winter term.

Dated at Roxbury this 29th day of November 1884.

Richard R. Davidson
George F. Leavenworth (by R.)
George P. Leavenworth (by R.)
} Examining Committee.

Emma Warner was granted a certificate to teach third grade in Good Hill District School No. 4 during the winter term. Dated November 29, 1884, this document was signed by three members of the Examining Committee. In its earliest days, each of the town's eight school districts had its own schoolhouse, but this school is the only remaining one-room schoolhouse in Roxbury. (RM.)

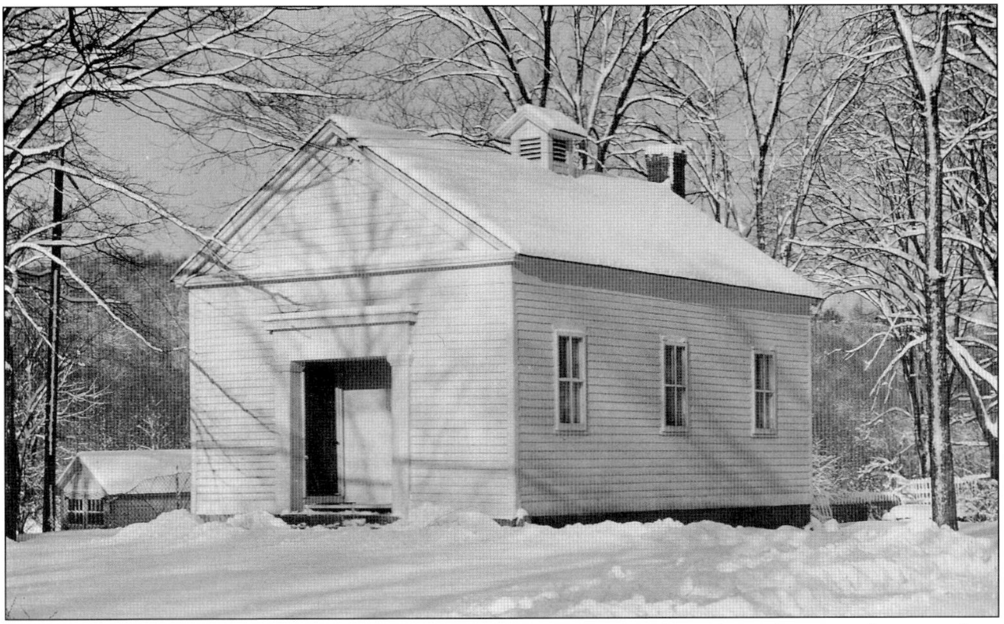

The Center School had only a small wood stove for heat when this photograph was taken in the winter of 1927. Students brought wood for the stove and the boys were expected to build a fire. The school was once opposite the Seth Warner Monument on South Street, but later moved next to the Christ Church on Wellers Bridge Road. There it stands today as the Christ Church Parish House. (RM.)

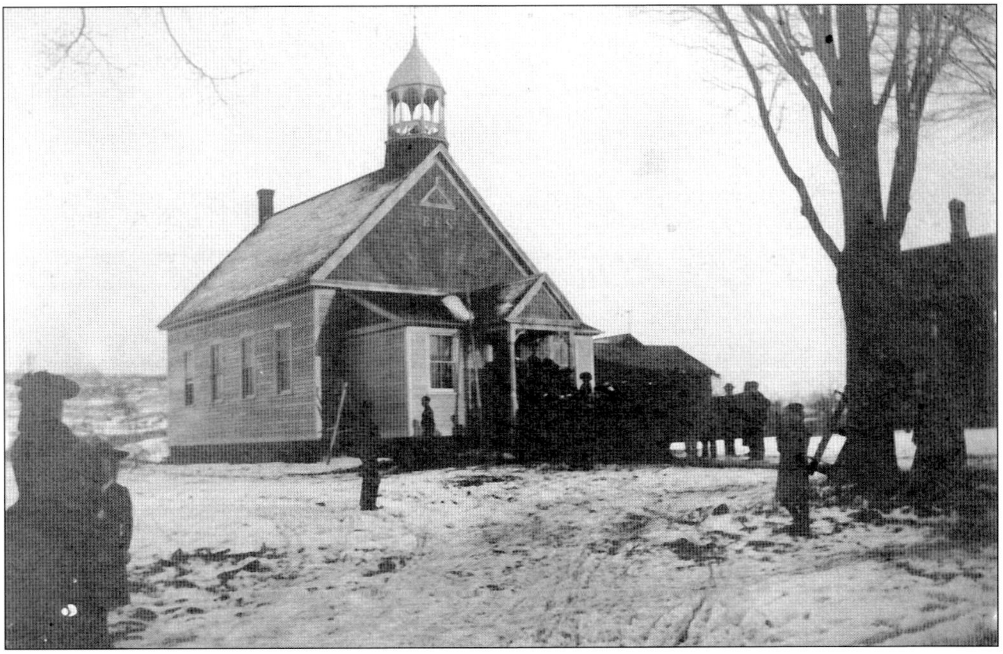

The Booth Free School was named for Hervey Minor Booth (1813–1893), its original benefactor who, in 1890, donated $10,000 to open a school in the Congregational Church Chapel. Later, students moved from the chapel to this one-room schoolhouse on South Street. This building, dated 1903, had a belfry, but no electricity, no running water, and no bathrooms. (RLT.)

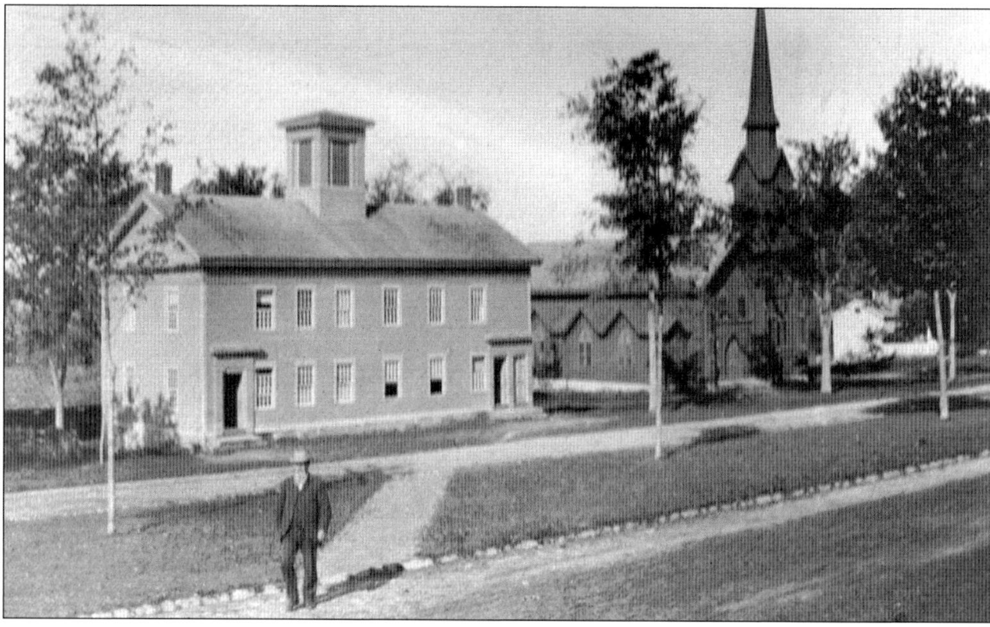

Constructed in 1854, the Grange Hall served as a Bridgewater schoolhouse until purchased in 1900. Here, a pedestrian crosses Main Street South. To his back are the Grange (left) and St. Mark's Church (right), with "The Green" behind him. The Girl Scouts planted a Christmas tree there during the Great Depression. It still graces the green today and is decorated and lit for the holidays. (BHS.)

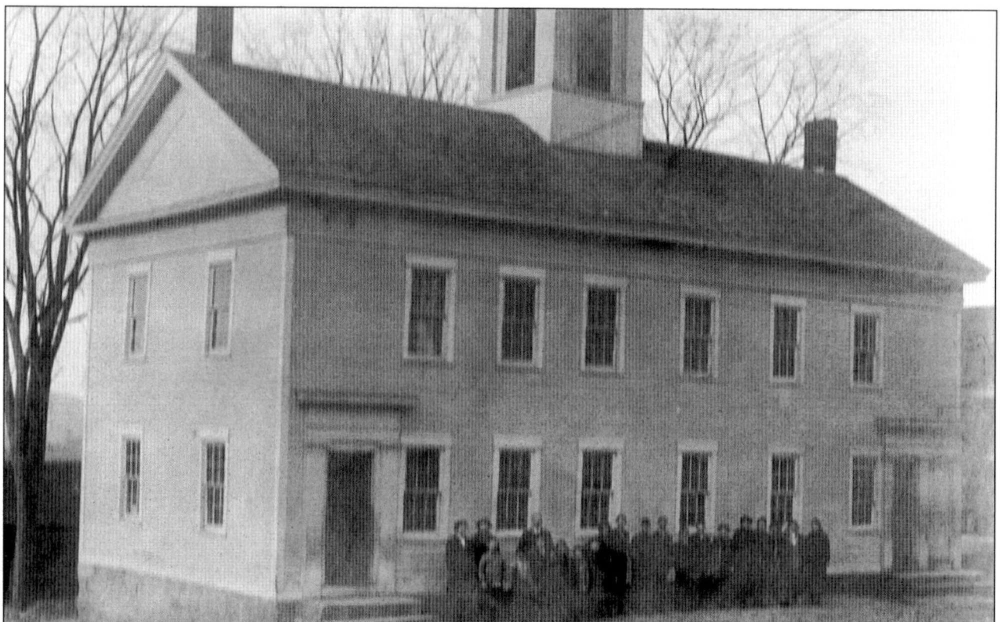

Although now known to most residents as the Grange, this building began life as a two-room schoolhouse. Eventually, the lower floor was used as a schoolroom and the upper floor as a men's club. The Town of Bridgewater also used it for meetings. It remained in use as a school until 1900, when the Grange purchased the building. In this image, the student body gathers for a group picture. (BHS.)

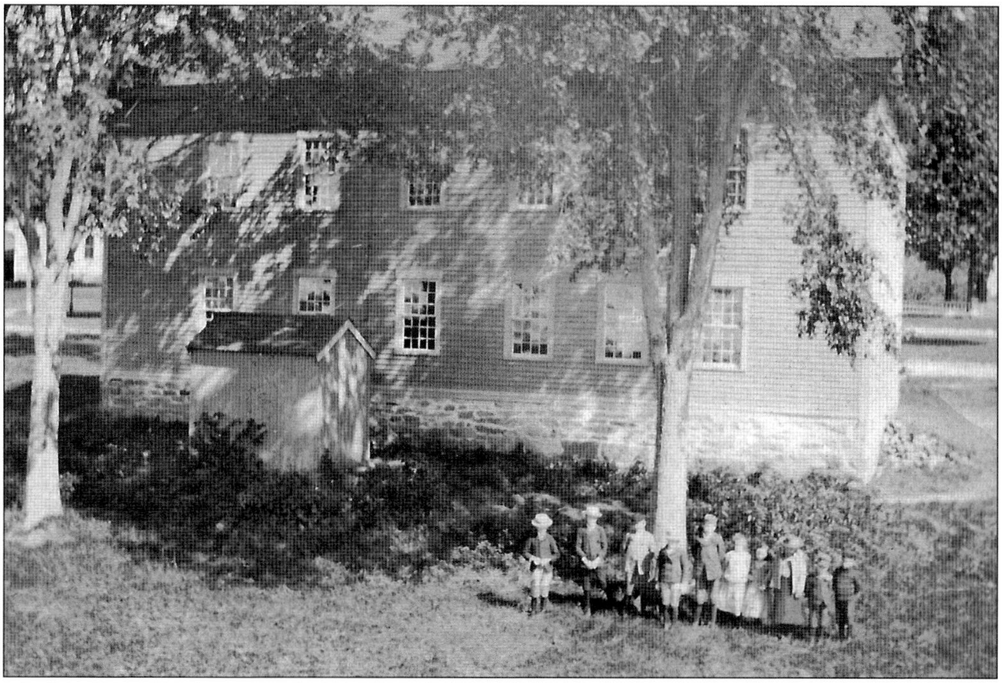

This recess-time photograph shows one of the seven groups of children who formed the student body of Bridgewater. The children stand behind the Center School on Main Street—today's Grange. (BHS.)

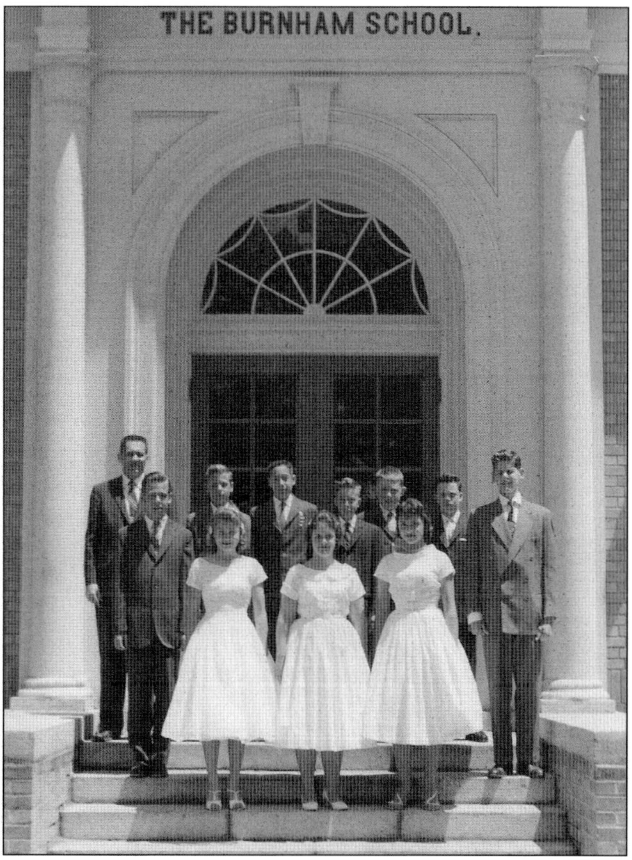

These smiling graduates stand on the steps of Burnham School in 1958. Schools from Bridgewater, Roxbury, and Washington formed Region 12. Today, a consolidated Shepaug Valley Middle School and High School is located in Washington. (Julie Stuart Seger.)

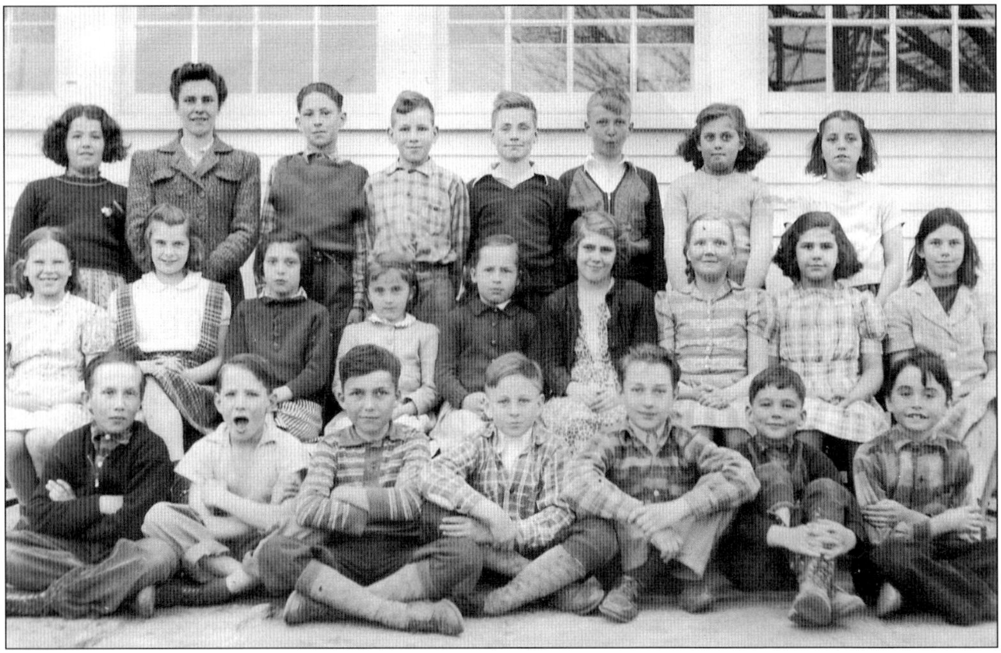

Teacher Madeline Beigneux, second from left in the back row, no doubt had her hands full with this group of Booth Free School fifth graders in 1942–1943. At the time, the school had only three classrooms for all grades. Beigneux later married Joe McGovern, a local farmer. Her sister, Adriane, became an accomplished portrait artist and still lives in Connecticut. (RM.)

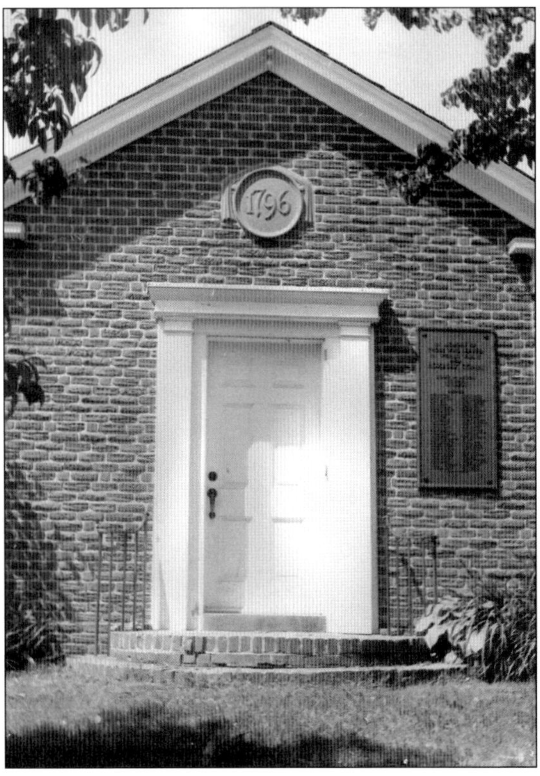

When a fire raged in the Old Town Hall, volunteers grabbed buckets of water and doused the flames. Afterwards, Roxbury officials realized that all the town's records could have burned. Herman Beardsley, a cattle farmer, and First Selectman Allen S. Hurlburt donated money and land to build this brick fireproof hall of records. Today, as the Roxbury Museum, it houses a collection of photographs, artifacts, and memorabilia. (HMLM.)

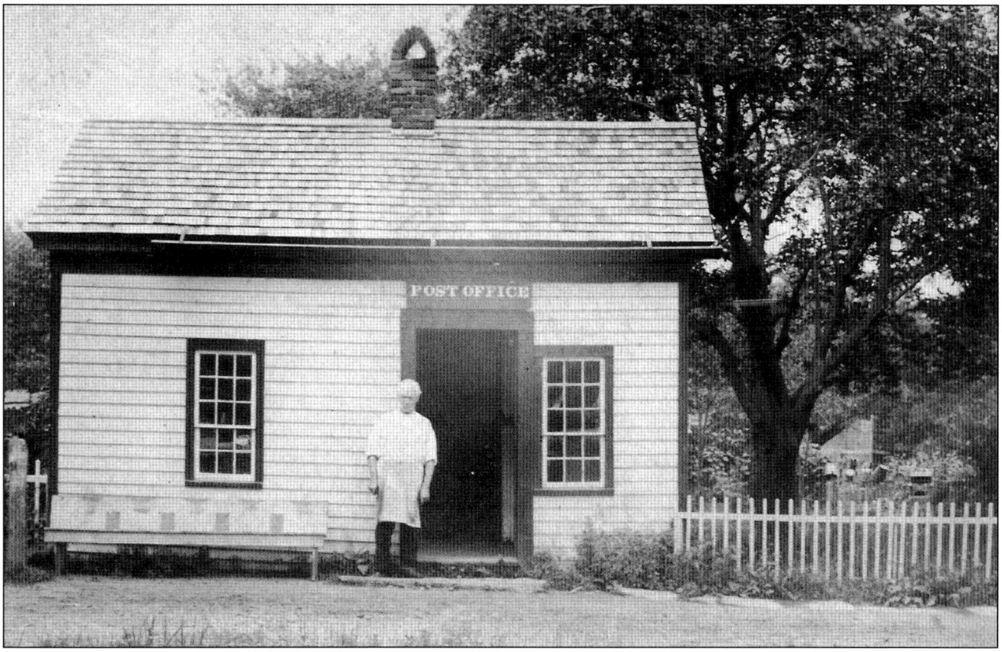

The Bridgewater Post Office on Main Street was a meeting place for many years. The walk to get the mail became a social event, catching up with the local news and getting letters from loved ones who were too far away to see frequently. A post card was found sent from one lady in the north end of town to another in the south. (BHS.)

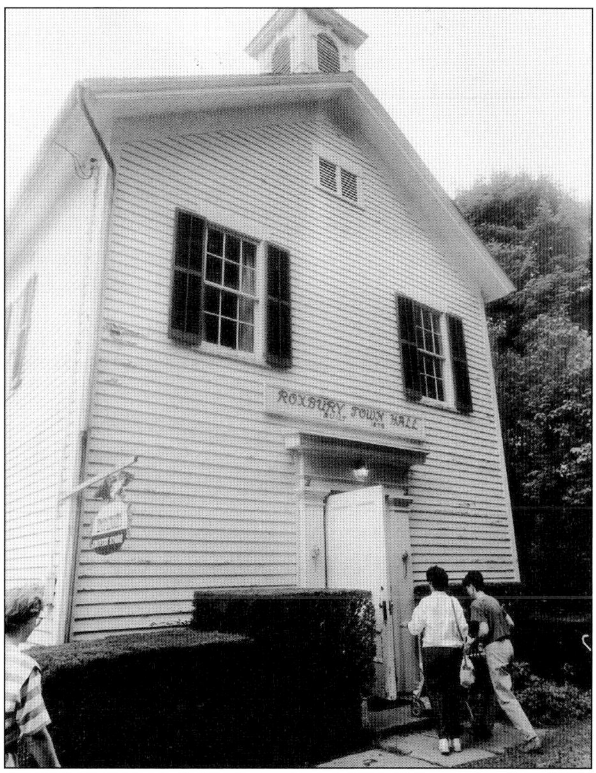

The Old Town Hall became a country store during an Old Roxbury Days celebration. During its renovation in 2004, men jacked the building eight feet off the ground and built a new foundation to replace the 100-year-old stone sill. A state grant, secured by the town, funded the preservation and renovation of this historic building. Today, it is a modern center for seniors and land trust offices. (RM.)

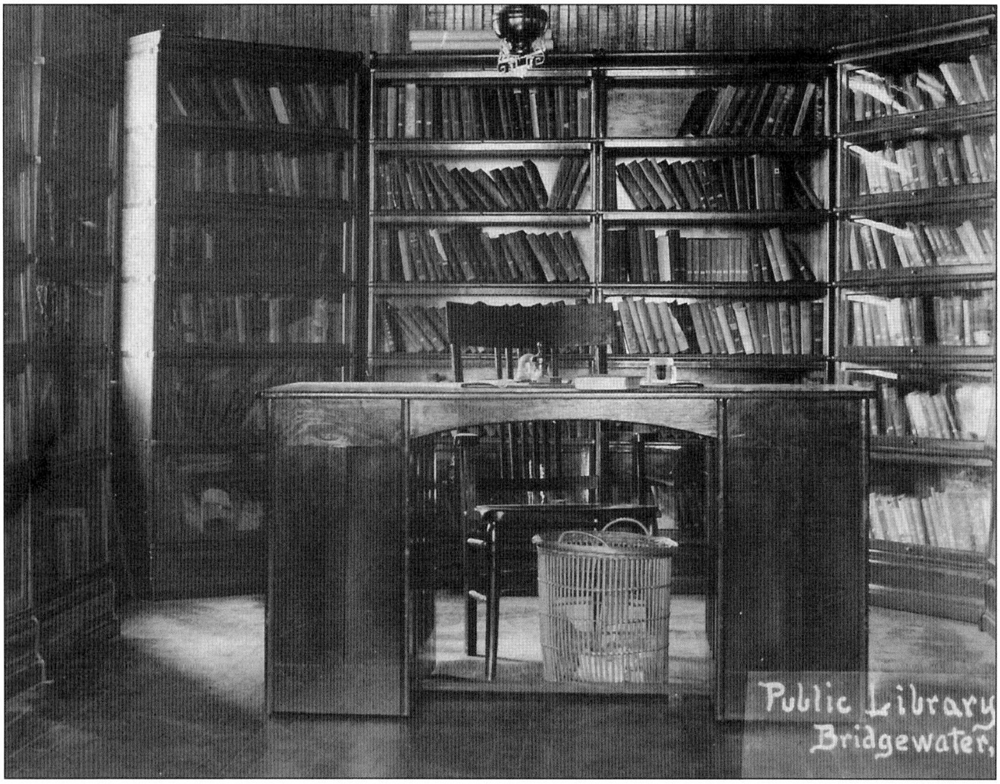

Prior to 1904, there was no public library in Bridgewater. Capt. Nathaniel Randall shared his own private collection of books with friends and neighbors. Each church had books that were circulated. Finally, in 1904, a grant from the Connecticut State Library Bureau allowed a library room to be set aside in the town hall. The current library was dedicated in 1926, a result of a bequest from Capt. William Burnham. (BHS.)

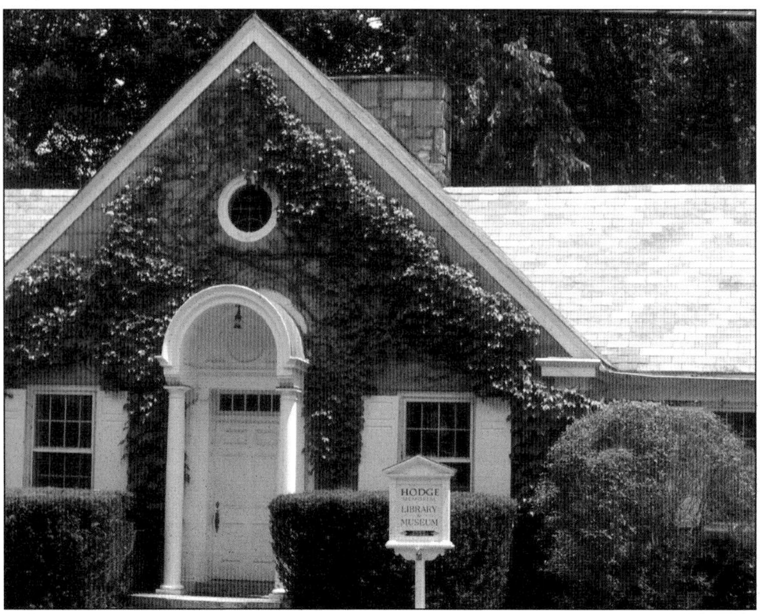

The Hodge Memorial Library and Museum, built in 1937, is now a museum. Roxbury's first libraries were in a general store and the town hall until Charles Watson Hodge (1856–1963), a prominent Roxbury benefactor, left funds for a library to be built in memory of his father, Albert Lafayette Hodge (1822–1920). He specified that builders use stone from Mine Hill. (HMLM.)

Four

FARMING

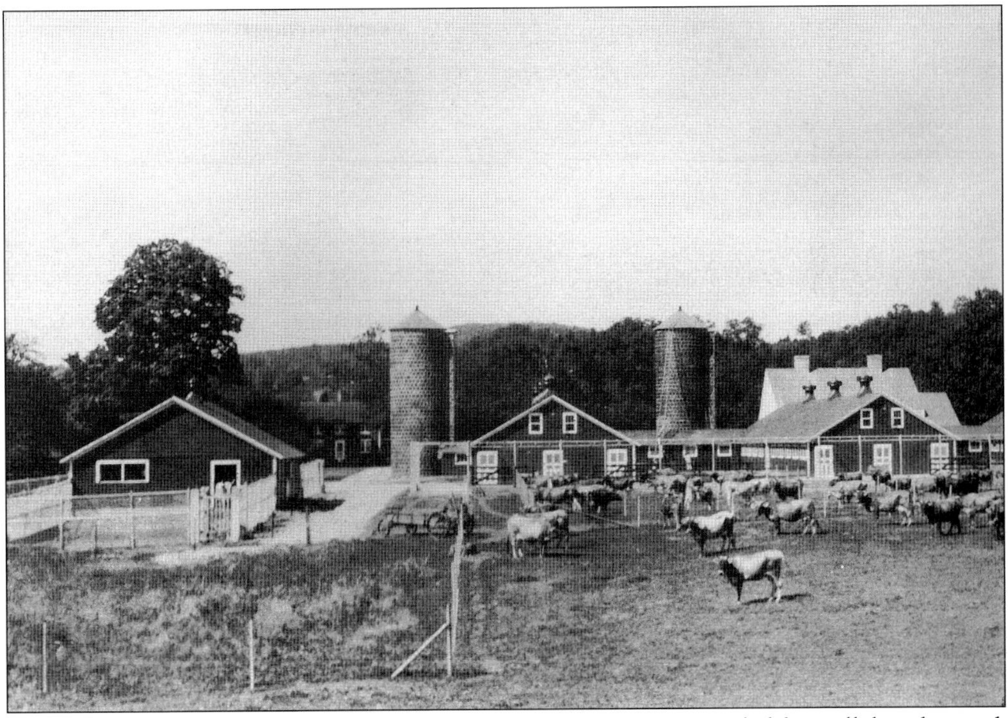

A brochure promoting Judd's Bridge Farms said it was "completely guarded from all dirt, dust and other city impurities. No hard surfaced road comes within two miles of the farm. A wall of staunch, heavily wooded hills insures the absolute cleanliness of the very air itself. The purest of water, so important to a dairy, comes from the finest possible sources—artesian well and springs." (RM.)

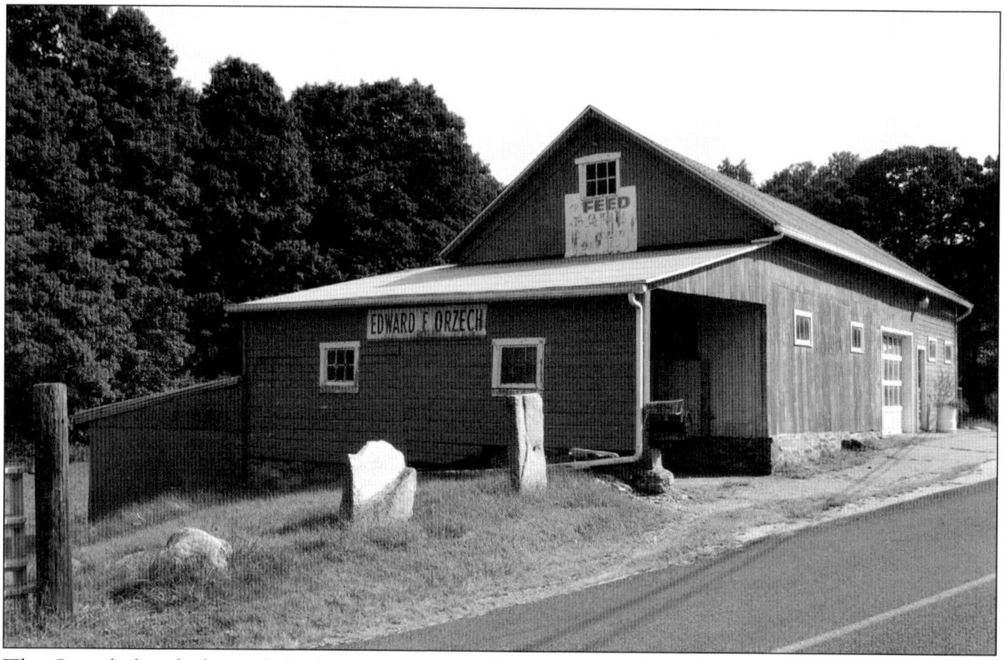

The Orzech family farmed the land and operated a dairy farm from 1927 until 2008. The Roxbury Creamery bottled their milk and shipped it to New York City. Before he died in 2008, the last owner, Edward Orzech, sold most of his land to the Roxbury Land Trust, keeping 30 acres to grow corn and operate a feed and farm supply store out of his bright blue barns. (Jeannine Green.)

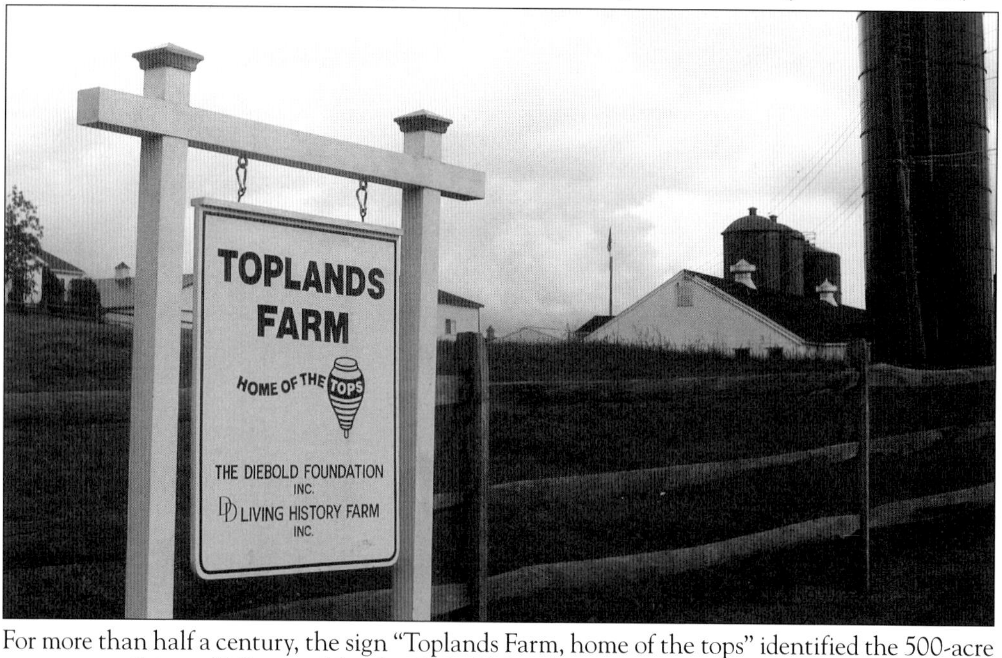

For more than half a century, the sign "Toplands Farm, home of the tops" identified the 500-acre property on Painter Hill owned by the Diebold family. In 2008, the family added The Diebold Foundation and DD Living History Farm. Today, barns house a collection of antique tractors and agricultural farm implements from the Roxbury Historical Society, and the fields are dotted with donkeys, chickens, goats, and Scottish Highland cattle. (Jeannine Green.)

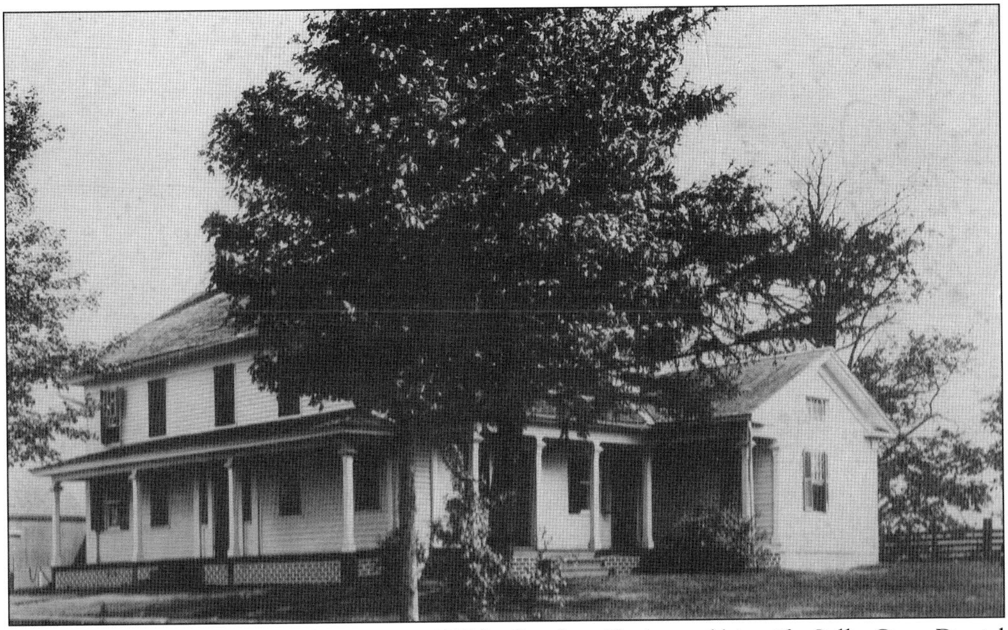

Hilltop Farm was built in Bridgewater in 1813 by Stephen Keeler and his wife, Sally. Capt. Daniel Keeler, his son, added to the property. By 1849, his farm was so successful that it won "Best Farm" in Litchfield County. The Keelers had extensive real estate holdings. Keeler Road was named for them. Their home, "Nine Hearths," on Keeler Road, was purchased by Daniel's brother, Hiram, in 1856. (BHS.)

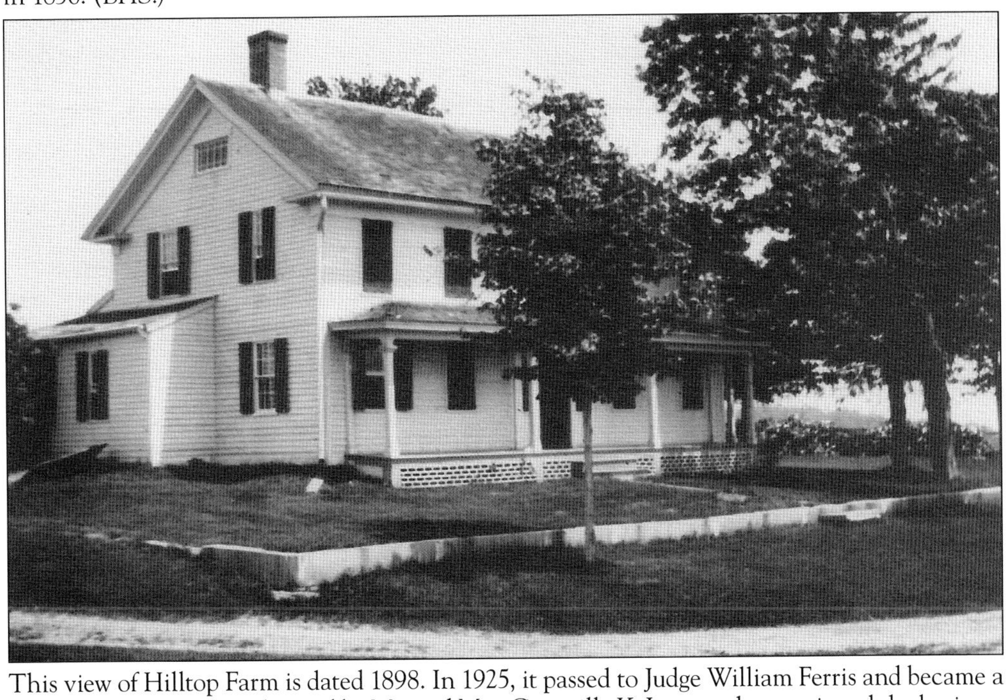

This view of Hilltop Farm is dated 1898. In 1925, it passed to Judge William Ferris and became a boardinghouse. It was inherited by Mr. and Mrs. Granville K. Lester, who continued the business as a "country inn." It subsequently became a health facility under two owners and, finally, was transformed into the Bridgewater Senior Center. (BHS.)

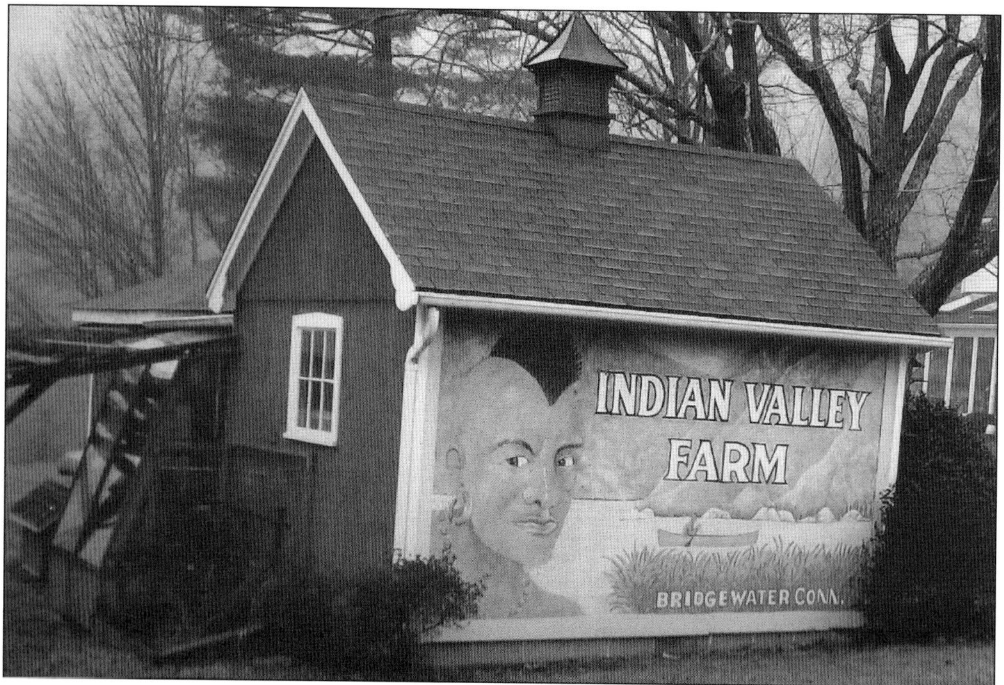

Indian Valley Farm in Bridgewater remains much as seen in this photograph. Behind these buildings lies Lake Lillinonah. The "new" street, Lillinonah Lake Road, constructed at the time of the flooding of the Housatonic River, is behind the photographer. (Dan Coppolo.)

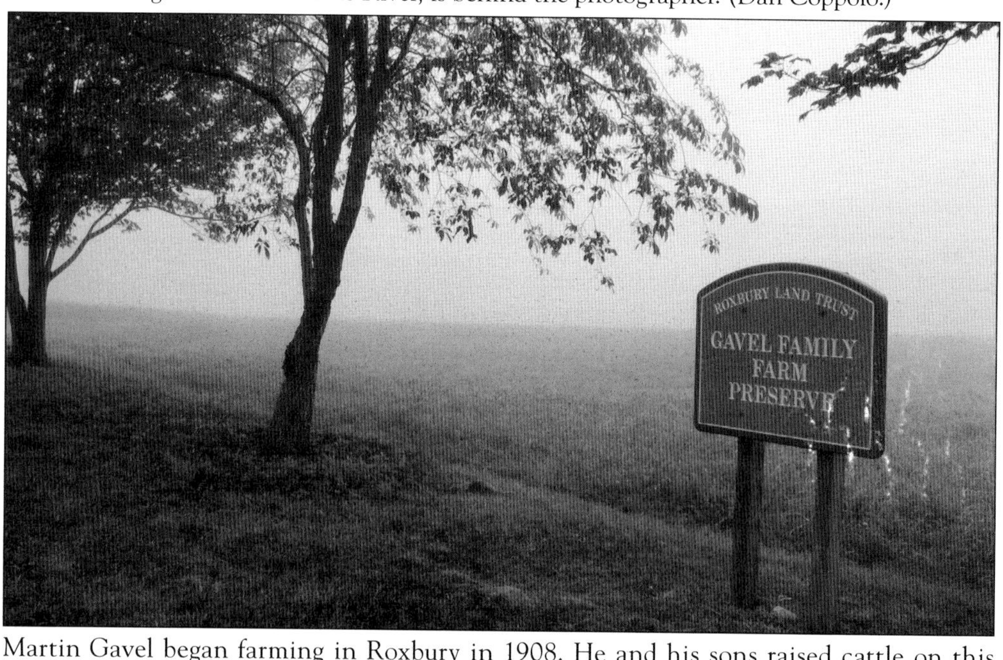

Martin Gavel began farming in Roxbury in 1908. He and his sons raised cattle on this land, and his sons, Frank and Henry, delighted neighbors when they hopped on their motorcycles and headed across the fields to round up the herd. In 2001, the 200-acre stretch became a Roxbury Land Trust preserve, ensuring that this parcel of earth will remain farmland until the end of time. (Jeannine Green.)

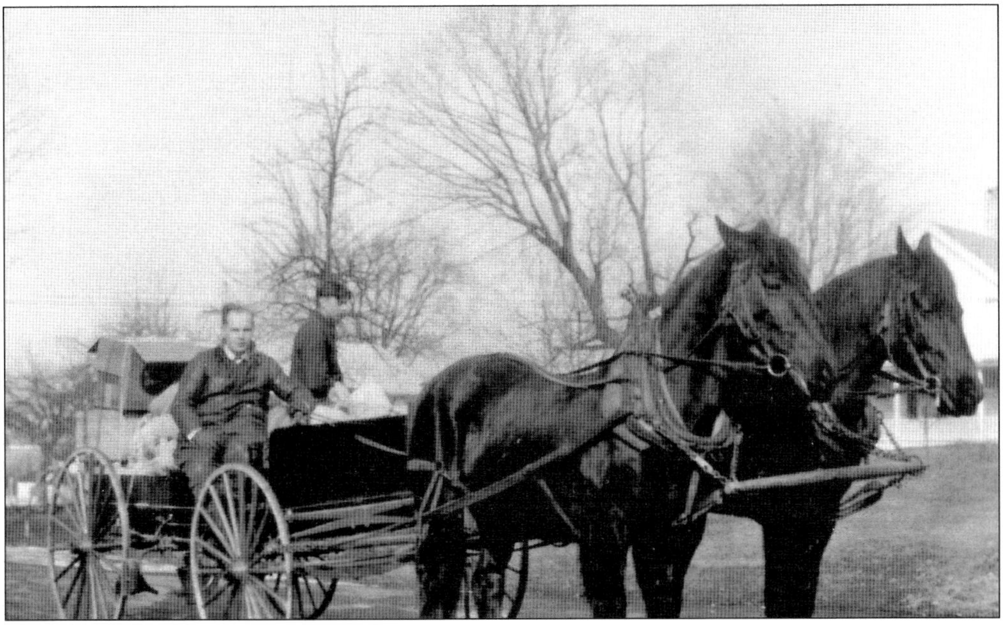

Workhorses on farms were used during the 1920s and 1930s to pull heavy loads. Two men in a cart drawn by two horses have a full wagon that must have been a heavy load, since each horse is wearing a collar to distribute the weight around its neck and shoulders. By the 1940s, tractors were used on farms, and many workhorses lost their jobs. (MML.)

A bearded man with a woman and small child are atop a horse-drawn wagon filled with hay. A couple and another woman stand next to the wagon. The man is in work clothes, and has his arm around the waist of a woman dressed in finer clothes. The woman on the right poses in a long gown with a belt and a ribbon. (Cathleen Hurlbut Bronson.)

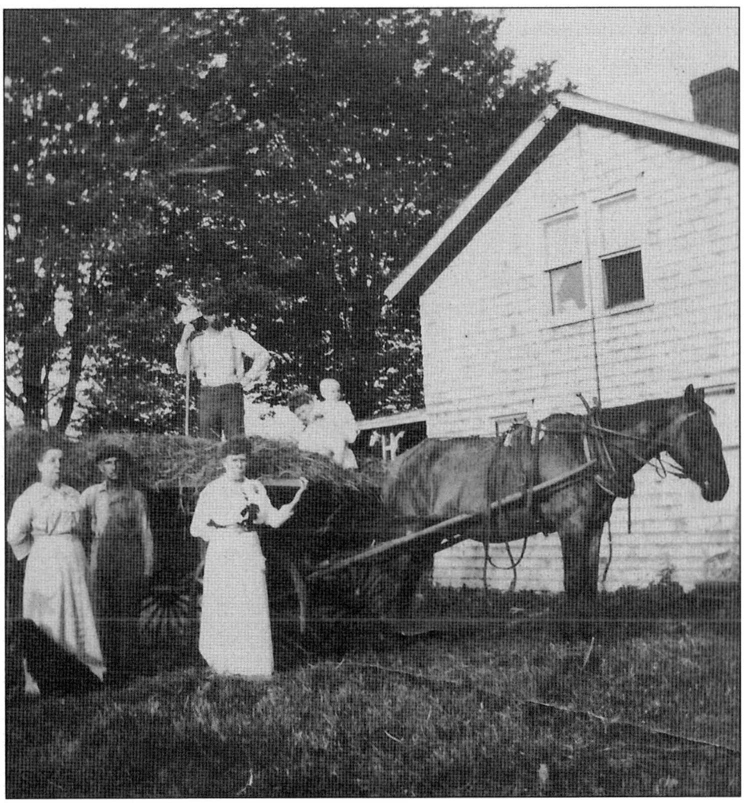

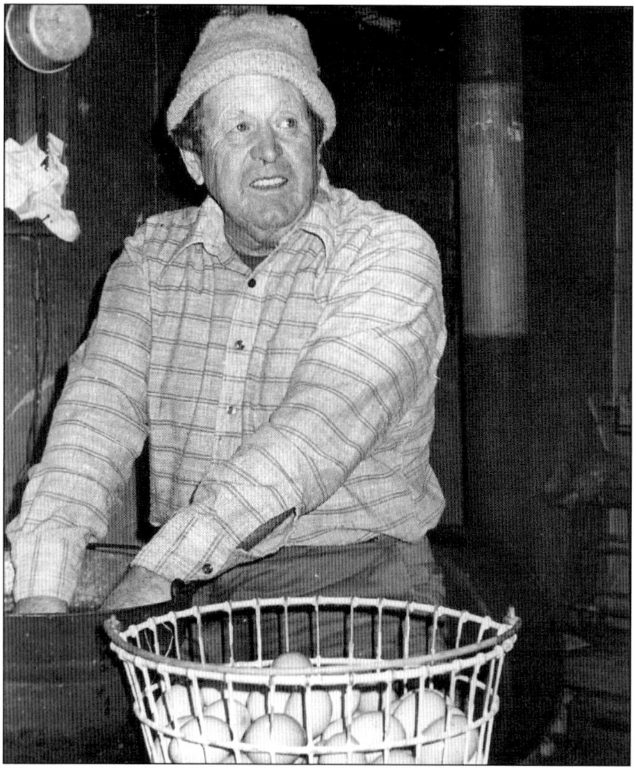

Lewis Elmer Hurlbut (1909–1992) raised over 3,000 chickens and operated a farm stand known as Maple Bank Farm. He owned the only farm in Connecticut that has been in continuous operation since the 1700s. It started as a six-acre land grant from an English king and grew to over 150 acres. This photograph by Laura Booth is dated October 6, 1981. (Cathleen Hurlbut Bronson.)

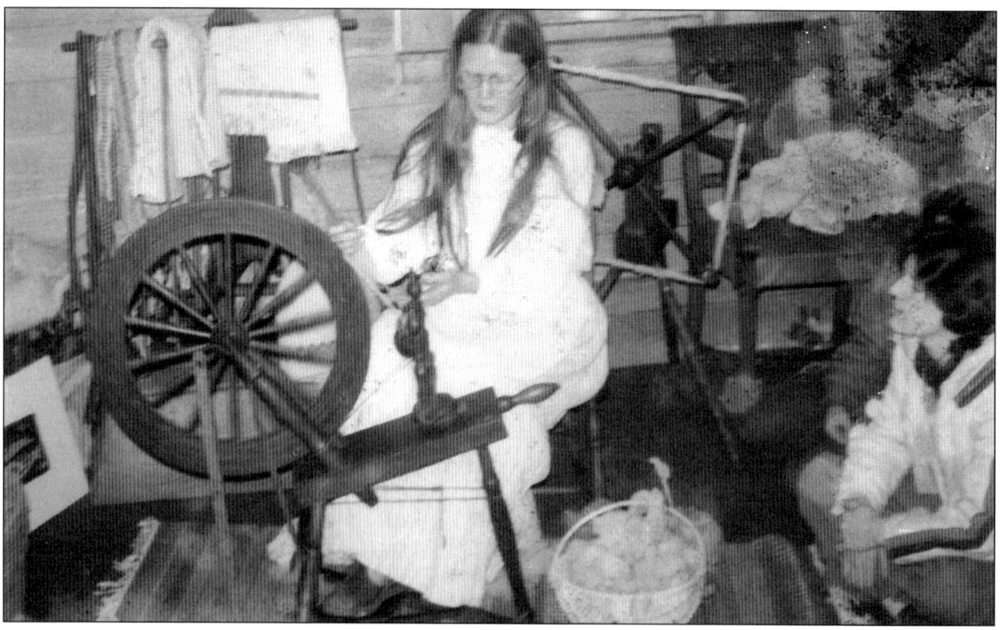

Spinning is a ballet of hand-and-eye coordination carefully feeding fibers to be spun into thread. The musical hum and buzz of the spinning wheel have disappeared from today's households, but in this undated photograph, Cathy Bronson of Roxbury, dressed in the traditional long gown of Colonial women, demonstrates her skills at a museum in Washington, Connecticut. (Cathleen Hurlbut Bronson.)

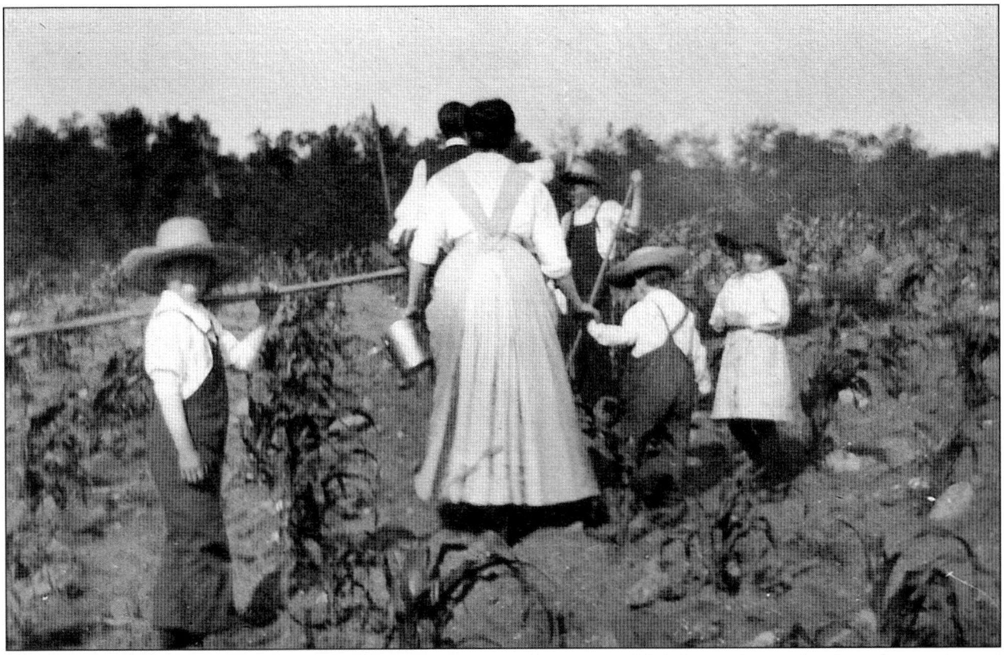

In this undated photograph, a family sets out to tend a cornfield. The father is leading his wife and family to the fields. He appears to be wearing a vest; the woman is wearing a long dress. Both are hatless. The boys are dressed in overalls and hats, and they carry tools. The mother carries a pail, possibly for water, and is prepared to look after the younger children. (Cathleen Hurlbut Bronson.)

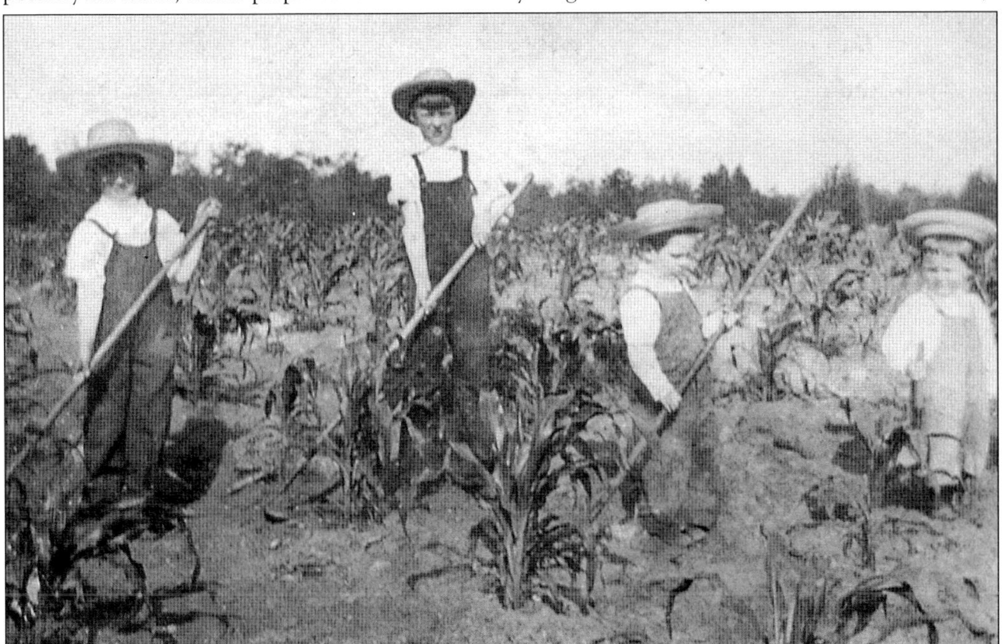

Everyone pitches in when it comes to farm work. The young farmers in this photograph, taken around 1914 are, from left to right, Harry Wilkinson, Henry Hurlbut, Lewis Hurlbut, and Alden Hurlbut. Dressed in work clothes and broad-brimmed hats, they do their part by hoeing, digging, and picking in their family's Roxbury corn field. (Cathleen Hurlbut Bronson.)

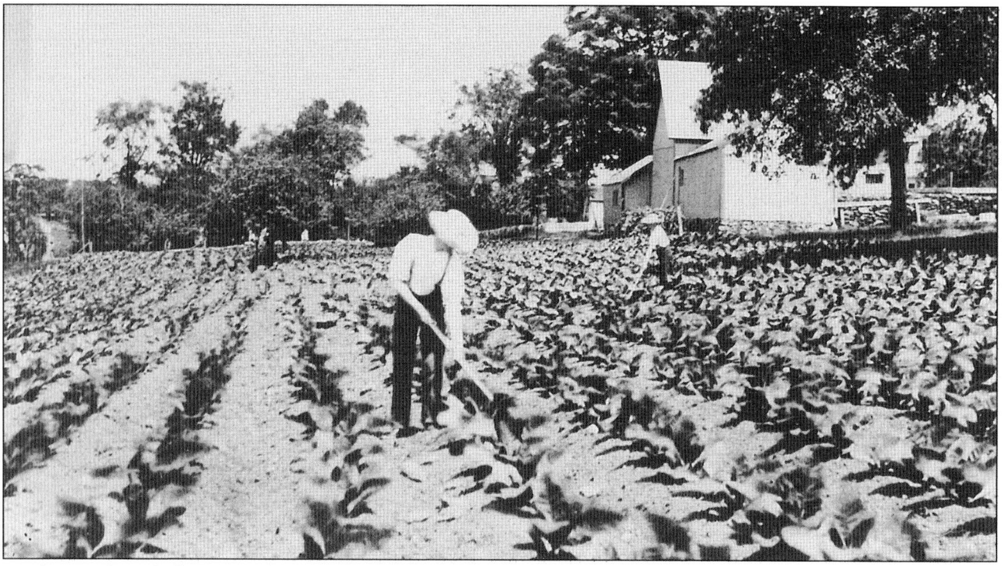

In this undated photograph, a man in work clothes and a broad-brimmed hat hoes rows of tobacco plants in a field on South Street. Tobacco was such a lucrative business that, in 1878, a local newspaper reported that Roxbury had produced nearly $30,000 worth in the previous season. Locally grown tobacco was of a fine quality and was used to wrap cigars, not the shade-grown crop seen in other parts of the state. (RLT.)

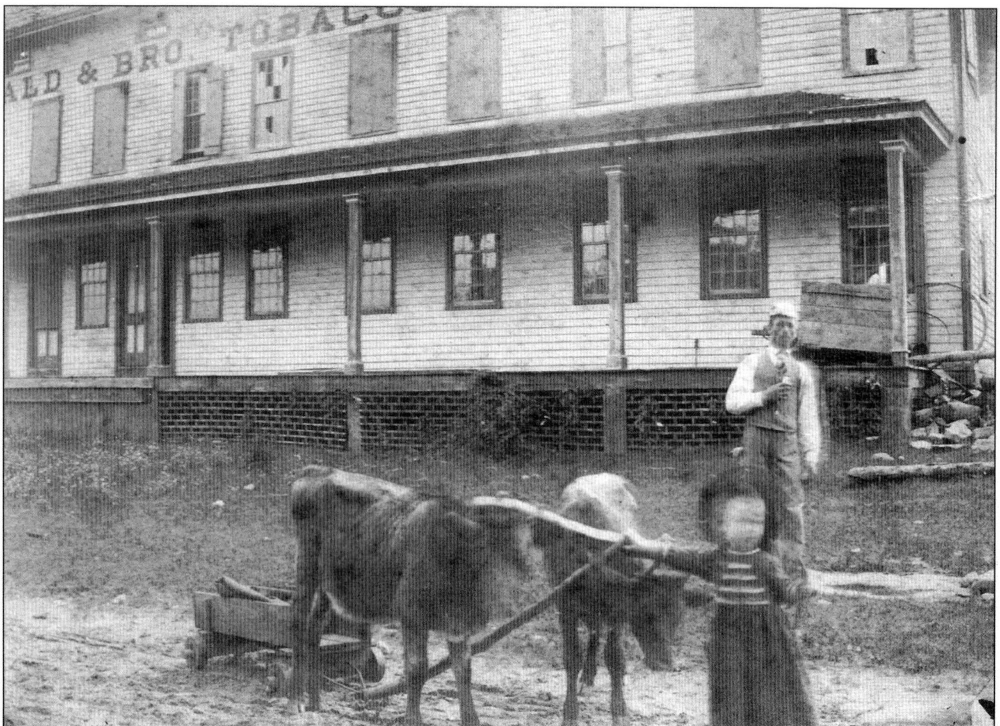

Young William S. Carlisle is pictured leading his yoke of baby oxen while his father looks on. The building pictured was the Rosenwald Tobacco Warehouse on Clapboard Road between Keeler Road and Route 67 in Bridgewater. It was one of three warehouses owned by Edward Rosenwald and family. (BHS.)

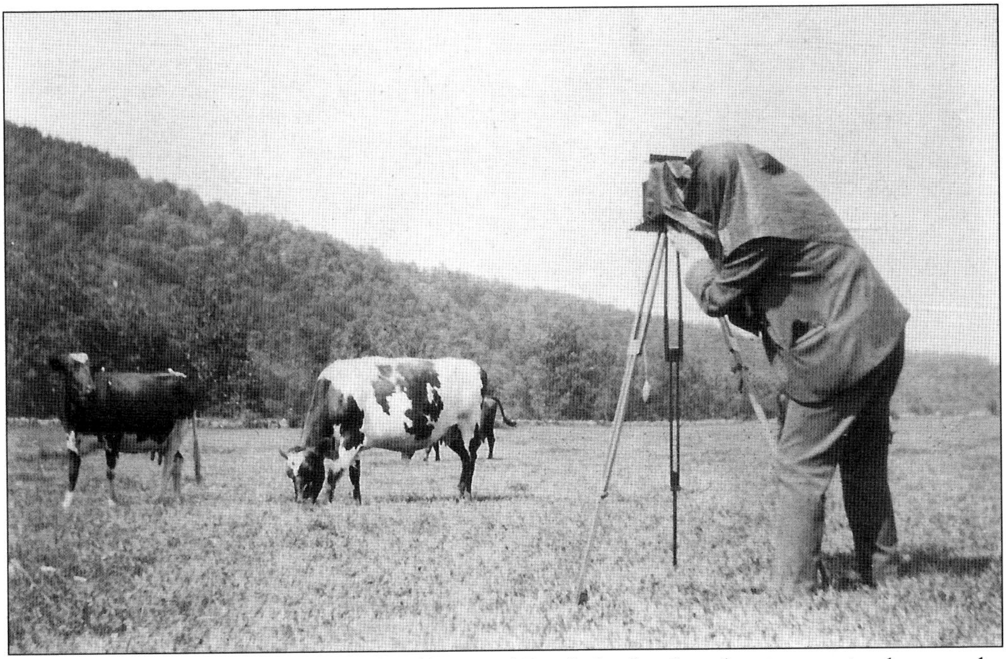

Austin H. Gillette's sons, Andrew W. Gillette and Frank A., developed an interest in photography in the late 1800s—a rather expensive hobby at the time. Their pictures of Bridgewater and Roxbury give residents today a time capsule of the way the towns were. Here, the caption reads, "The Photographer Photographed." (BHS.)

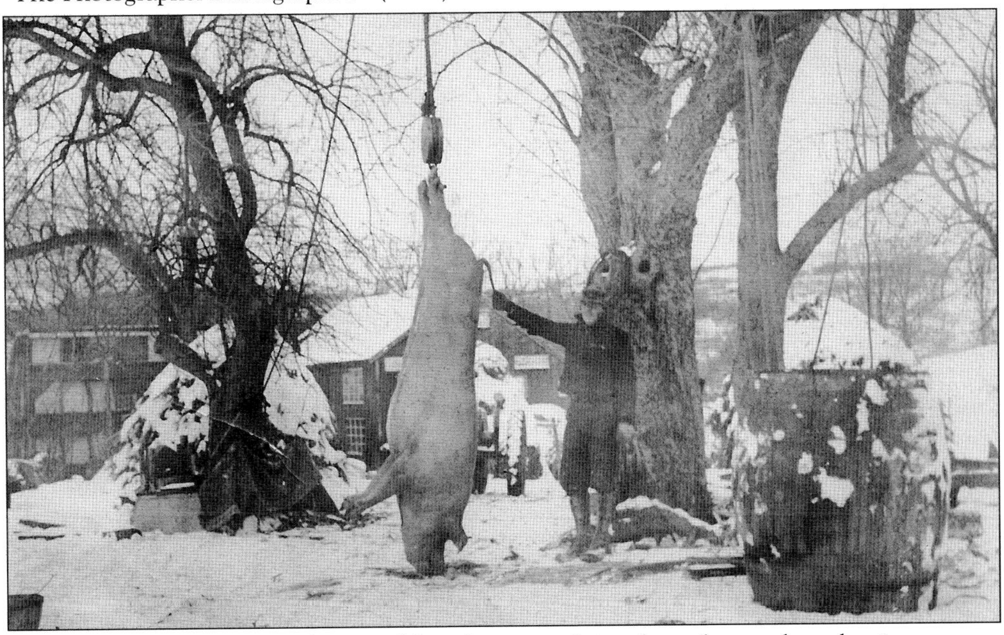

Farmers' almanacs were popular pamphlets that gave advice about the weather, planting seasons, and bits of traditional lore. One bit of advice about the annual December hog slaughtering was to avoid a waning moon; otherwise, "the pork would shrink and wither away in the barrel." This undated Roxbury winter scene shows a man with a hog hanging from a tree; a large barrel of water hangs nearby. (Cathleen Hurlbut Bronson.)

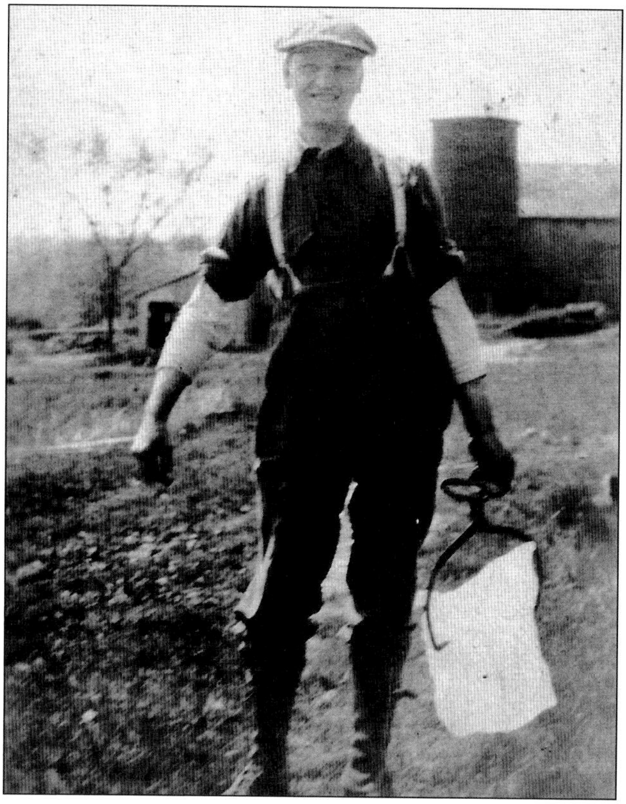

Ice tongs were a common sight in the days before refrigeration. Men cut ice from local ponds and stored it in icehouses on their properties. Because natural ice was used to preserve dairy products, ice cutting became an important seasonal occupation. In this undated photograph, Albert Johnson, of the Hurlbut family, carries a block of ice to the family icebox. (Elinor Hurlbut.)

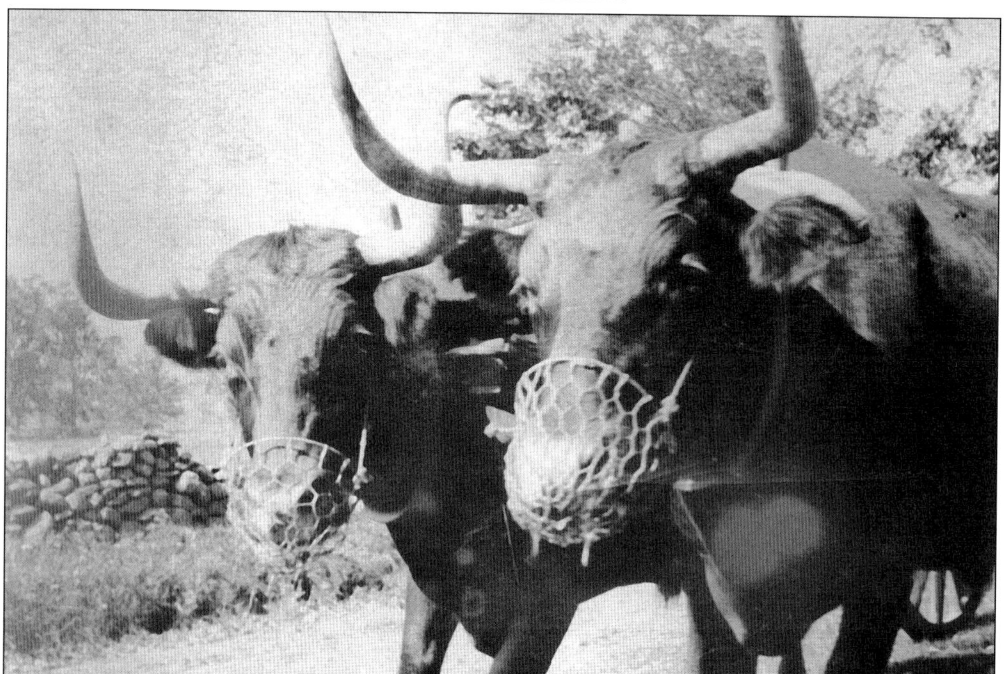

These fine oxen were the property of John Keeler, a relative of Col. Hiram Keeler. The family's original farm on Keeler Road in Bridgewater was called "Nine Hearths." (BHS.)

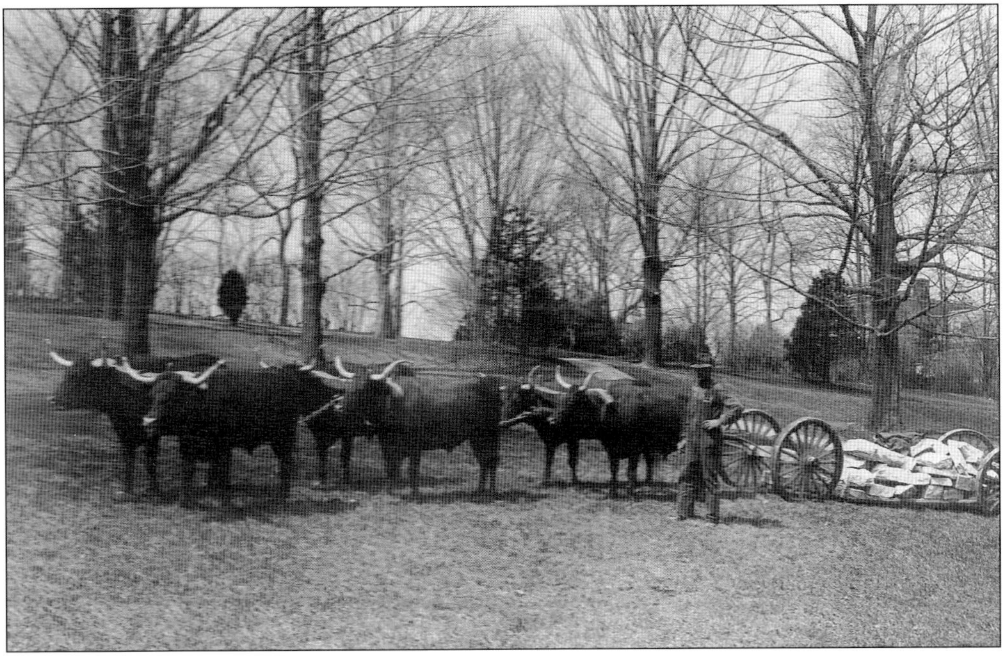

Percy Peck Beardsley (1891–1968) was a farmer, cider-maker, and World War I hero who fought alongside Sgt. Alvin C. York in the Argonne Forest in France. In this undated photograph, Beardsley is driving his prize-winning Devon oxen—possibly to the Danbury Fair for another blue ribbon. (Elinor Hurlbut.)

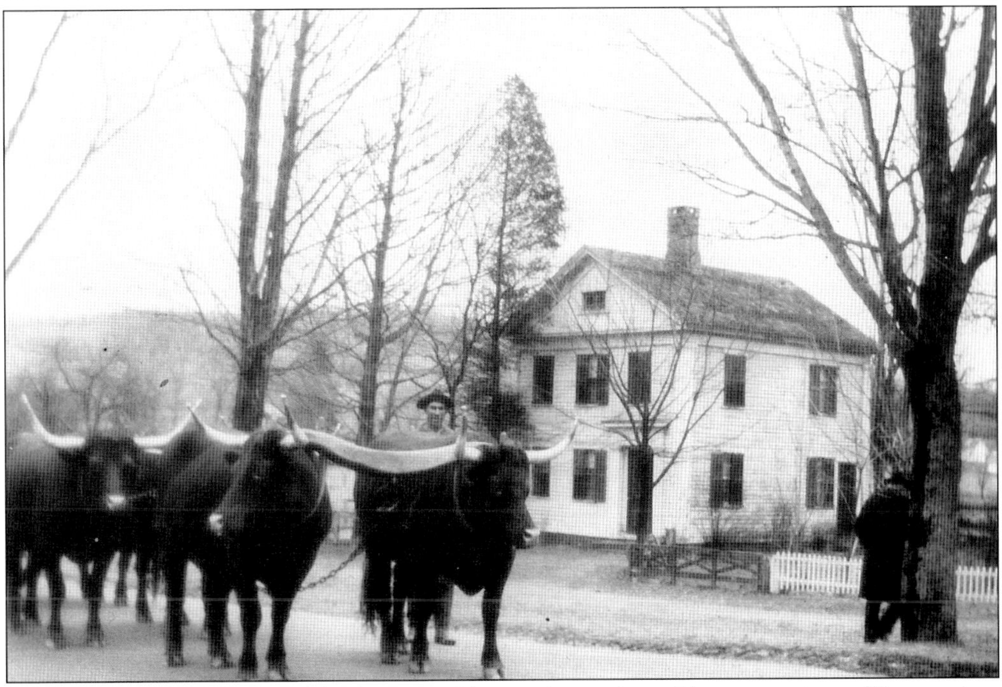

Nathan Thomas "Nate" Beardsley (1868–1943) was a descendant of five generations of Connecticut Yankees. In this 1934 photograph, he is leading a string of ruby-red Devon oxen from his farm on Good Hill Road through Roxbury, perhaps to win more blue ribbons at a country fair. (HMLM.)

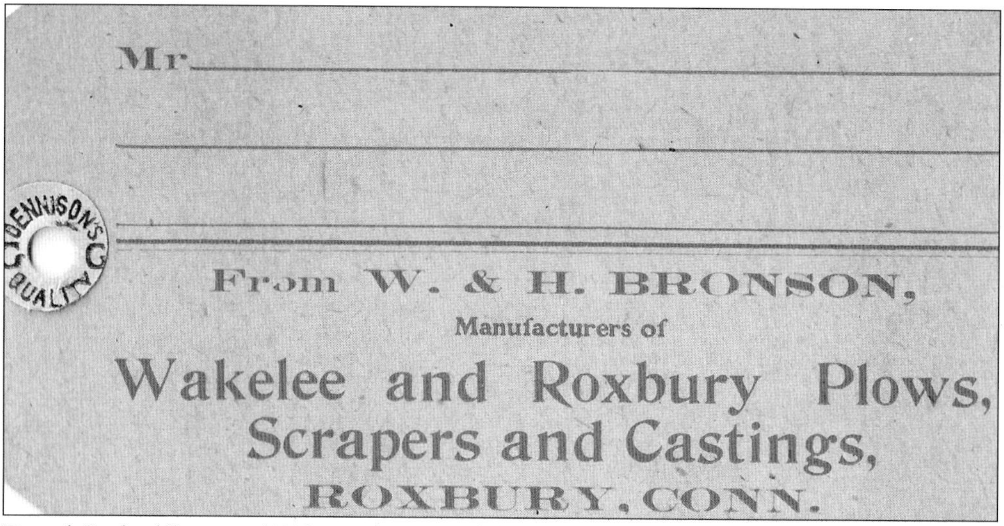
Mr.

From W. & H. BRONSON,

Manufacturers of

Wakelee and Roxbury Plows,

Scrapers and Castings,

ROXBURY, CONN.

Daniel Gaylord Bronson (1813–1878) invented the Bronson plow —a walking plow for one man, drawn by one or two horses. After his death, his sons William and Henry continued their father's foundry. In 1897, they bought the Wakelee Plow Company in Southbury, Connecticut. The plows and scrapers manufactured at his foundry on Squire Road were sold throughout New England. (David Gaylord Ryerson.)

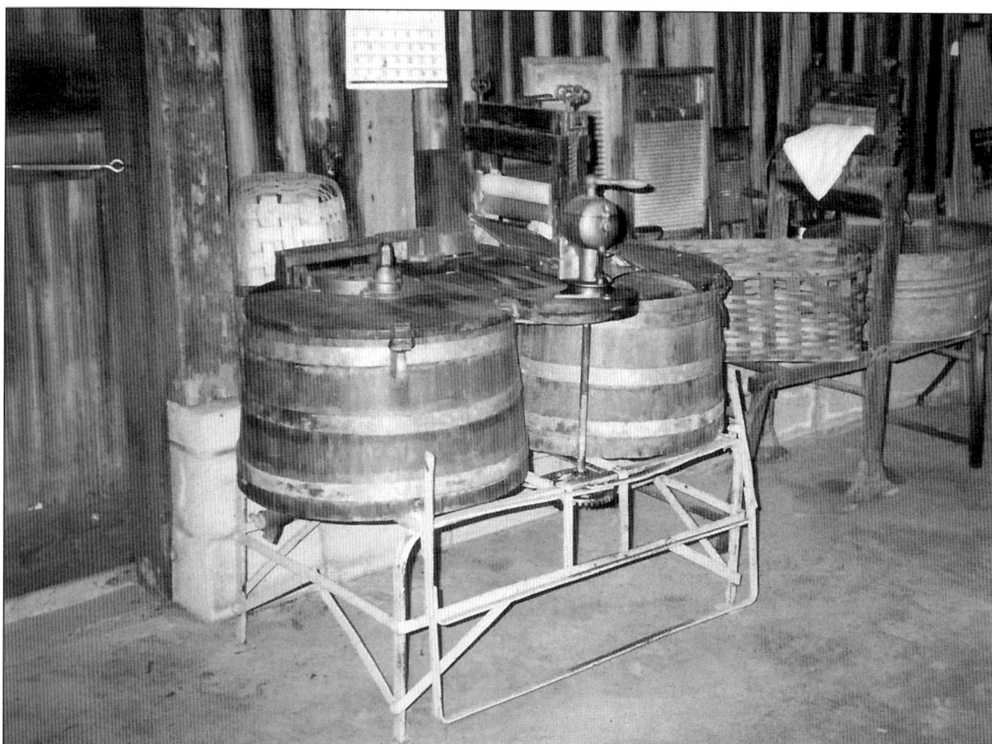

Before the days of top-load and spin dry, women spent the day washing clothes, first with the washboards seen in the background, and, later, with contraptions like the ones in this photograph. These old-fashioned hand-powered washing machines with wringers are on display in Roxbury's Historical Society Barn at Toplands Farm. (RM.)

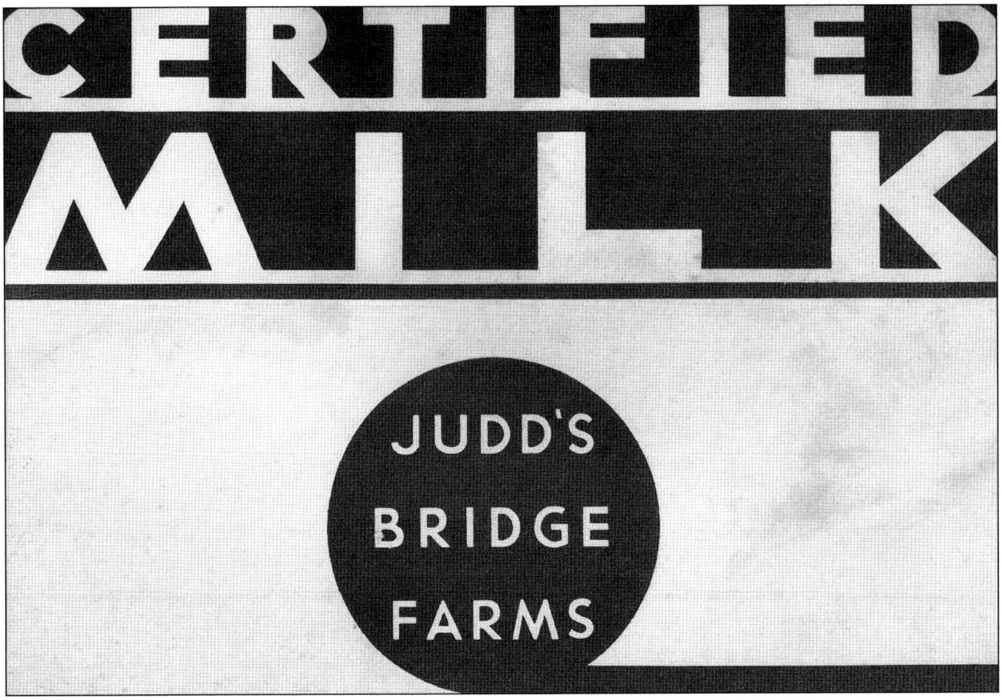

The owners of Judd's Bridge Farms were proud of their certified milk, produced the day it was delivered to its customers. Not only was the milk produced at the farm from the healthiest of Brown Swiss and Jersey cows, it was also pasteurized and bottled at the farm. The owners, therefore, had control over every quart. Their motto was "Be Healthy—Drink Milk—Be Wise—Drink Certified!" (RM.)

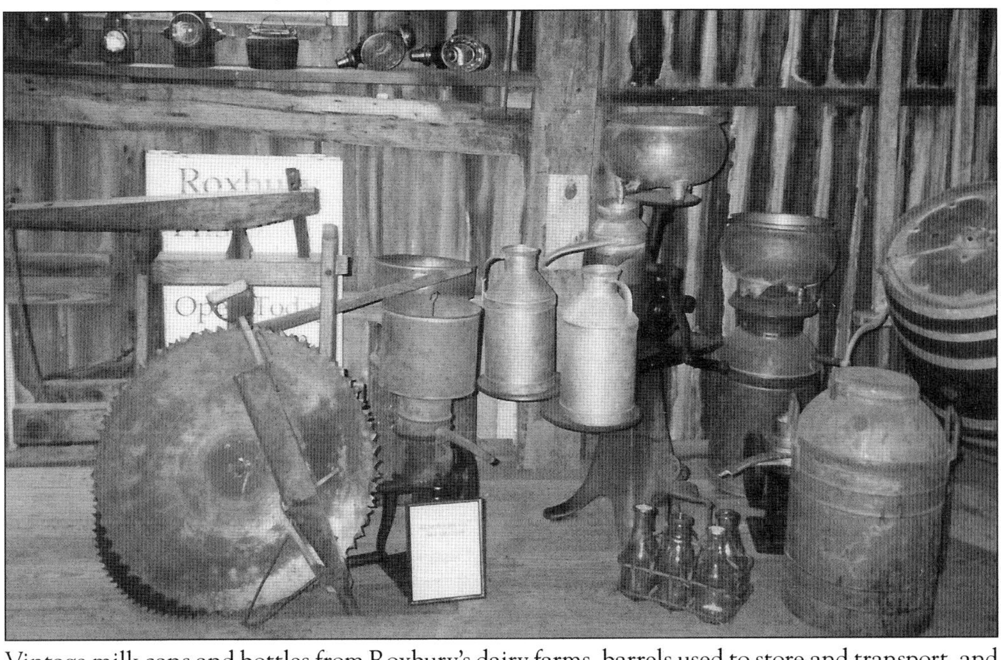

Vintage milk cans and bottles from Roxbury's dairy farms, barrels used to store and transport, and a variety of saws are on display at Roxbury's Historical Society Barn at Toplands Farm. (RM.)

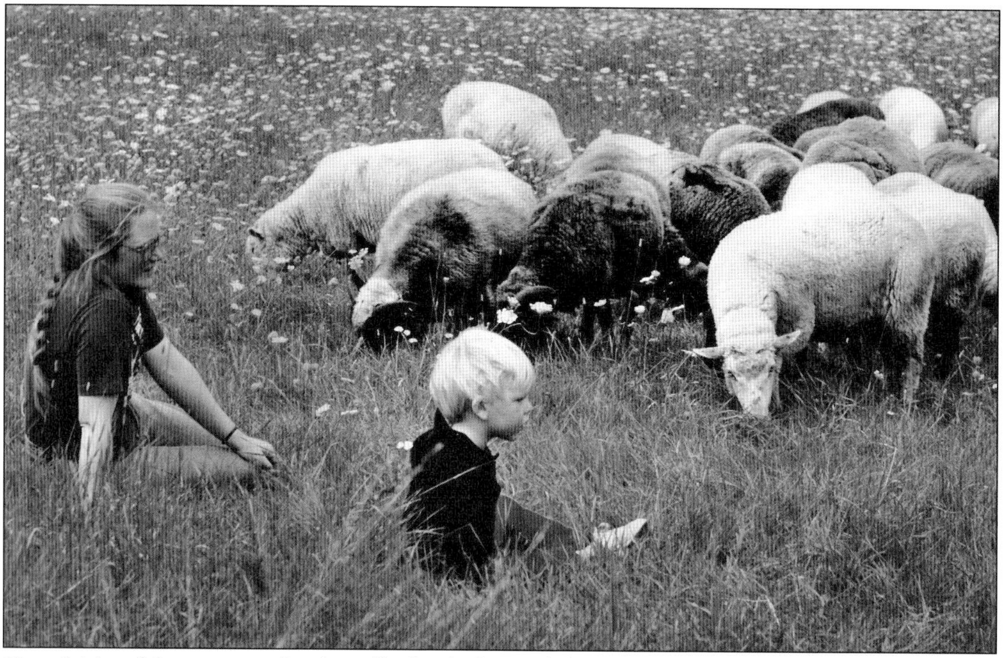

Out of sight of the camera, a border collie herds sheep while Cathy Bronson and her son, Christopher, enjoy the field of flowers at Maple Bank Farm. The Bronson family raises sheep, chickens, vegetables, and flowers on their Roxbury farm. Corn, blueberries, apples, and other goodies are available at their farm stand. (Cathleen Hurlbut Bronson.)

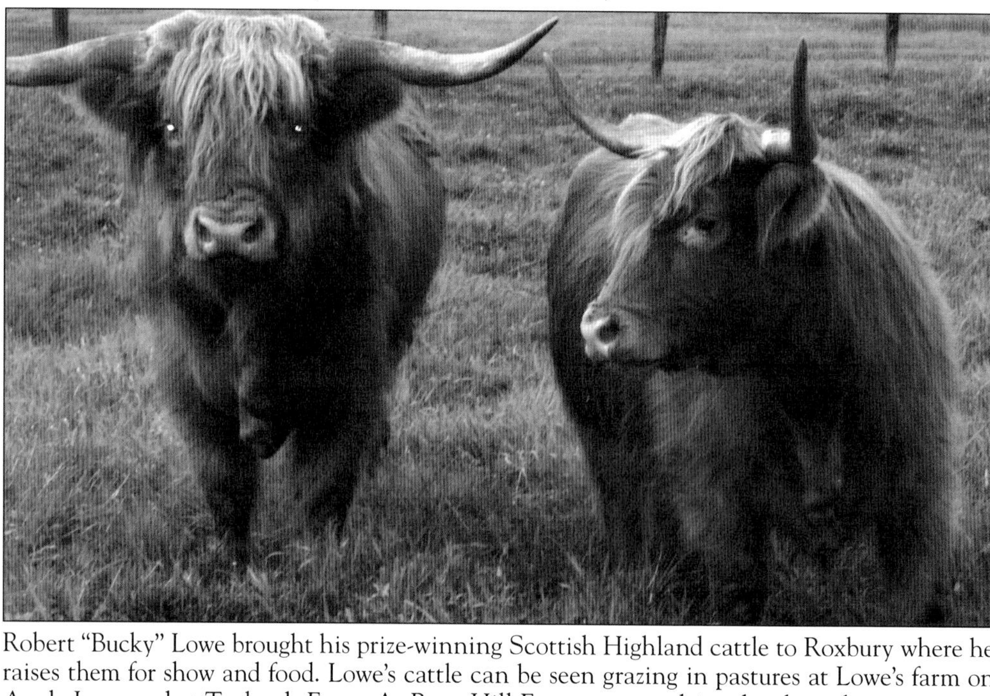

Robert "Bucky" Lowe brought his prize-winning Scottish Highland cattle to Roxbury where he raises them for show and food. Lowe's cattle can be seen grazing in pastures at Lowe's farm on Apple Lane and at Toplands Farm. At Race Hill Farm, many a driver has been known to stop and gaze over the fence where Laura and David Miller care for their red-coated, long-horned gentle giants. (Jeannine Green.)

Five

ON THE MOVE

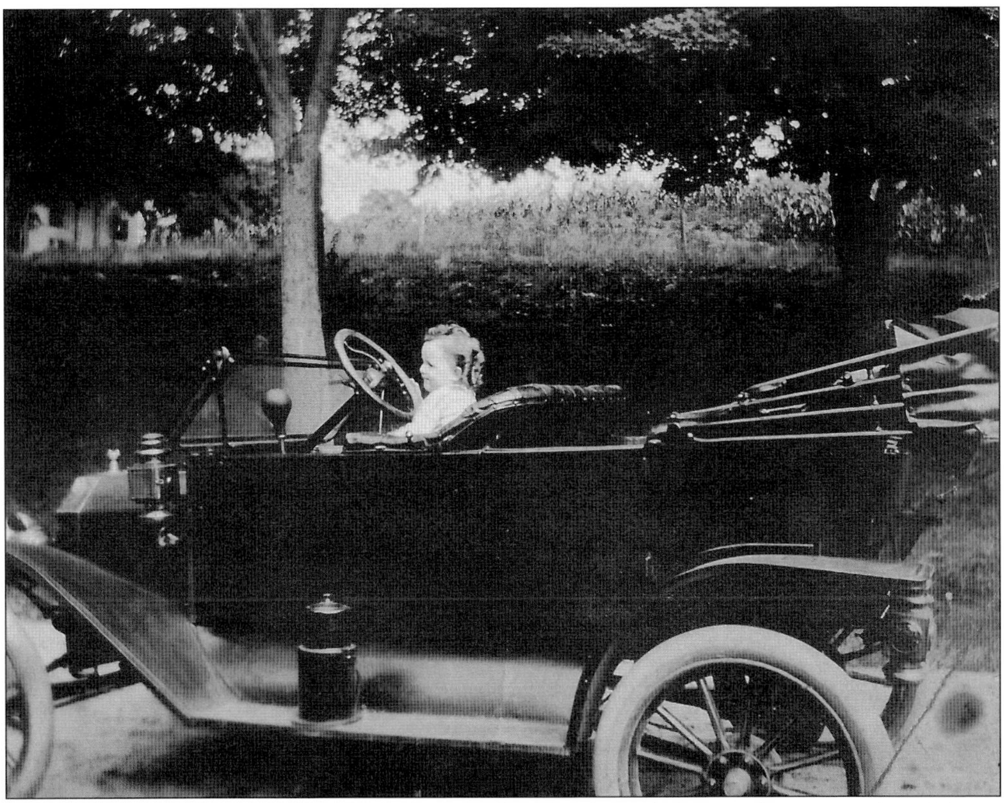

Alden Hurlbut, a descendant of Roxbury's founding family, is the young driver seated in a Morris automobile in this July 1913 photograph. (Elinor Hurlbut.)

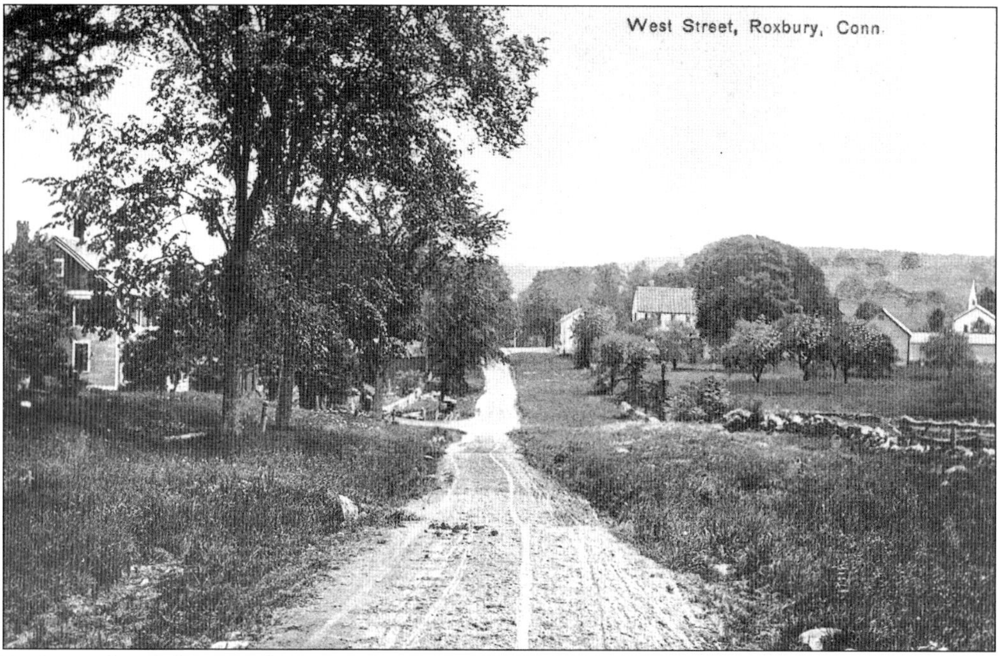

In this undated photograph, West Street was a dirt road. Now named Wellers Bridge Road, it runs downhill from Roxbury's Center to a main highway leading to Bridgewater and New Milford. Another name for this road was Sanford's Hill, named for a family that owned property along this road for more than a century. (RM.)

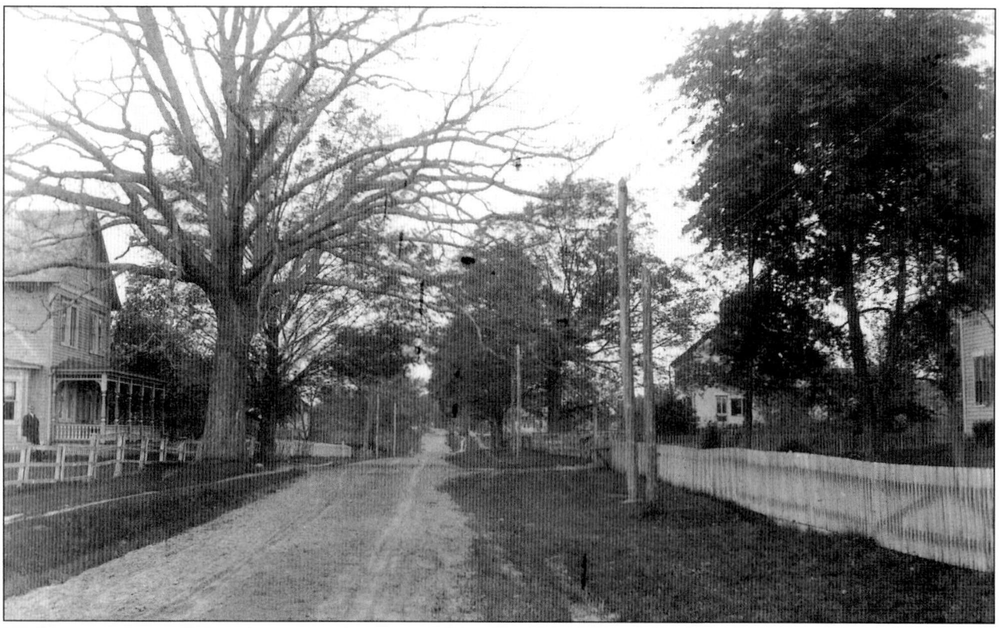

Today, it is named South Street, but in earlier days, it was called Christian Street, and in 1894, a local newspaper called it the longest street in Roxbury. It was once the center of trade and commerce, with a cobbler's shop, meat market, and blacksmith shop, as well as a foundry and casting shop. Part of it lies in the historic district, and it is lined with 18th- and 19th-century homes. (RM.)

Route 133 is also known as Main Street North and Main Street South—its dividing line lying at the stop sign in the center of Bridgewater. At the time this picture was taken, Route 133 was the access to Southville, a division of Bridgewater at the foot of the southern hills of town, on the banks of the Housatonic River. (BHS.)

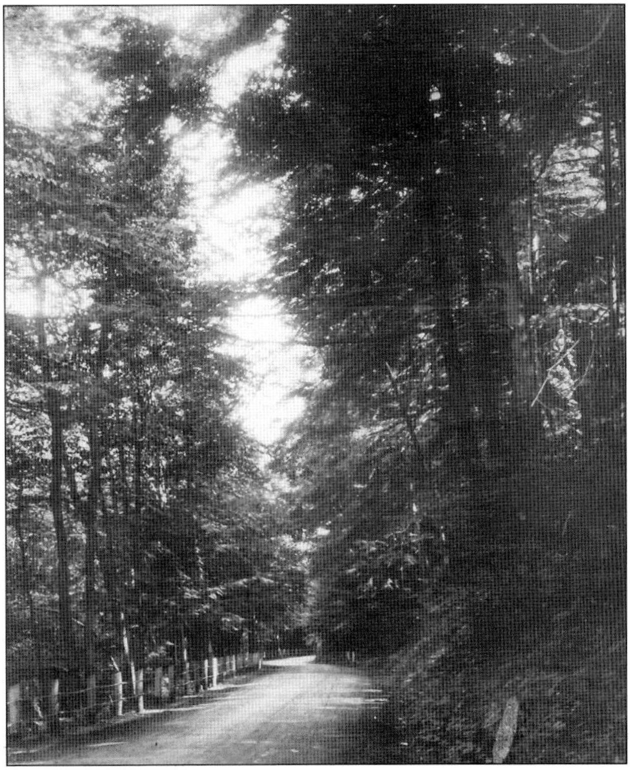

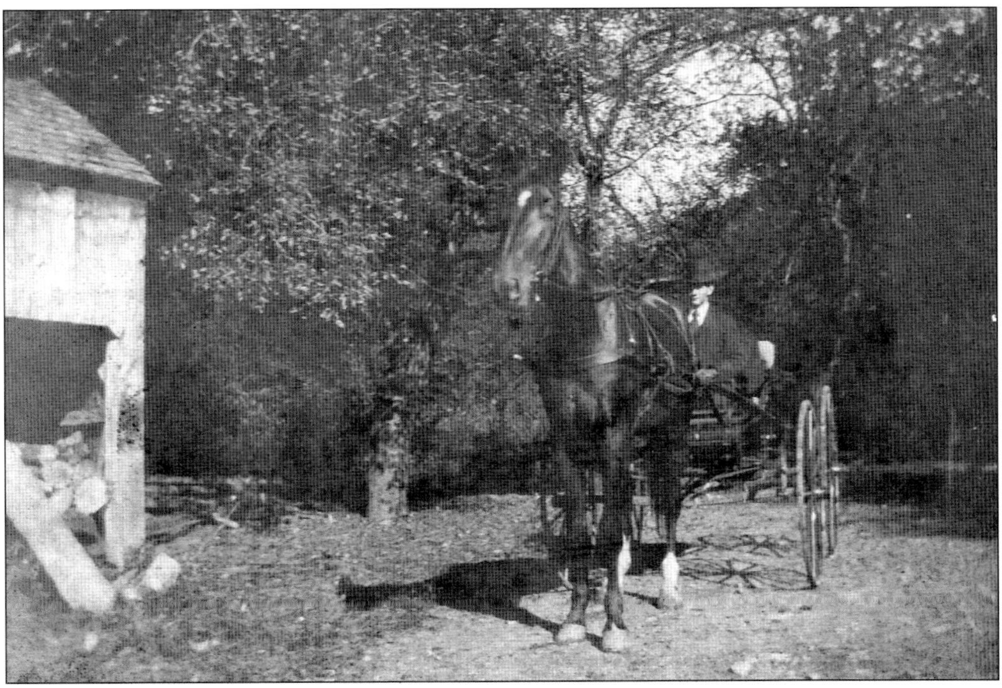

Charles A. Northrop proudly drives his horse and wagon through Southville in this image. A descendant of Grant Northrop, who moved from New Milford in 1853 to purchase a 100-acre farm, he remained active in Southville and Bridgewater businesses throughout his lifetime. (BHS.)

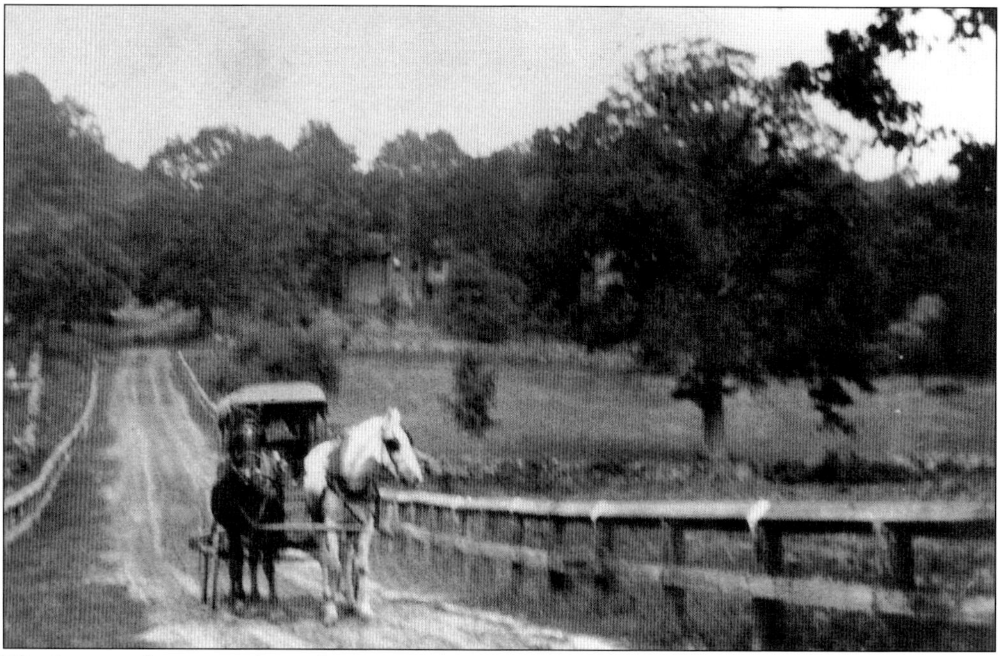

The horse and carriage shown here were used as postal delivery and for passengers between New Milford and Bridgewater. Even though the trip was about 10 miles, in the days before automobiles, this was a full-day trip. Often travelers stayed with friends or extended family overnight, as they did not want to be on muddy trails after dark. (BHS.)

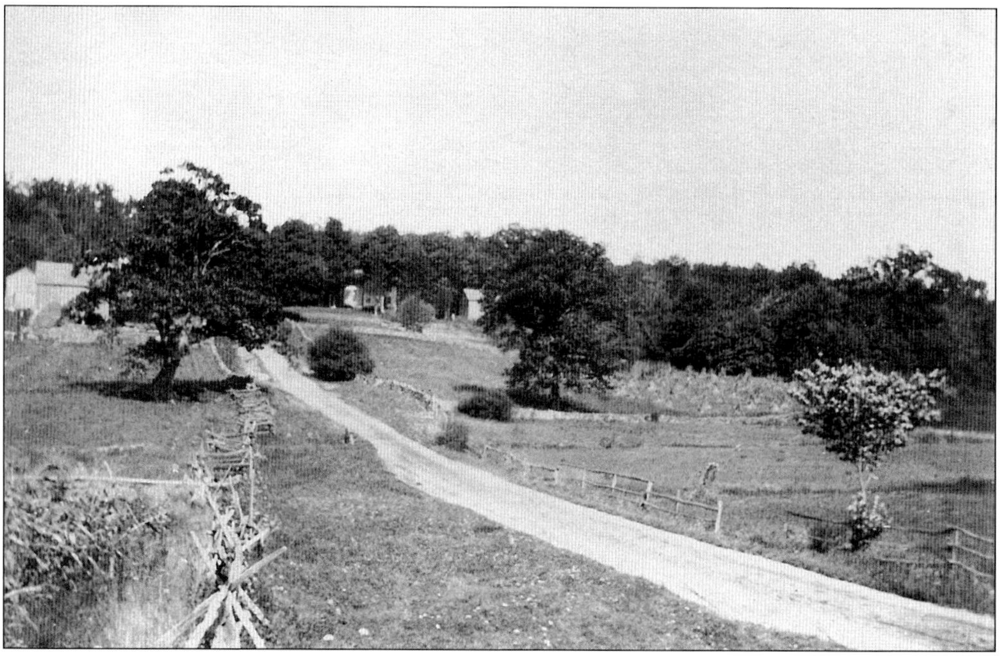

In these pictures of pre– and post–Civil War Main Street, the Bridgewater homes of the Sturdevant family are on either side of the road. Builders of spinning and wagon wheels, they deeded land to their son as a wedding gift. The only condition made was that their son, their blacksmith, set up his smithy before the wedding. He did—in the house he built for his bride. (BHS.)

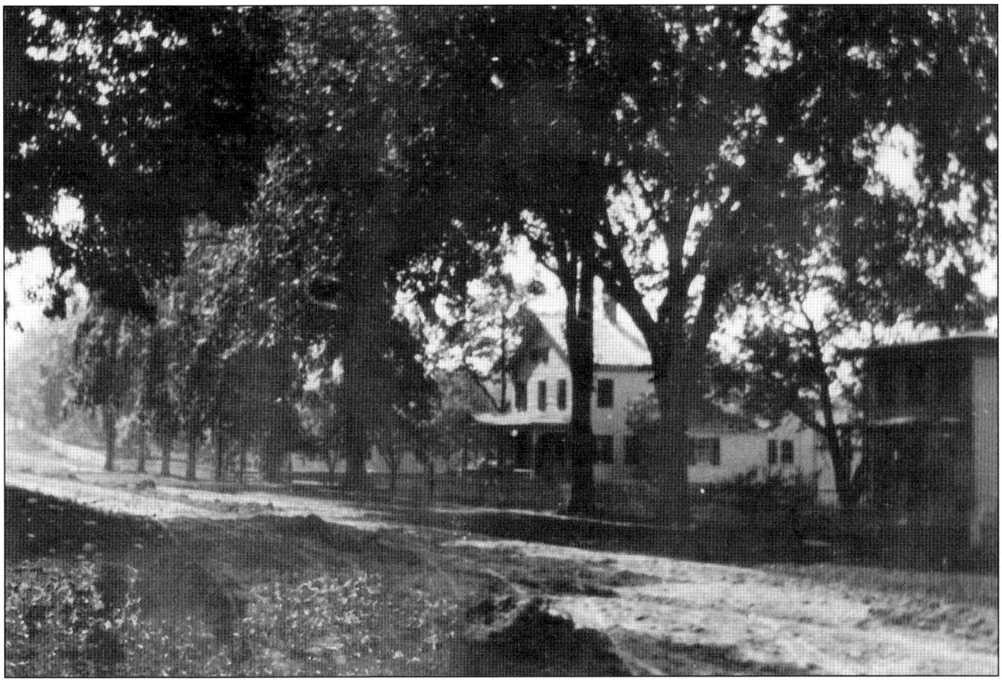

This image shows Main Street opposite Town Hall in Bridgewater. The view now reflects the same building constructed by C.B. Thomson, now housing a village store, post office, and bank. (BHS.)

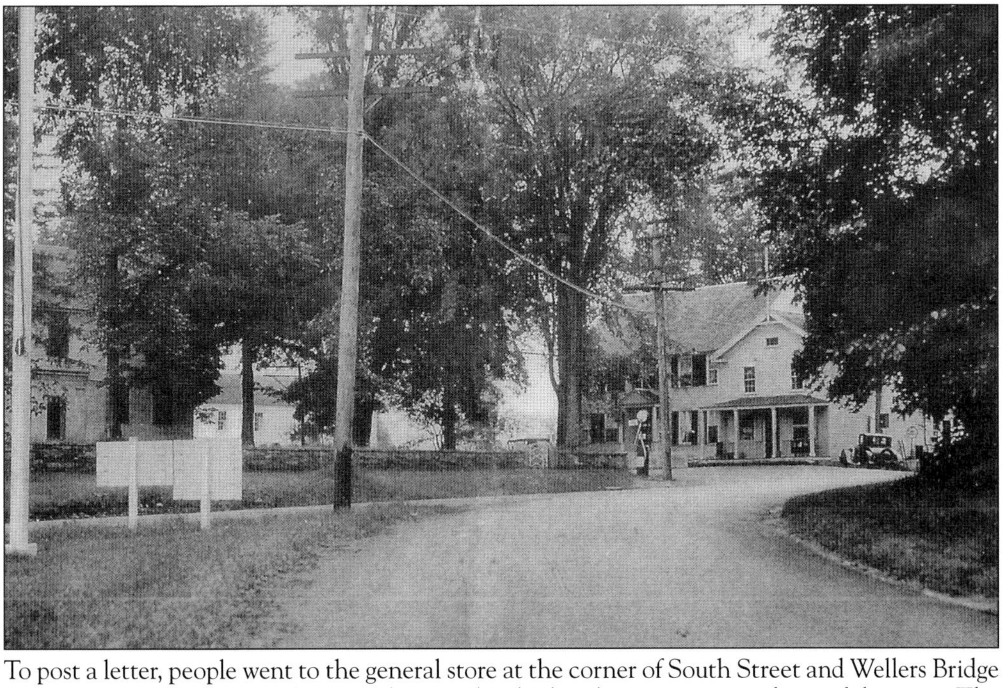

To post a letter, people went to the general store at the corner of South Street and Wellers Bridge Road shown in this undated postcard. Note the shed with a gas pump in front of the store. The store, pump, and post office are gone now, but the late-Georgian house to the left of the store, built around 1784, still stands. (RM.)

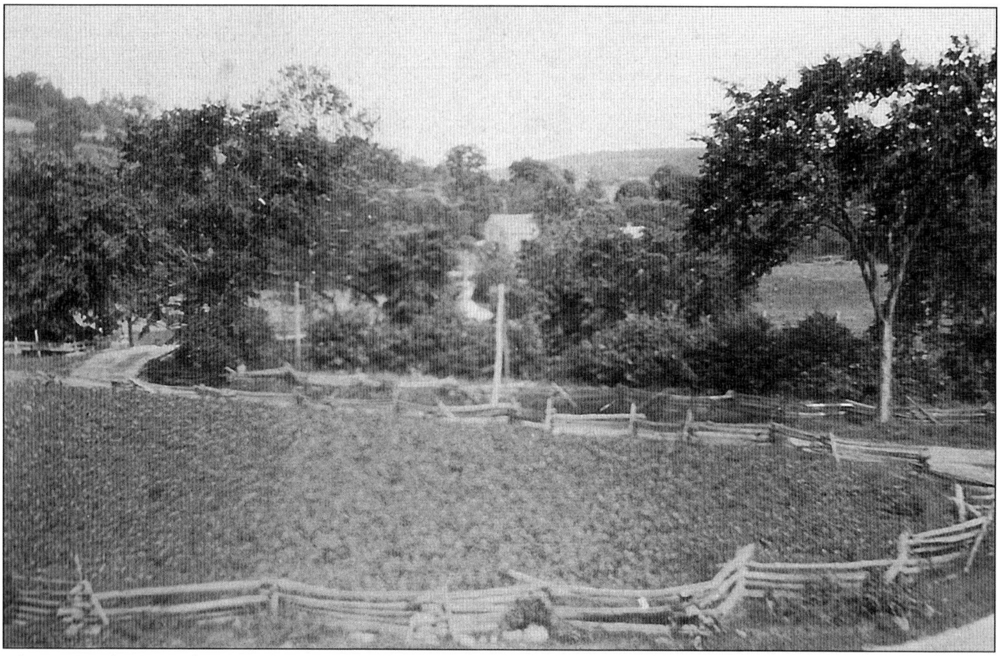

Photographer Andrew W. Gillette captured this image of Wellers Hollow in the early 1900s. In earlier days, each town appointed a fence viewer to see that farmers kept their fences mended and their cattle and hogs penned in, not wandering on the town green or destroying neighbors' crops. This photograph gives some idea of how many miles of fences a viewer had to monitor. (BHS.)

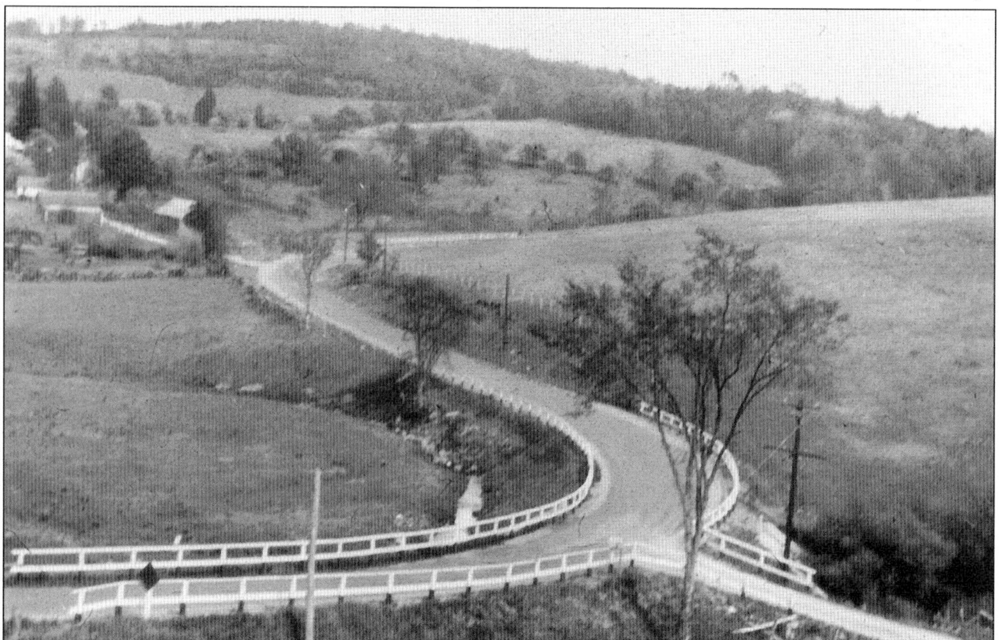

Southbury Road, Route 67, sweeps downhill from Roxbury Center to the hills of Southbury. At the corner of Squire Road, the road curves over Jack's Brook, intersects with Rucum Road, and then climbs uphill to Southbury. This photograph was taken in 1934, and the landscape looks much the same today. (HMLM.)

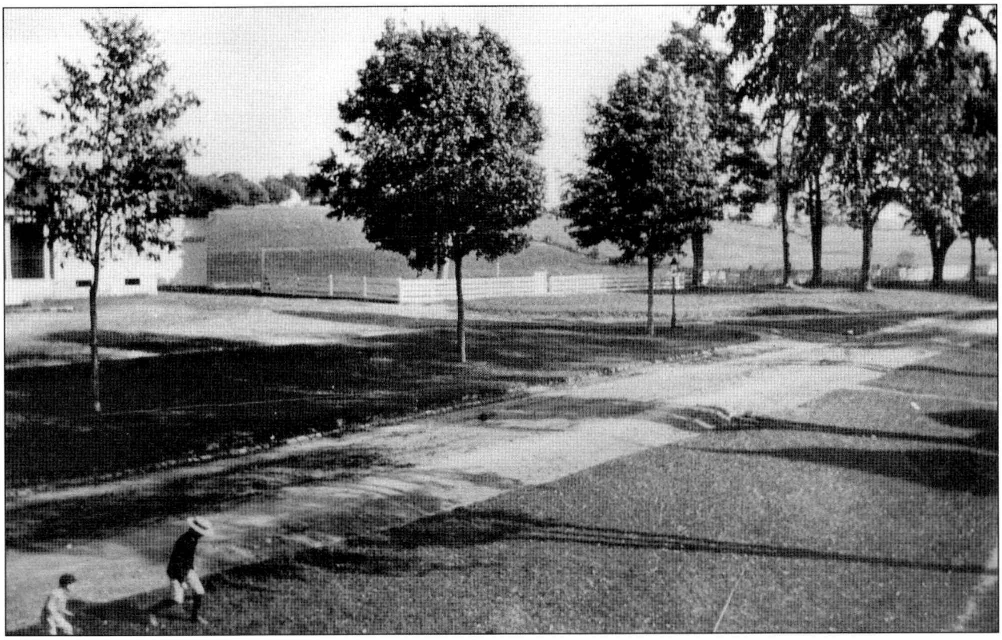

In this view of the center of Bridgewater in 1900, C.N. Hatch's General Store is shown with open land behind the fence. That area became the site of major town buildings—Bridgewater Town Hall, The Peck House (home to the Bridgewater Historical Society), the Burnham Library, an elementary school, and the firehouse. (BHS.)

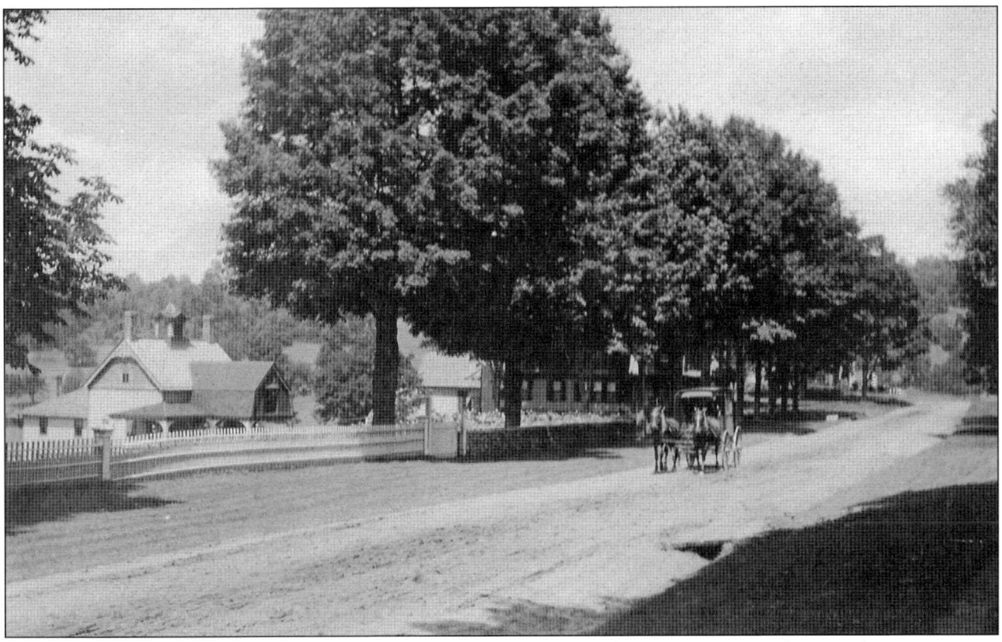

A 1900 carriage passes the home of C.B. Thompson, Bridgewater's most famous businessman. His home was a testament to his success, beginning his business with the "Little Giant Pocket Scales" in 1879 at age 27, followed by "nickel-plated shears." His use of the mails caused constant disagreements with the US postal inspector. When he died in 1942 at age 90, he was still at odds with the Post Office. (BHS.)

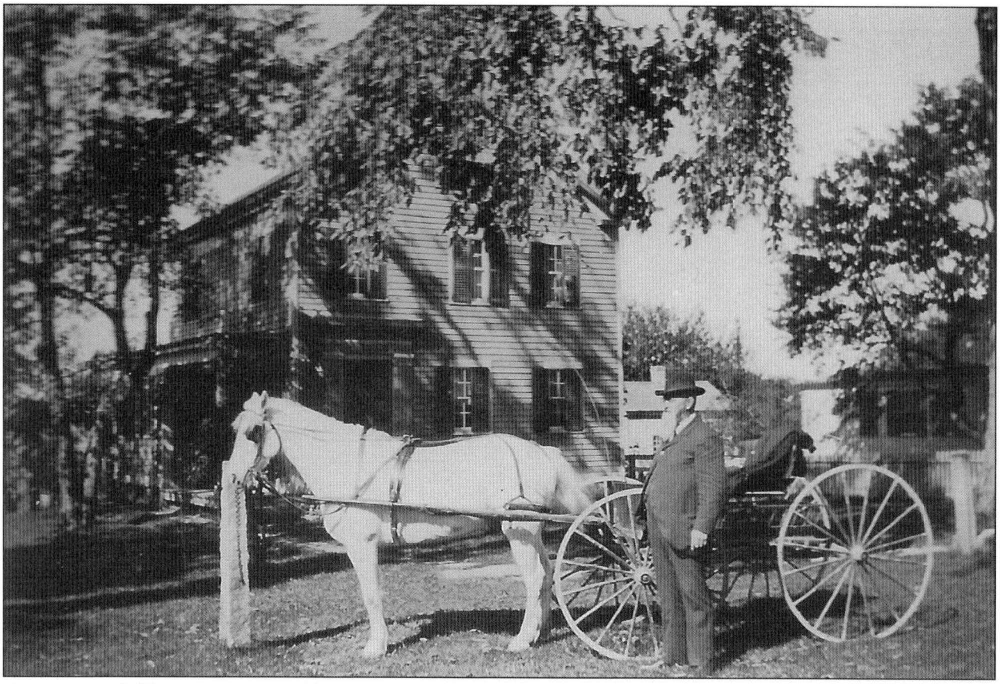

Austin H. Gillette is pictured here in his spindle buckboard in front of his Bridgewater home in 1901. According to the Carriage Museum Library, the "New-Style Spindle Wagon" was featured in the June and August 1895 editions of *Carriage Monthly*. (BHS.)

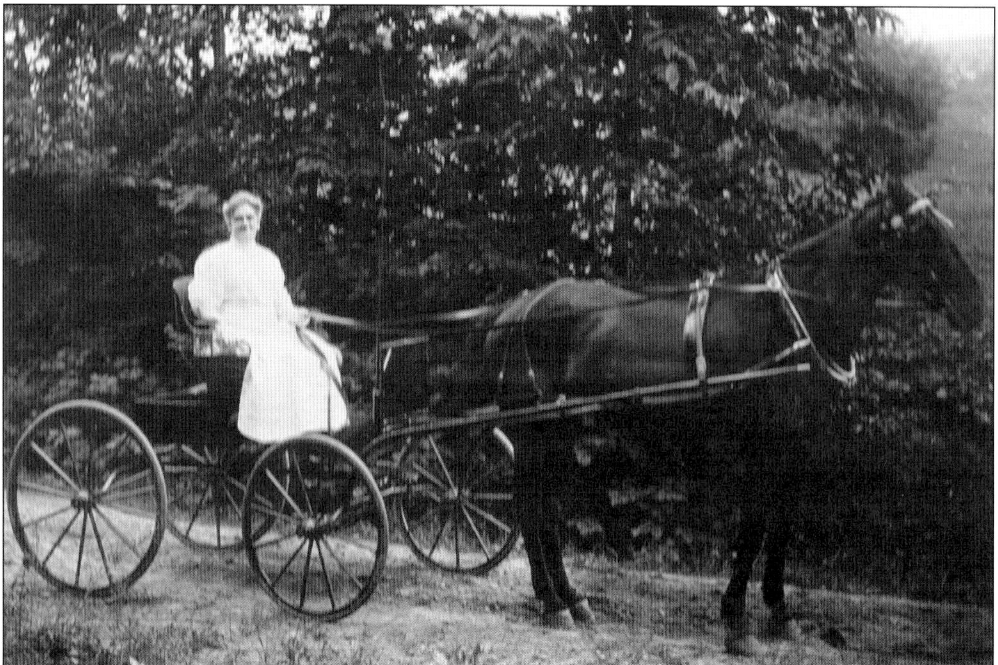

All decked out in her Sunday-Go-to-Meeting outfit, this Bridgewater woman sits in her buggy for the camera. The Bridgewater Congregational Church had a large structure for the carriages and horses of their worshippers. (BHS.)

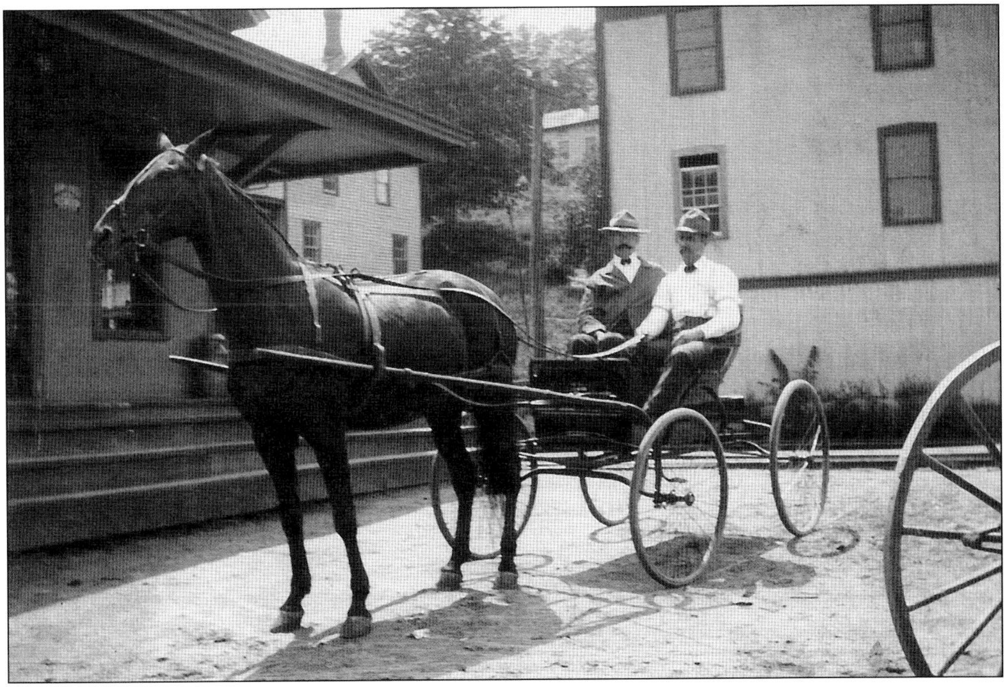

Two men in white shirts, bow ties, and hats seem ready for a ride in a one-horse buggy at Roxbury station. Perhaps one of the men is a driver picking up the other man at the station in this undated photograph. (RM.)

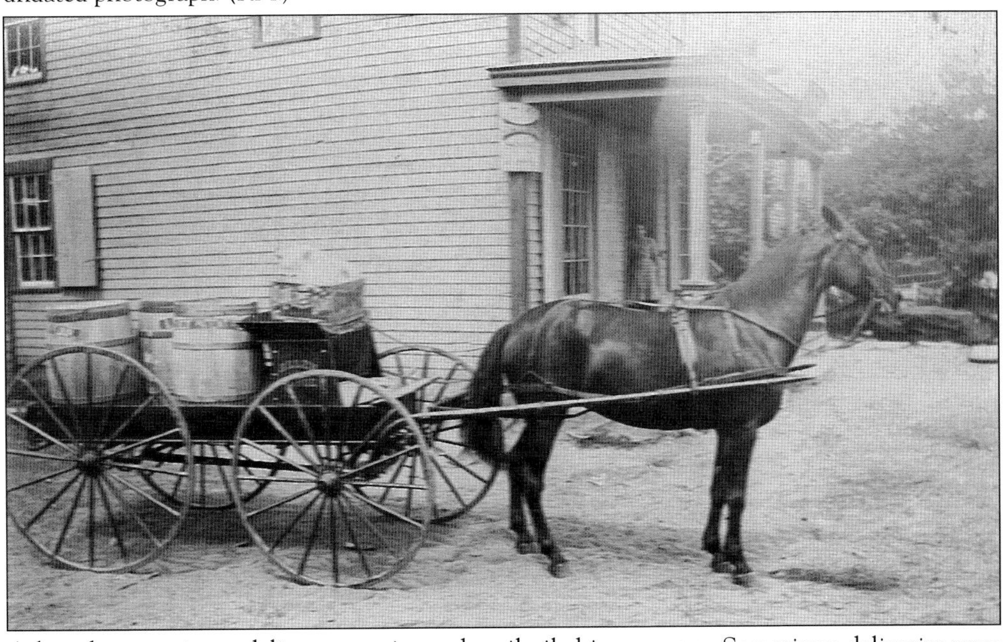

A lone horse waits to deliver groceries and mail piled in a wagon. Sometimes deliveries were done via stagecoach; other times by private carriers like the one here parked outside the Allen Joyce General Store at Roxbury Station. Allen Joyce was appointed postmaster at Roxbury Station in February 1891 and managed a general store for over 25 years. He died in January 1918, aged 55. (RM.)

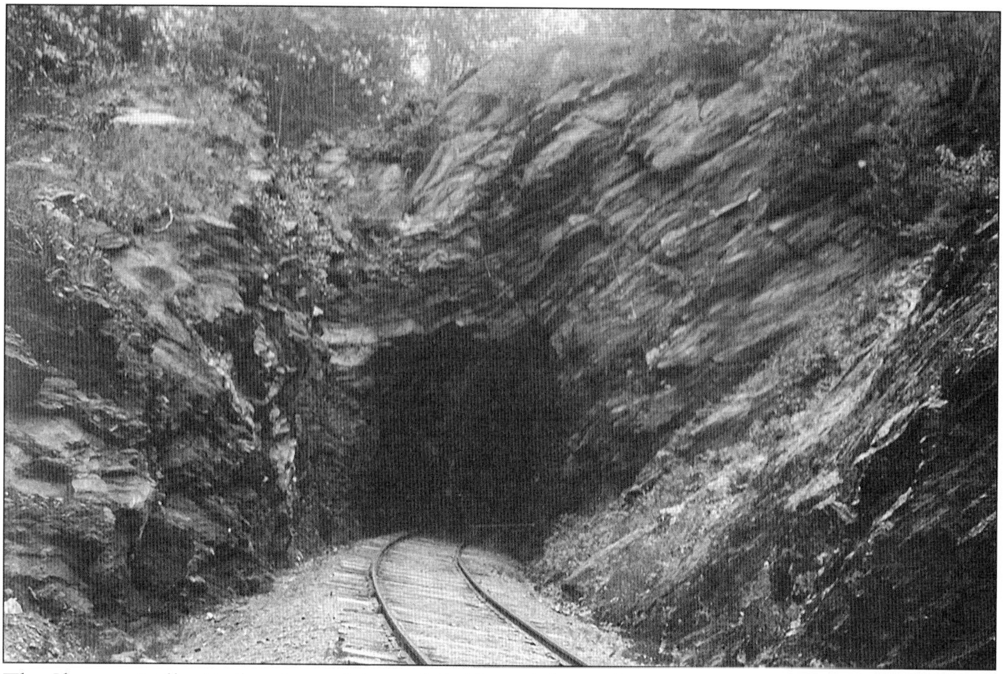

The Shepaug Valley Railroad raced through fields and chugged its way across rocky hills and through this tunnel carved into a mountain on its way from Roxbury to Washington, Connecticut, and points north. The tunnel is 30 rods long, has a bend in it, and is north of Judd's Bridge Farm. (RM.)

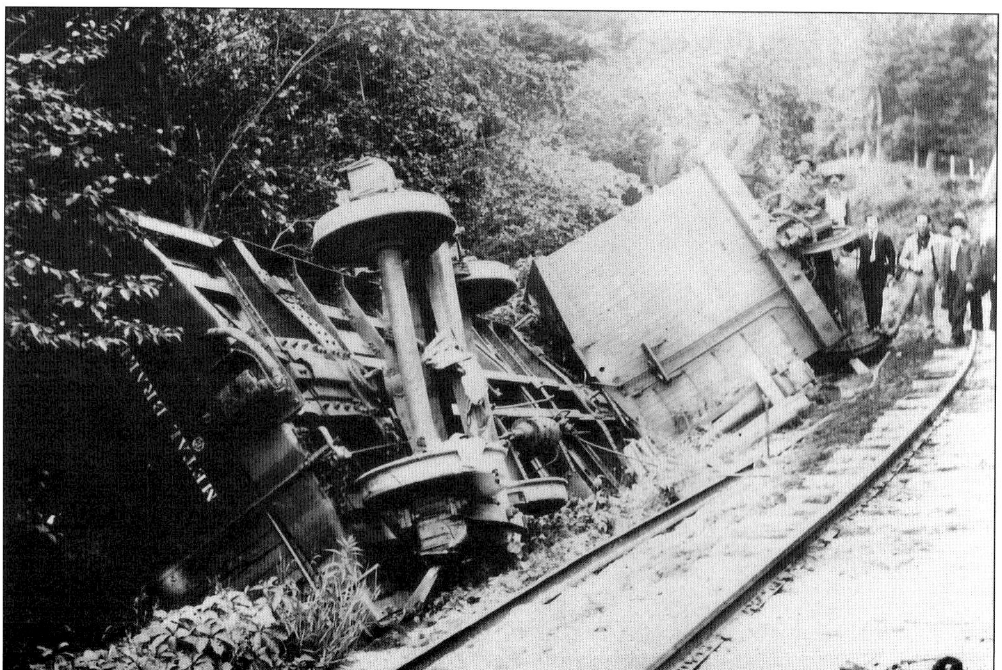

Accidents are bound to happen. In this photograph taken by Joseph West on June 24, 1906, Shepaug Valley Railroad cars—one marked "metal brakes"—derailed, upended, and toppled over. A group of men look on, no doubt trying to figure out how to get the fallen cars back on track. (RCC.)

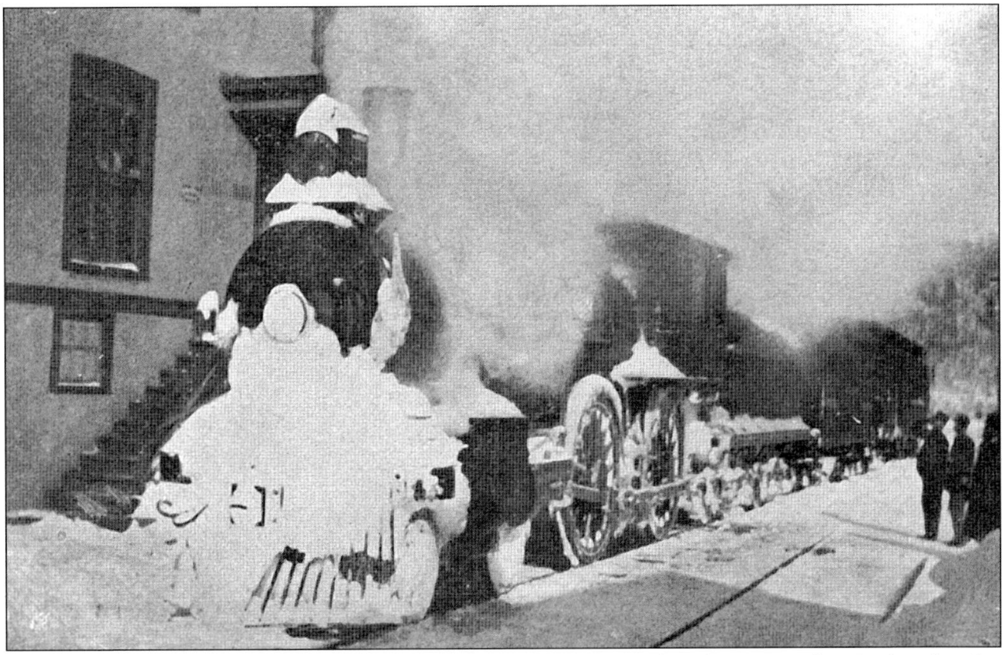

Three identical engines pulled passenger and freight trains on the Shepaug Valley Railroad—the *Shepaug*, *Waramaug*, and the *Weantinaug*. In this undated photograph, the name and engine number are hidden under snow piled high against the front wheels of this locomotive as it pulls into Roxbury Station. (RLT.)

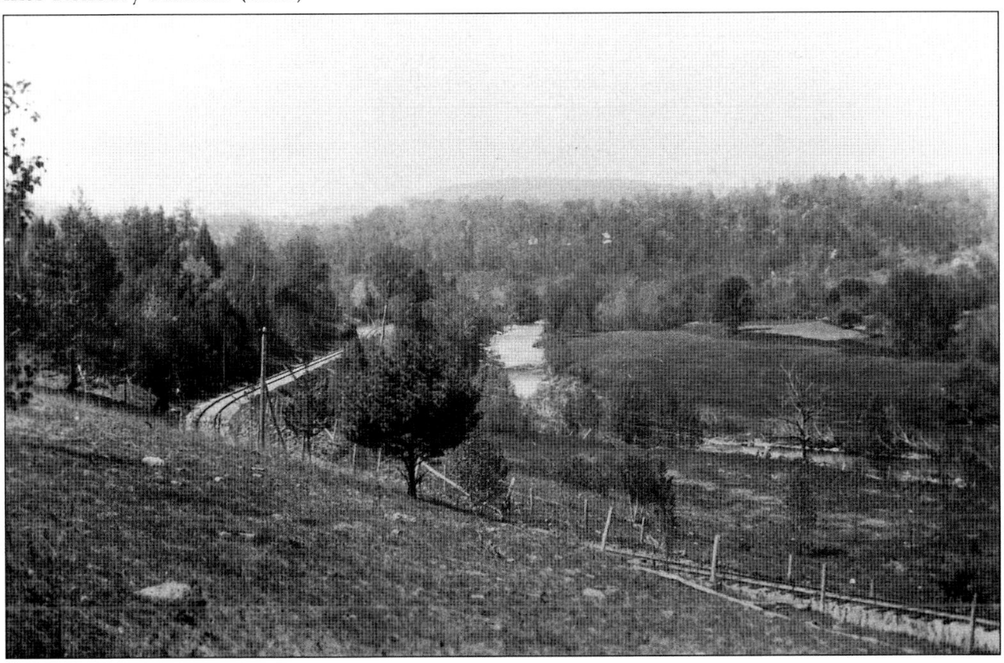

Shepaug Valley Railroad tracks followed the river through Roxbury from 1872 to 1948. Its passengers and freight traveled a labyrinth route from Hawleyville to Litchfield along 32 miles of track. They passed through scenic farmland, screamed through a 235-foot tunnel carved through solid rock north of Roxbury, and enjoyed 192 curves—about six per mile—along the route. (RM.)

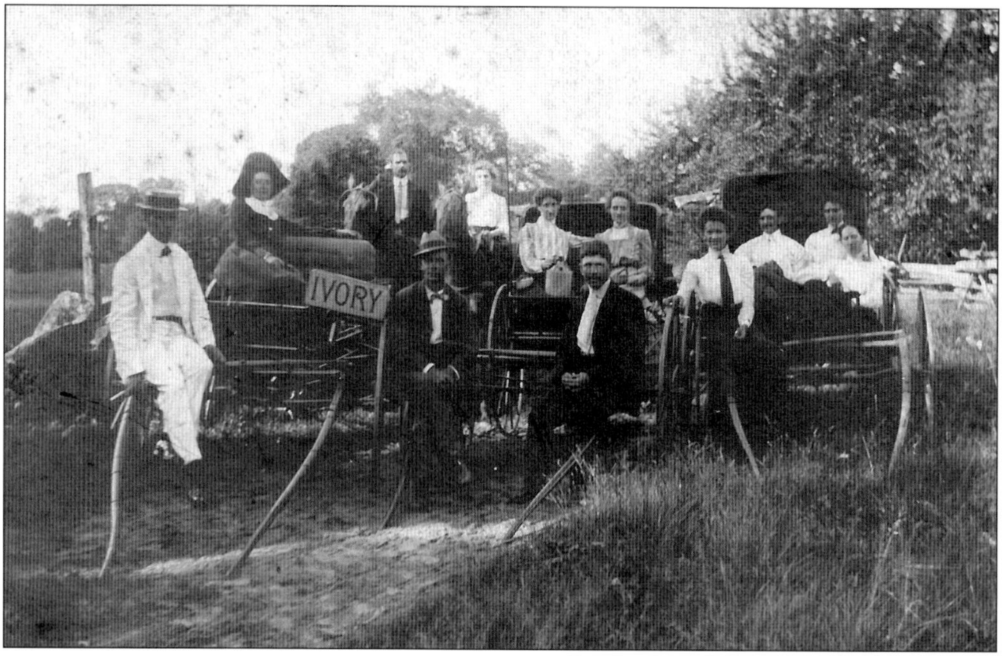

A group of young Bridgewater people pose here, sitting in wagons. One of their horses can be seen in the rear. The "Ivory" sign remains a mystery. (BHS.)

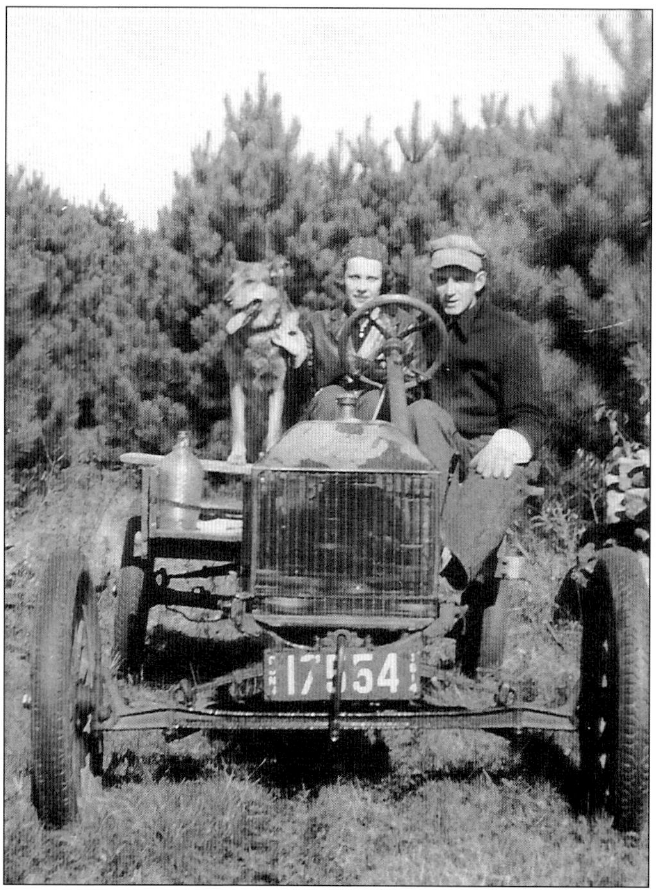

In this photograph dated 1938, a man, woman, and their dog take a leisurely ride through Roxbury's countryside in a 1913 Model T. (Elinor Hurlbut.)

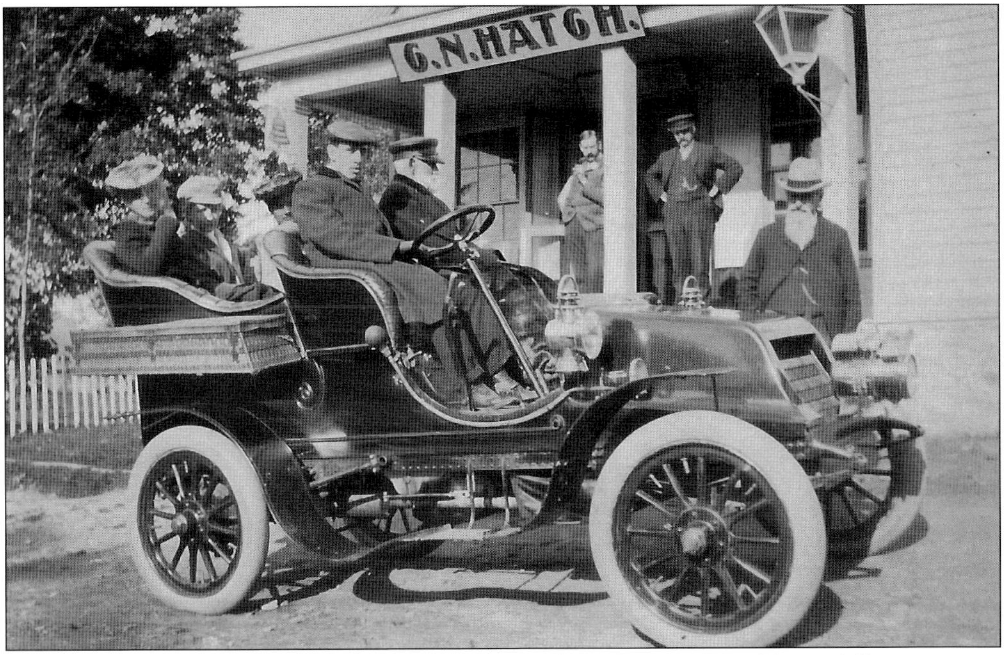

The general store seen here changed names frequently and was operated by 11 different owners over the years. It was originally built by Joel Sanford for his son, Charles G. Sanford, in 1838. The property passed through families well known in Bridgewater, including the Warners, Minors, Pecks, Gillettes, Malletts, and Hatches. (BHS.)

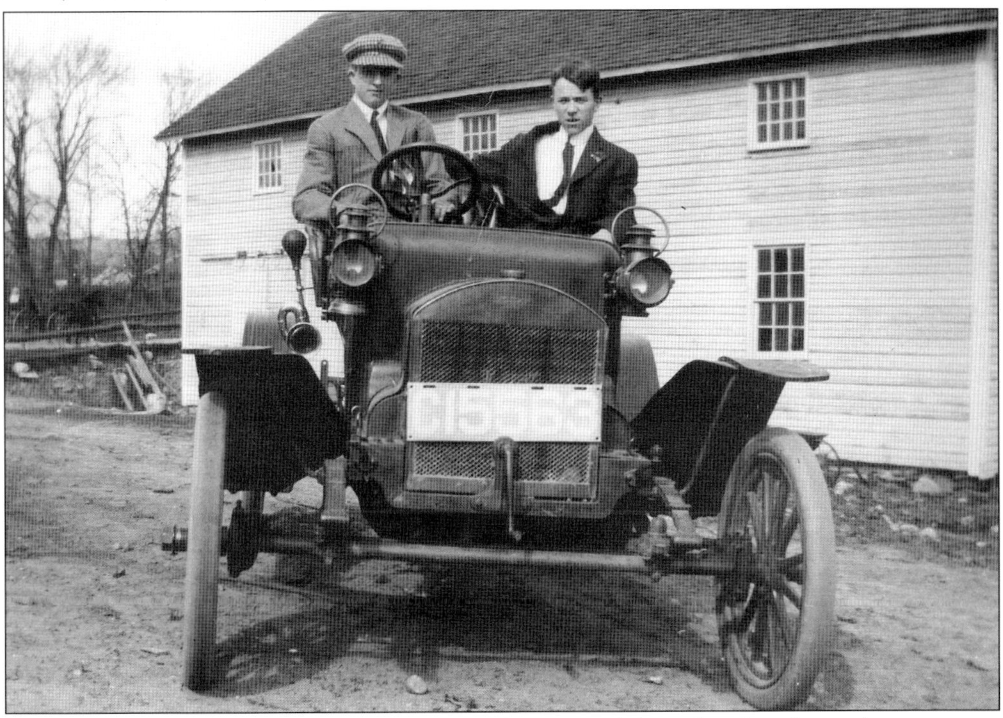

Carl Warner, shown here in a dark suit, sits in his automobile with a friend outside a creamery near the Still River. Warner's wife was Elizabeth Northrop Warner. (BHS.)

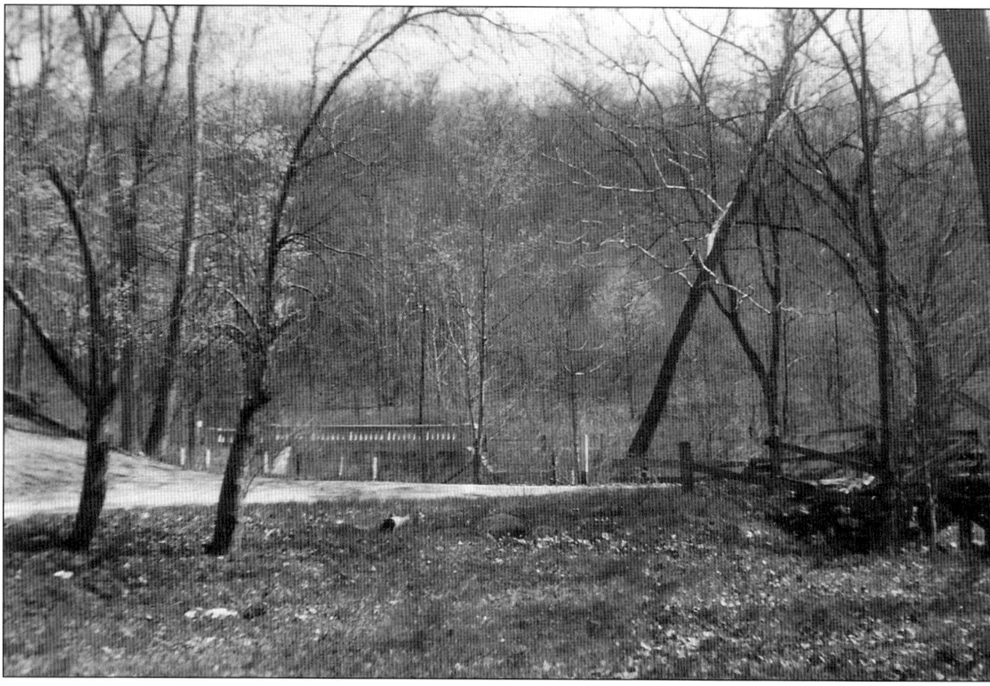

The old bridge over the brook in Southville was photographed by Abby Northrop on May 7, 1950. The Northrop family had long held interests in Southville, sometimes using abandoned buildings for storage. (BHS.)

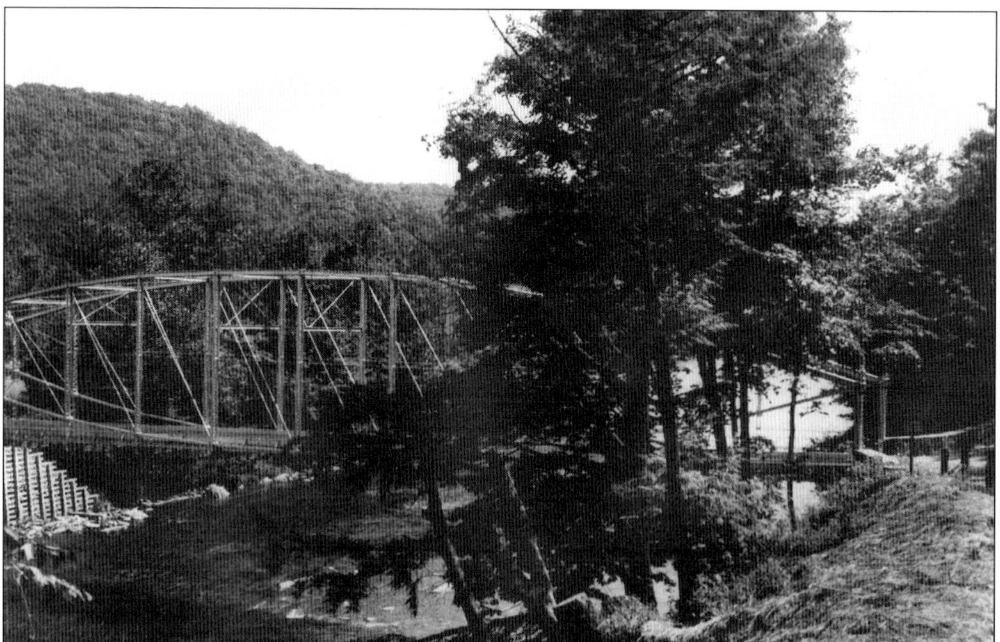

The first bridge over the Housatonic River was built in 1849. In 1880, a new toll bridge was built at Southville. Travel between Bridgewater and Brookfield was both difficult and expensive. A series of ferries was run by the Babbitt family. They also ran an inn, popular with traveling businessmen. A series of pulleys was sometimes used to transport livestock across the river. (BHS.)

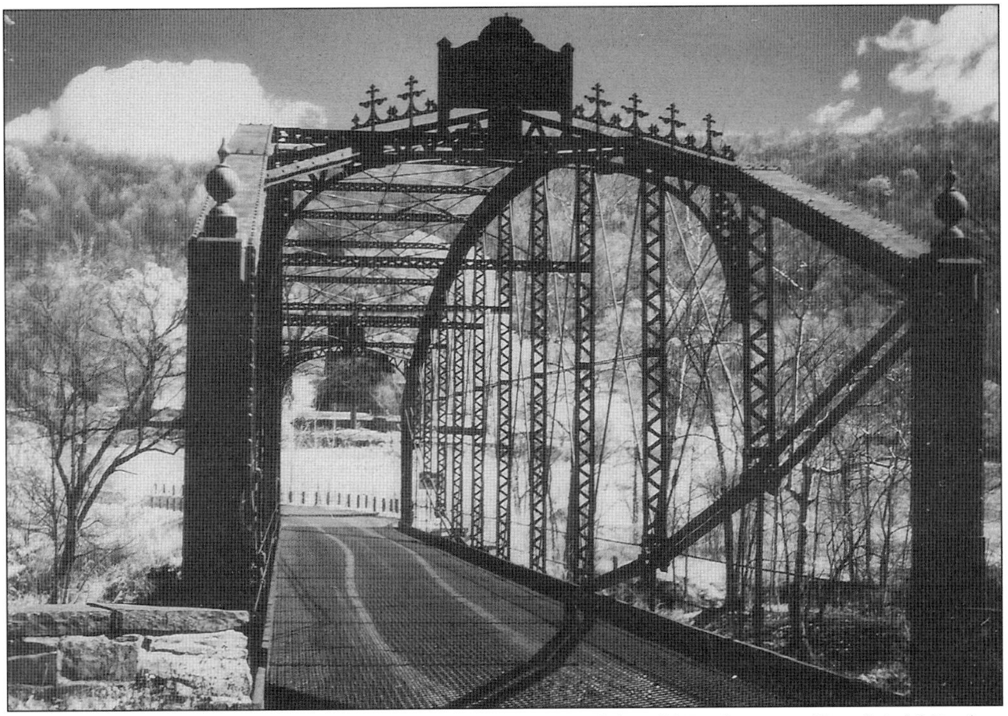

On a clear winter day, a photographer took this picture of the old Bridgewater/Brookfield Bridge. When it was demolished to make way for the new bridge over Lake Lillinonah, the cement pylons that were part of the foundation were removed and recycled. They were used at the Bridgewater Country Fair for many years in the Tractor Pull. (BHS.)

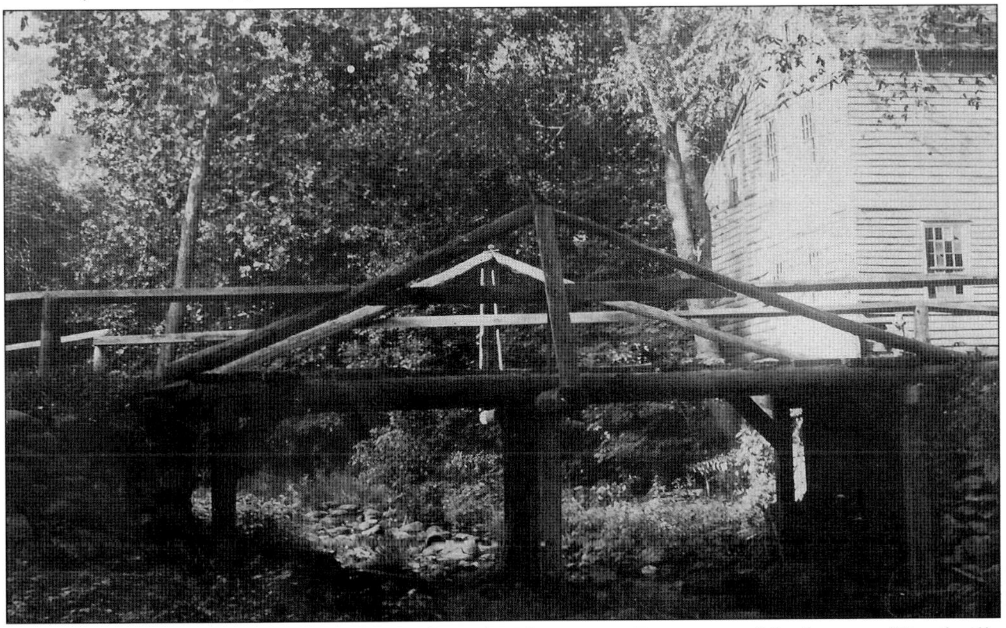

Spanning the Wewaka Brook, which travels to the Housatonic River, one of the homes of Southville is seen here. An 1880 map of Bridgewater and Southville shows 27 homes and businesses in the town. (BHS.)

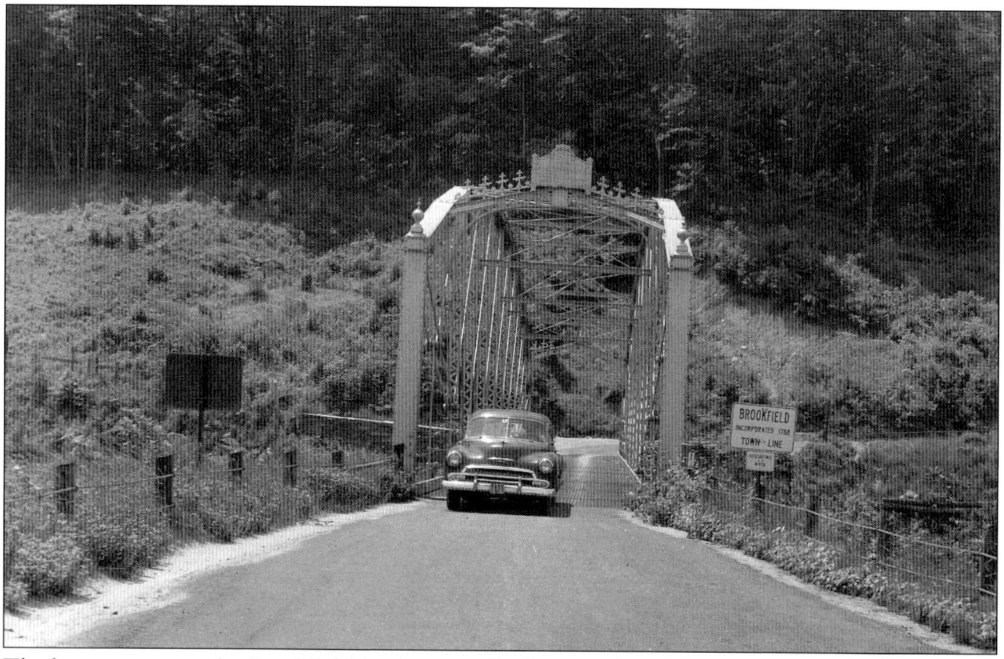

The last car to cross the Brookfield-Bridgewater Bridge was that of the Bridgewater first selectman, G. Douglas Johnson. This bridge was constructed in 1890. Johnson removed the iron sign that marked the entrance to the bridge, which had been built by the Berlin Bridge Company. That sign is still on display at the Captain's House, next to the Bridgewater Historical Society. (BHS.)

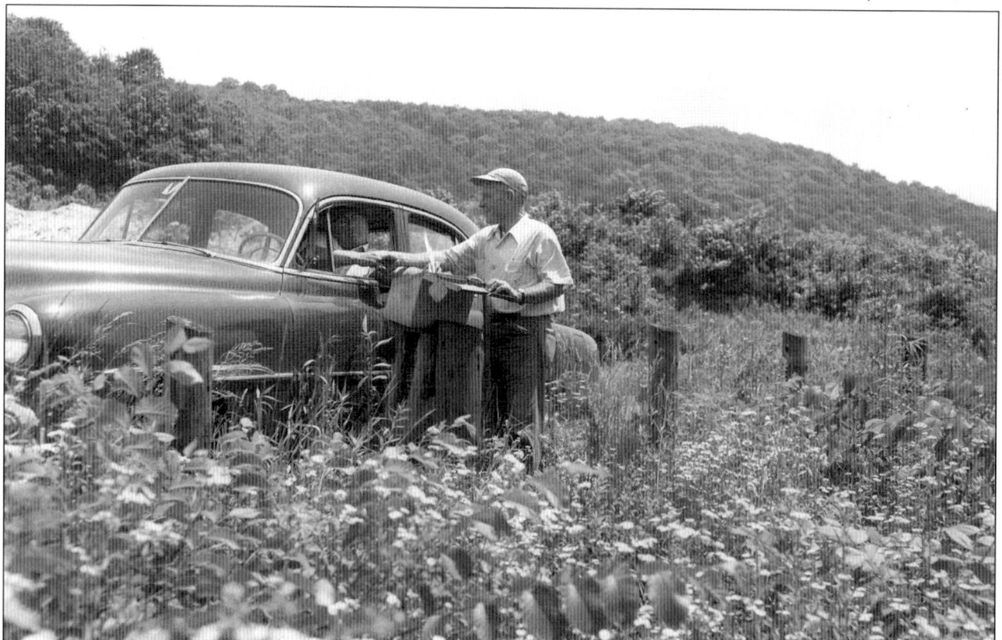

The last mail delivery to Southville was made by postman Paul F. Kominack on June 15, 1955. Here, he shakes hands with the Bridgewater first selectman, G. Douglas Johnson. Kominack began delivering the mail to Southville in a horse and buggy in 1917. This delivery, 38 years later, went to the town's only three remaining mailboxes. The final demolition was imminent. (BHS.)

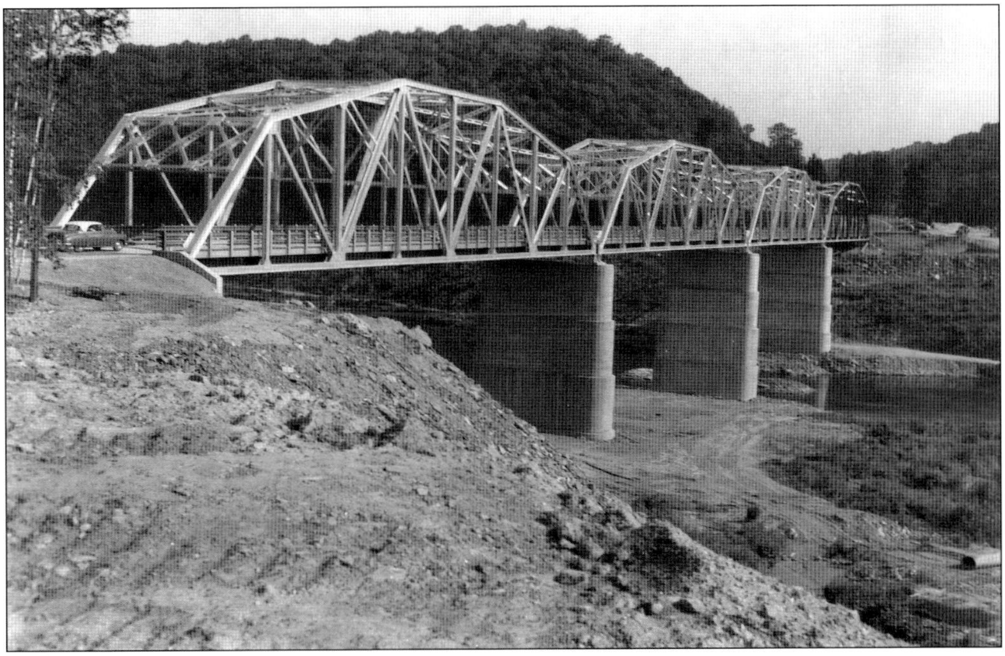

The completion of a new bridge over the Housatonic River was the last link in the Shepaug Hydroelectric Development Plan. By connecting waterpower plants along the river, Connecticut Light and Power Company created a system that generated about 117 million kilowatt hours of electricity when it opened in 1955. (BHS.)

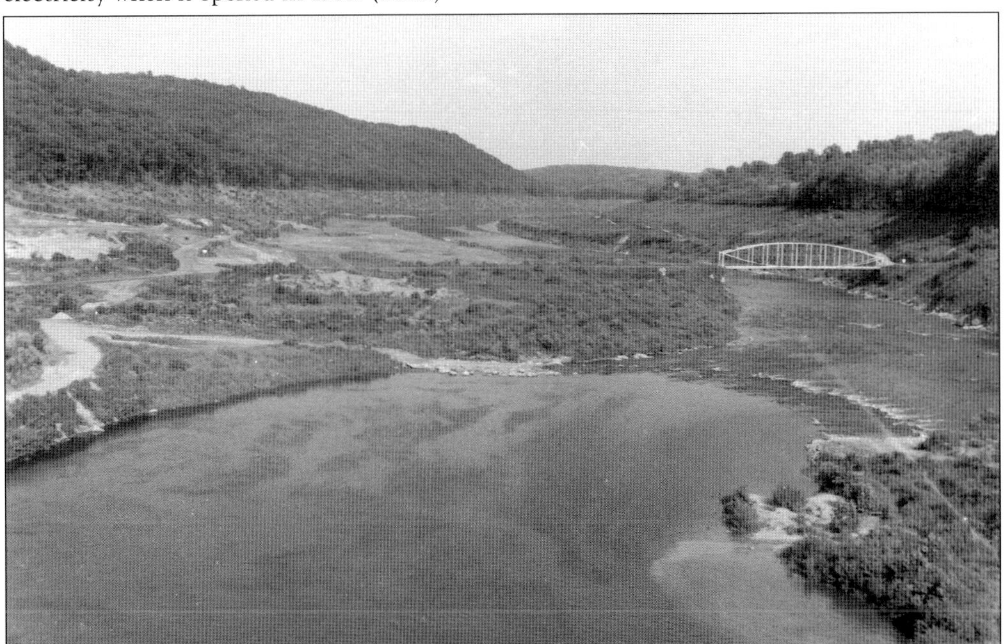

The Housatonic River winds between Brookfield and Bridgewater towards New Milford. At one time, fishing in the river was a major industry. Lamprey eel, bass, trout, and shad were caught here. Old-timers said that the flooding of the river to form Lake Lillinonah caused the fish to move to new locations. (BHS.)

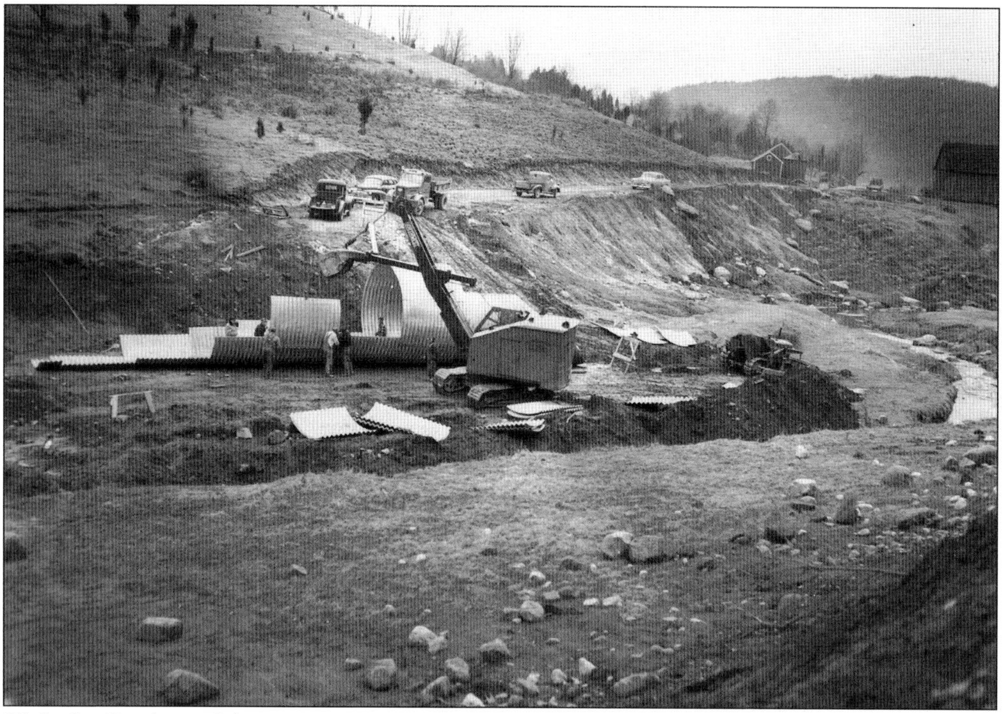

With the flooding of the Housatonic River and the creation of the lake, new roads needed to be constructed to provide access to Bridgewater businesses and homes. (BHS.)

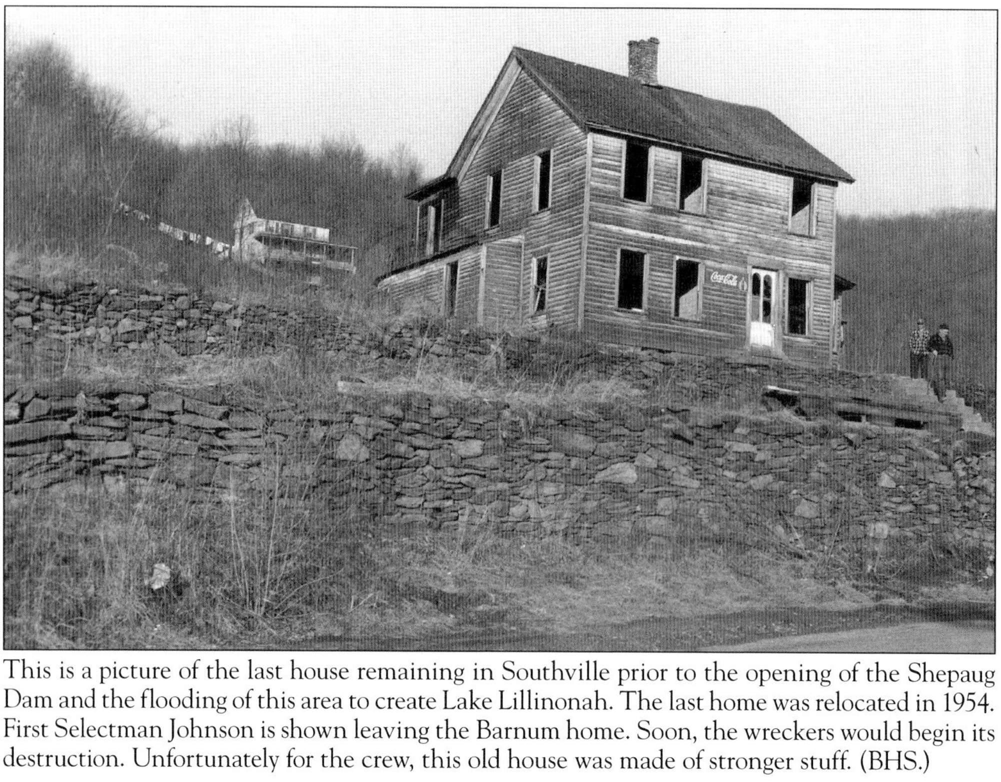

This is a picture of the last house remaining in Southville prior to the opening of the Shepaug Dam and the flooding of this area to create Lake Lillinonah. The last home was relocated in 1954. First Selectman Johnson is shown leaving the Barnum home. Soon, the wreckers would begin its destruction. Unfortunately for the crew, this old house was made of stronger stuff. (BHS.)

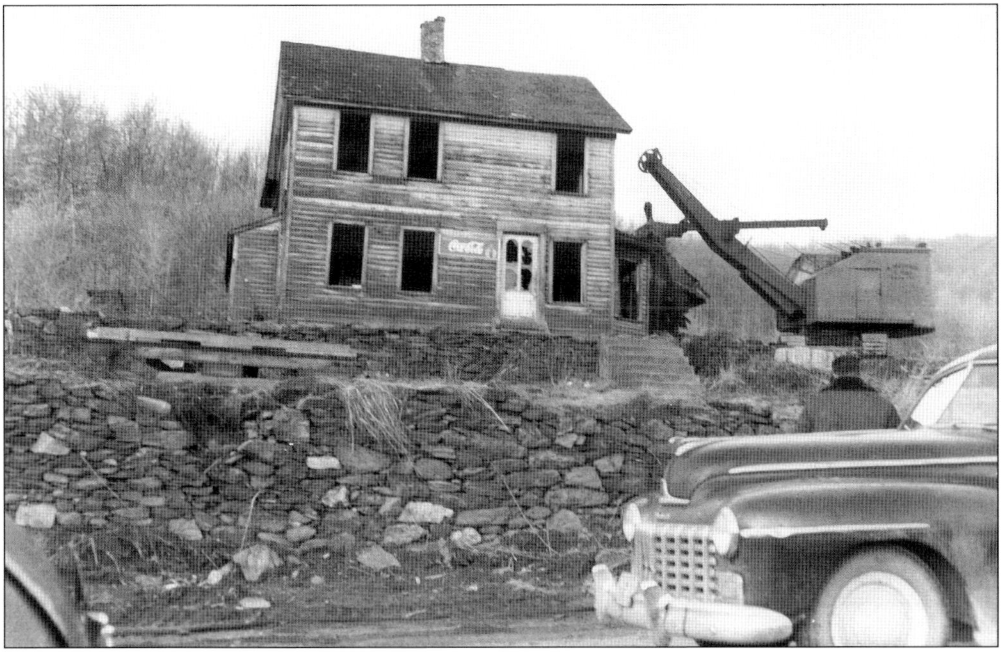

The wrecking ball and crane were in place for the demolition of this 130-year old home. The plan was to reduce the structure into two piles of easily burnable timbers. The wreckers were only successful in knocking down half of the house, built with wooden, pegged timbers and walls covered in plaster. (BHS.)

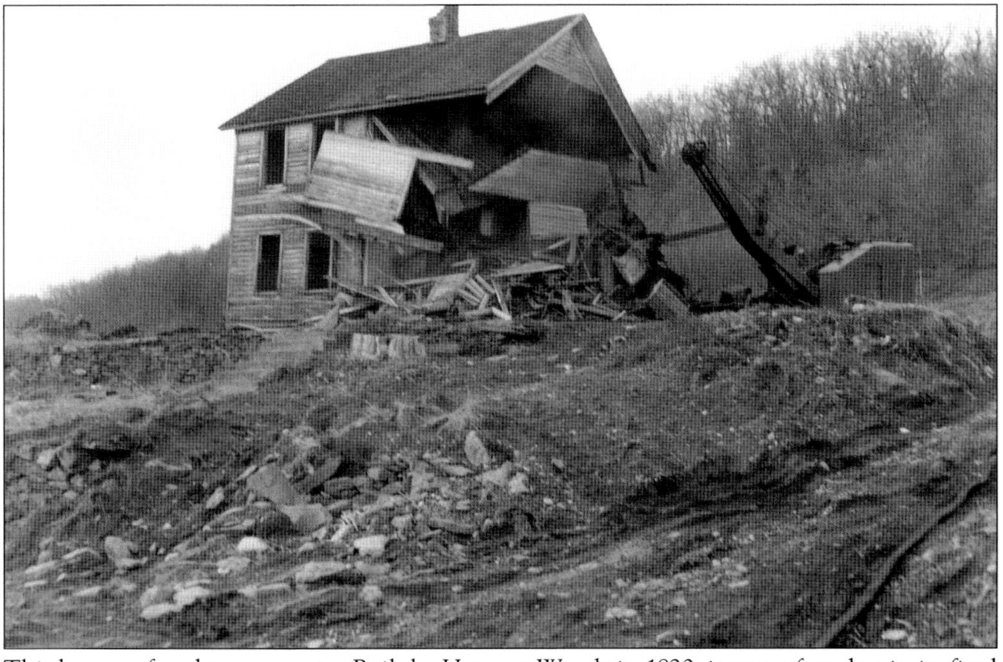

This house refused to cooperate. Built by Herman Woods in 1820, it was referred to in its final years as the Barnum House because of its last residents, two brothers who were referred to as "The Barnum Boys," even as senior citizens. They claimed to be relatives of P.T. Barnum. The last brother, Andrew, died on January 18, 1951, at the age of 78. (BHS.)

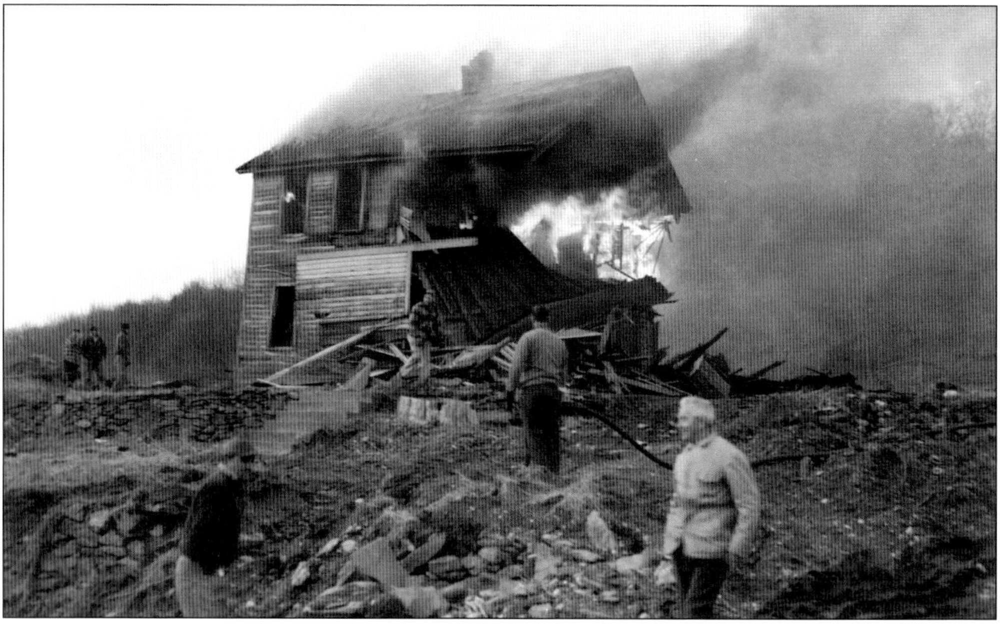

Once it became clear that the old house would not fall to the wrecking ball, plans changed. The Bridgewater Fire Department, authorized to set the house afire, made several attempts to get the fire going. A wooden rowboat was discovered in the cellar. Evidently, the Barnum Boys had built the boat down there, but had neglected to measure the size of the doorway beforehand, and they were never able to get it out. The firemen soaked the boat in kerosene and set it afire. (BHS.)

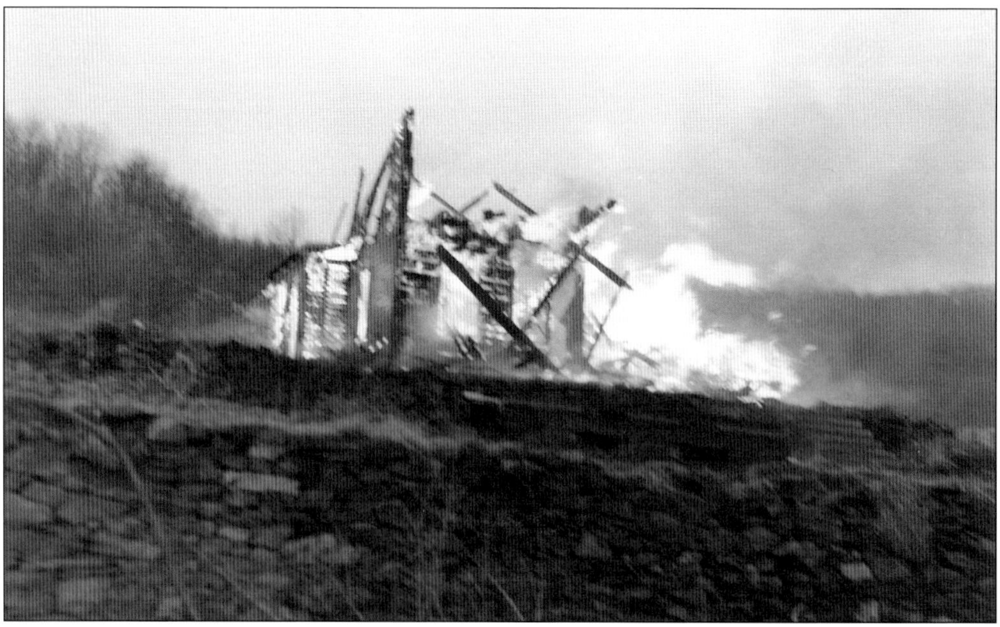

More than 75 Bridgewater residents came to see the destruction of the last of Southville's homes. As they stood watching the flames, they shared their memories of the Southville they knew. At one time, the village had been home to many businesses—including hat shops, an ironworks district, a boot and shoe factory, a tannery, a country store, and a textile factory—as well as churches, a post office, and a school. (BHS.)

Six

Earning a Living

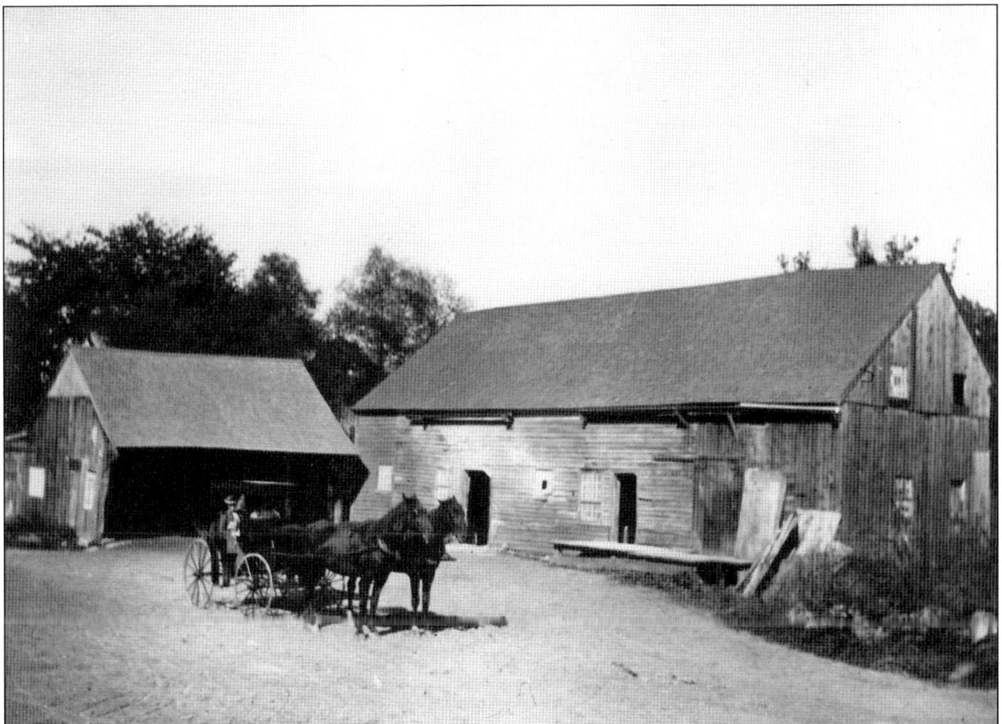

A passenger waits patiently as the Bridgewater Stage makes a stop at H.A. Hill's Mill in Roxbury. William Weston served as stage driver for many years. (BHS.)

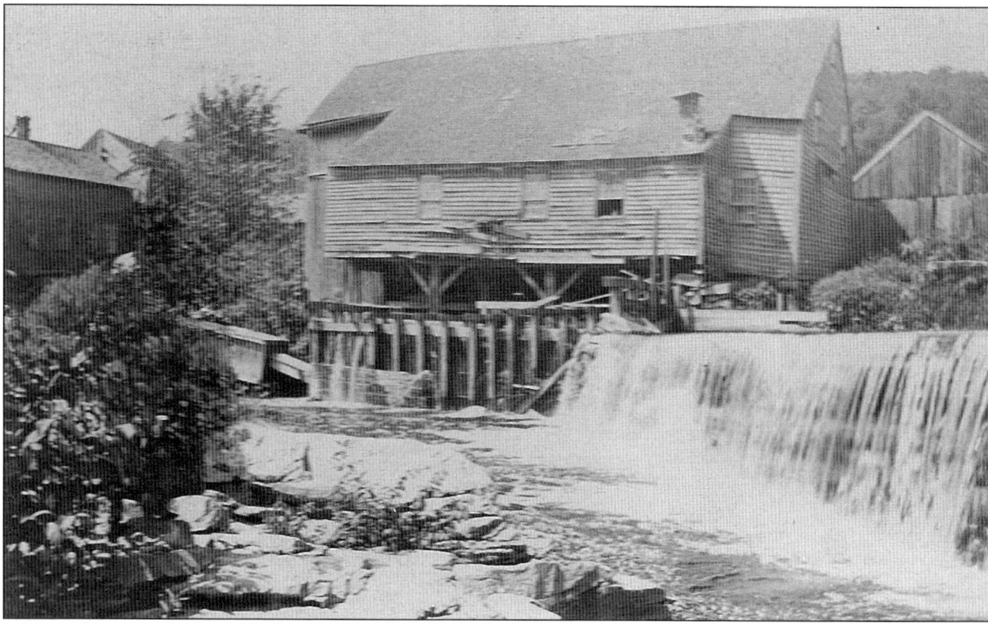

The title "Old Mill Roxbury" adorns this undated photograph. Waterpower was essential to farmers who carted their grain to the gristmill, their wood to the sawmill, and their cloth to the fulling mill. One of Roxbury's oldest mills is the John Trowbridge Mill on Baker Road near Fenn Brook. Stone arrowheads have been found on the property, suggesting that Native Americans lived on this site. (RM.)

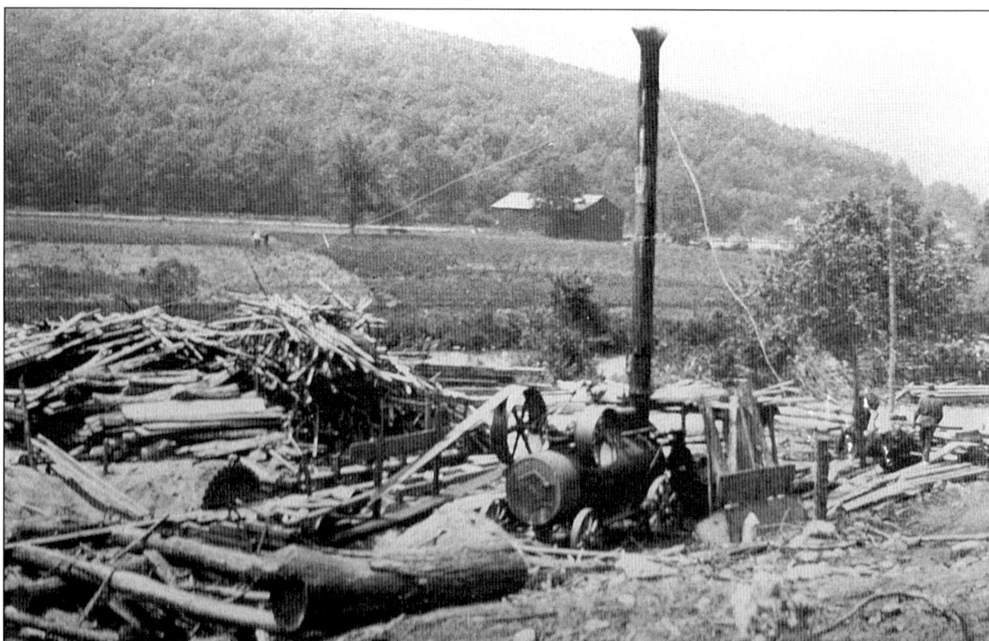

Albert Lafayette Hodge's sawmill on the site of the present-day Hodge Park on the banks of the Shepaug River is pictured in this undated photograph looking northwest. A tobacco barn can be seen across the open field. Other families operated sawmills, including the Bronson and Castle families, which operated sawmills on Jack's Brook. (RM.)

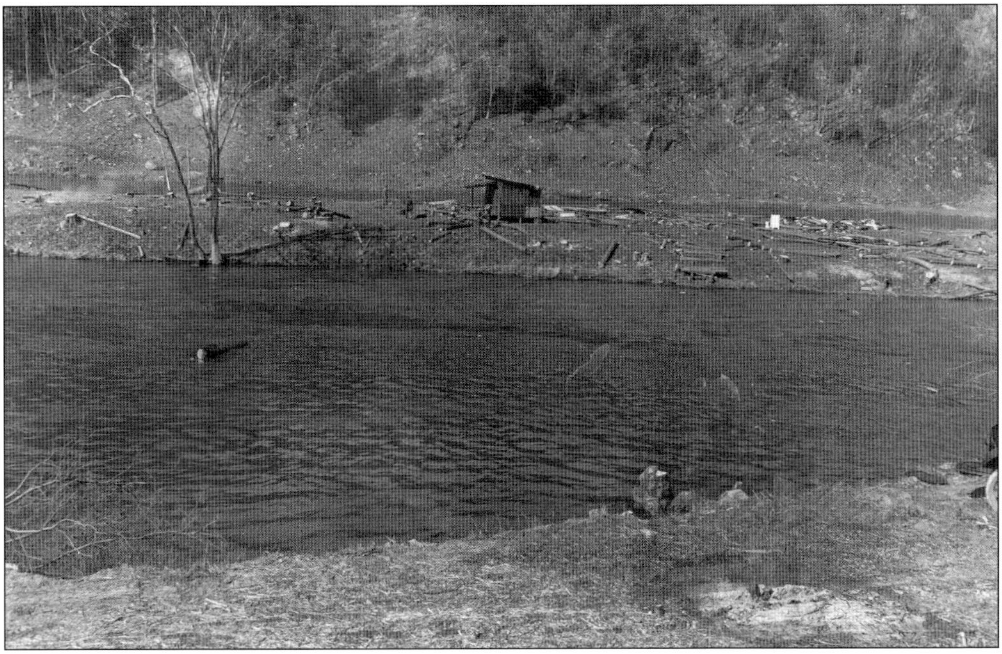

From 1646, Goodyear Island was used as a trading post. It marked neutral territory for Native Americans and settlers, who were safe to come here and barter. Later, it became a recreational area for both Bridgewater and New Milford. It is almost bare here, as logging and other demolition for the creation of the new lake are completed. (BHS.)

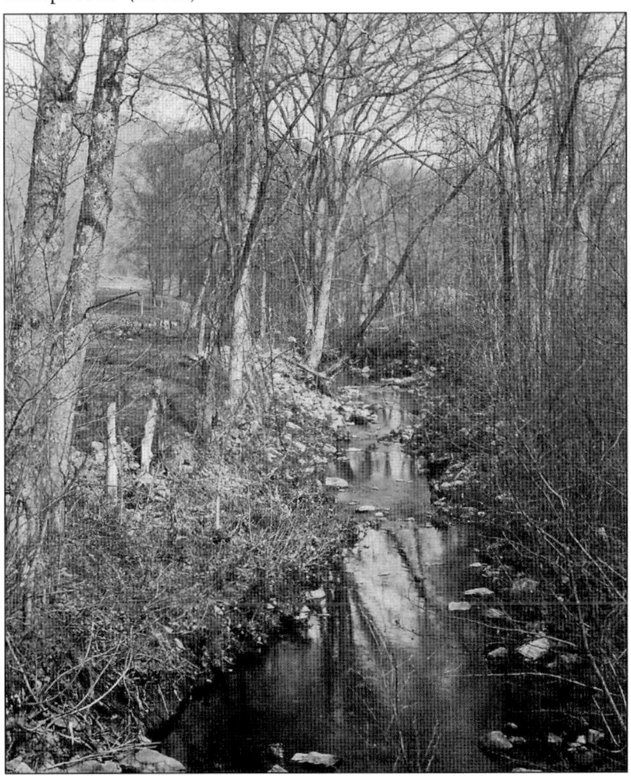

The Red Mill, located on Route 133 in southern Bridgewater, was powered by the Wewaka Brook as it traveled down into the Housatonic, and now, to Lake Lillinonah. One owner was Richard Boleslavsky. With his fellow countrywoman, Maria Ouspenskaya, famous as the Gypsy woman in Lon Chaney's *The Wolf Man*, they founded the American Laboratory Theater, precursor to The Actor's Studio. (BHS.)

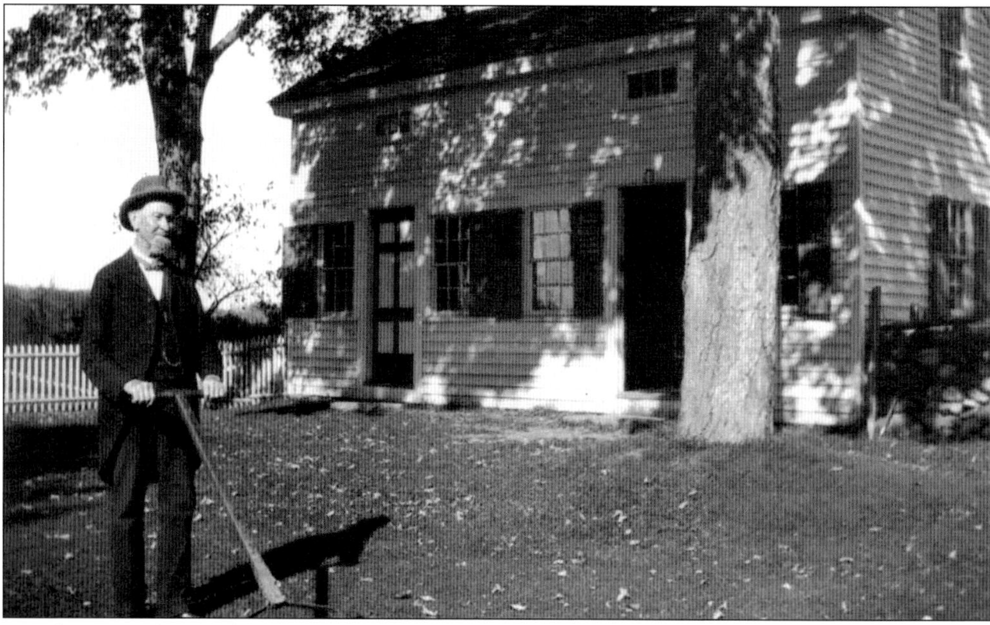

Smith R. Weeks was born in Bridgewater in 1818. His family built their home north of the Congregational Church around 1840. Weeks constructed his tailor shop near that home and was the town's tailor for nearly 50 years. He is shown here mowing his front lawn in 1898. This was one tailor who always showed his skills—sometimes wearing his own product, even for gardening. (BHS.)

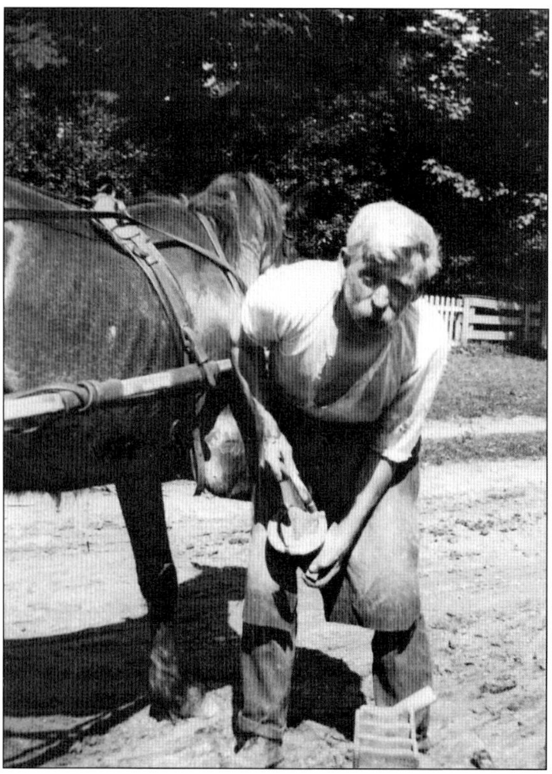

James Orr was Bridgewater's blacksmith. Born in December 1858, he and his wife, Mary H., lived with their three children, Isabelle, Ethel, and Walter, along with his wife's aunt and uncle, William and Martha Rice, and a boarder, Horace Brooks—all in a modest home on Main Street, next to his smithy. (BHS.)

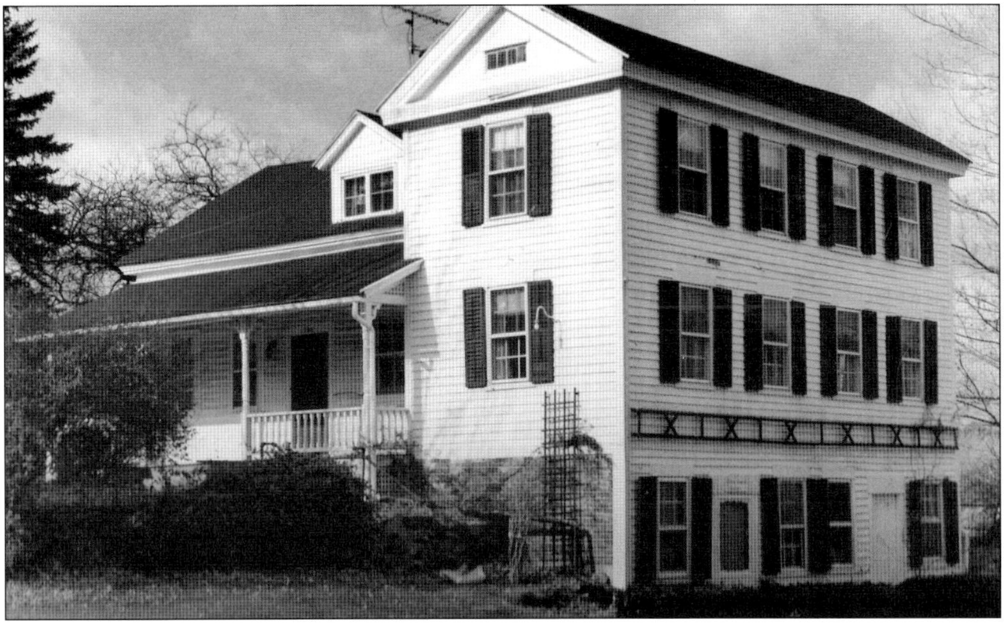

Built around 1740, Capt. Roswell Ransom's Tavern at One North Street was the site of many Roxbury celebrations. Tragically, in October 1787, a soldier was accidently killed during a militia training exercise. Captain Ransom continued to operate this tavern until 1796, Roxbury's year of incorporation, when he moved his family to New Haven. In 1846, the Greek Revival–style house became the Christ Church Rectory. (RM.)

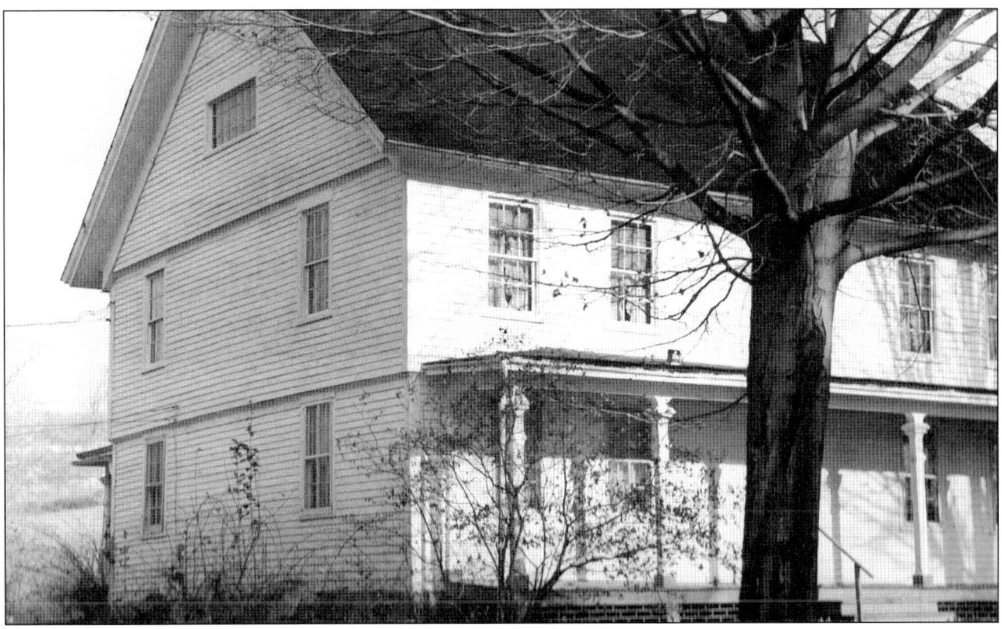

Stagecoach passengers no doubt welcomed a stop at the c. 1785 Burwell Tavern in Roxbury. The house at Four Southbury Road was bought in 1839 by the Thomas family who held it for over a century. The best known of the large Thomas clan was Harvey Thomas, who raised and sold horses and drew his neighbors' attention when he drove his trotters and sulky down Church Street. (RM.)

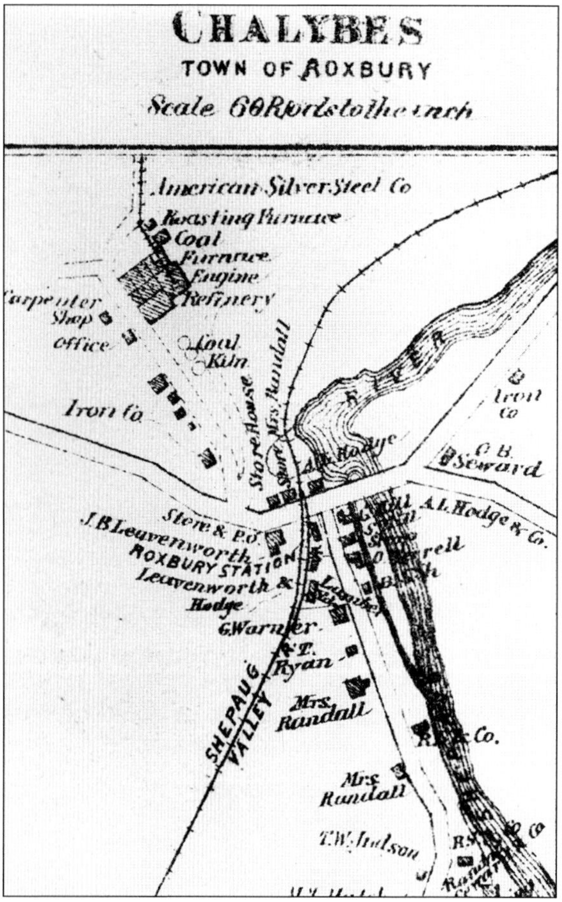

Chalybes was a boomtown when hundreds of miners, stonecutters, masons, and other laborers from Europe settled here. This map of Chalybes from the 1874 *Beer's Atlas of Litchfield County, Connecticut* shows the vast mining operations with furnaces, railroads, and the village. The name Chalybes was given in 1867 by Dr. Horace Bushnell, but the Greek name caused a stir. The village later became known as Roxbury Station. (MML.)

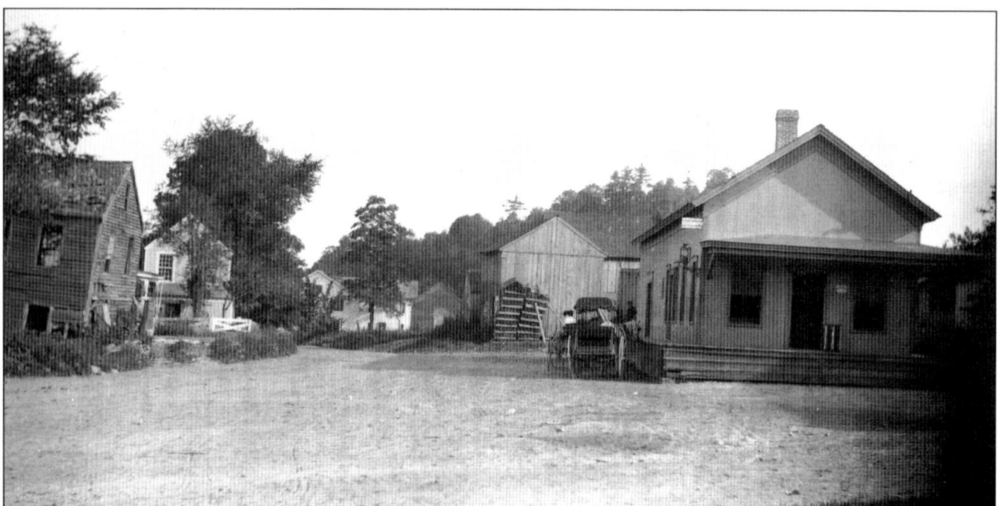

This 1905 photograph depicts Roxbury Station at Mine Hill where mail arrived on the Shepaug Valley Railroad, which operated a spur through the village. A post office, hotel, gristmill, boardinghouses, tavern, creamery, general store, and lumberyard were all built in the area to serve the hundreds of workers in the mines and quarries. (RM.)

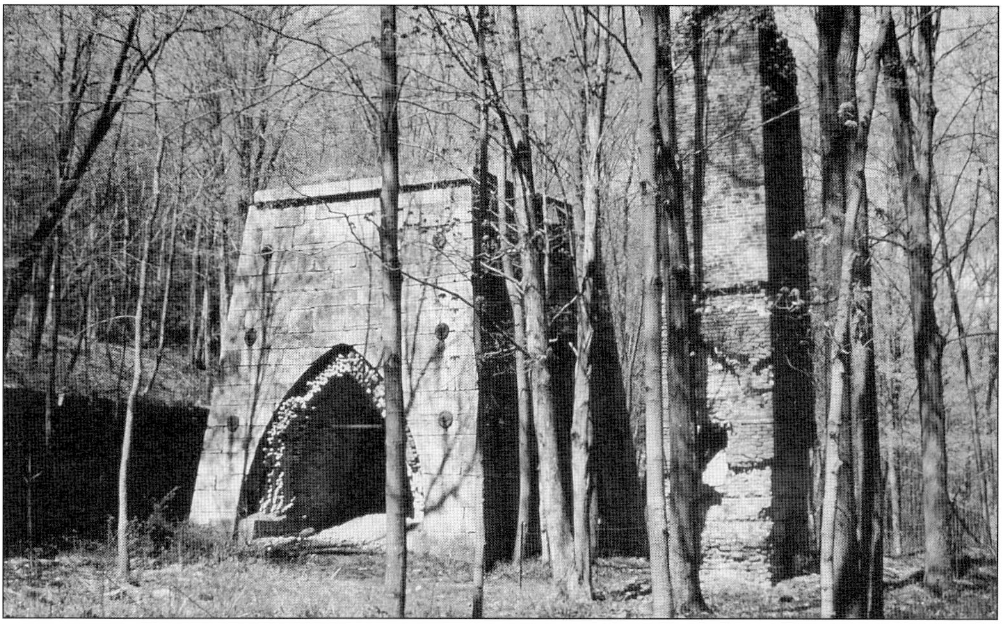

Mine Hill was first worked in 1751 for silver and, in the 1800s, saw a short but intense experiment with iron and steel. This National Historic Landmark in Roxbury has Connecticut's most extensive ruins of the iron ore industry that once thrived here. A 3.5-mile walk takes visitors past a blast furnace, roasting ovens, tunnels, shafts, and granite quarries. This image shows two ore-roasting kilns for siderite. (RLT.)

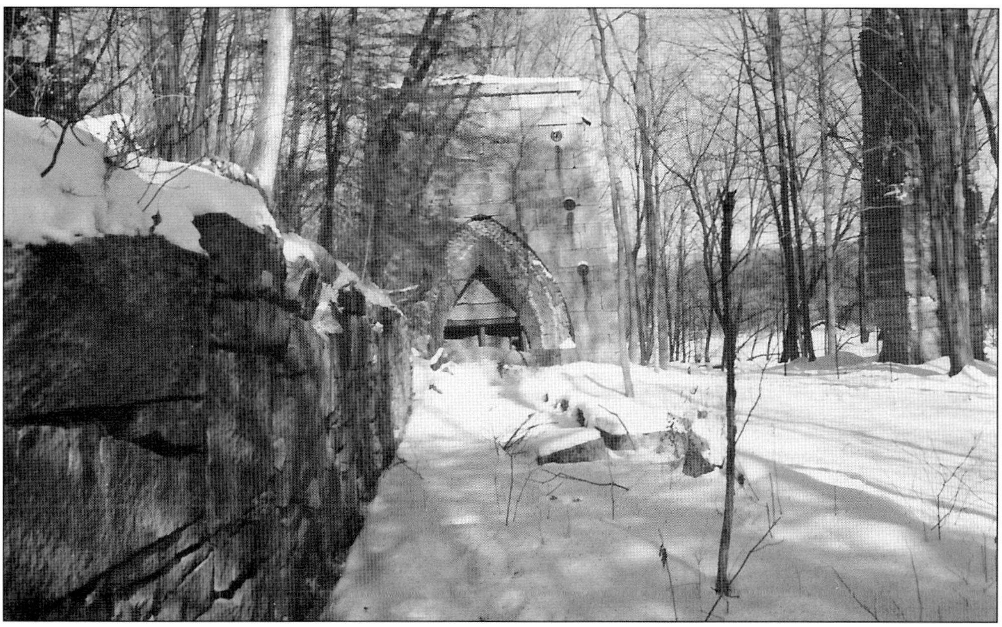

The blast furnace was at the heart of Mine Hill's iron-making venture. After a long and complicated process of mining, transporting, roasting, and hand sorting, workmen shoveled prepared ore and charcoal into the top of the blast furnace to transform the ore into molten metal. Impurities were drawn off, and the molten iron was tapped to run into channels in a sand casting bed, where it cooled into iron pigs. (RLT.)

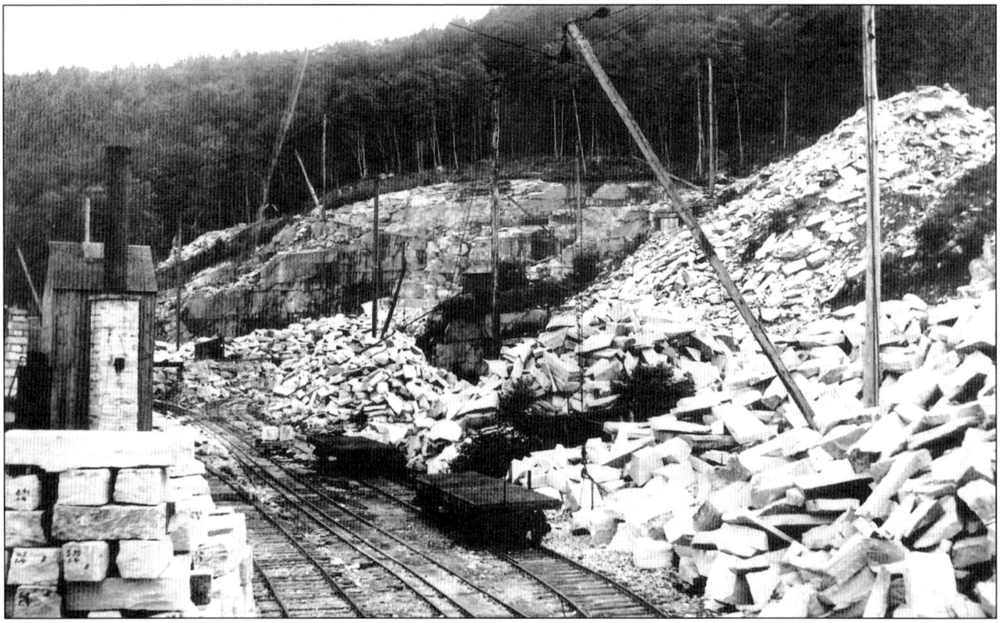

In 1817, Yale University professor Benjamin Silliman commented that he was more impressed with the "light, agreeable gray" stone he found at Mine Hill than he was with the iron and silver ore. He described the granite as "singularly perfect." The narrow-gauge rail in this image ran through the upper quarries, and the cut granite was loaded onto railroad cars and hauled away on the Shepaug Valley Railroad. (RM.)

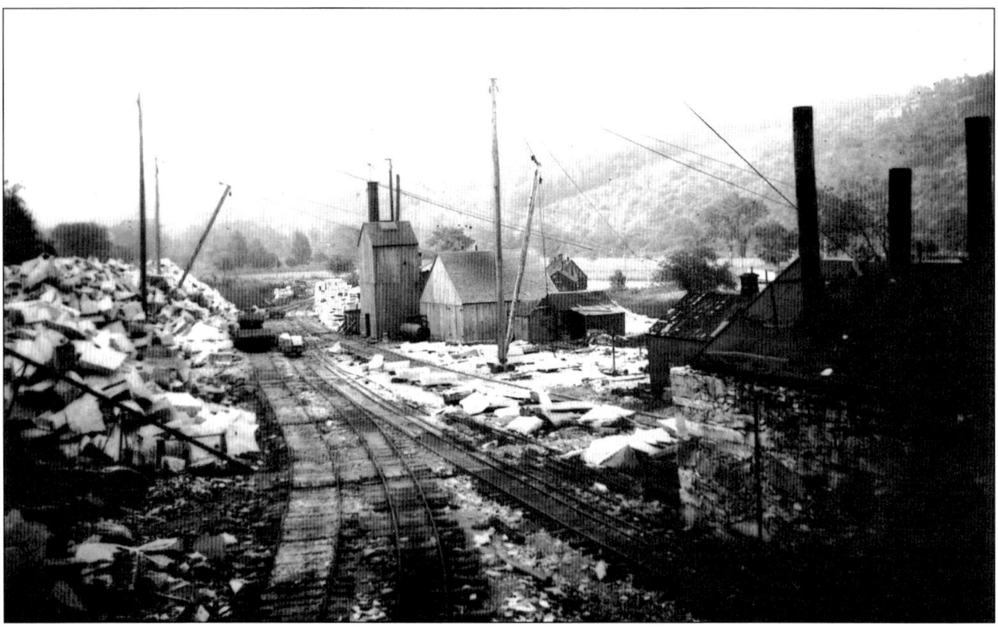

Stoneworkers walked on a suspension bridge across the Shepaug River to reach the Rockside Quarry at Mine Hill in Roxbury. This 1905 Joseph West photograph shows cut granite ready to be hauled down the mountainside on narrow-gauge rails where it was shipped to Bridgeport, New York City, and other locations. Before the Shepaug Valley Railroad opened in 1871, oxcarts carried the rocks downhill. (RM.)

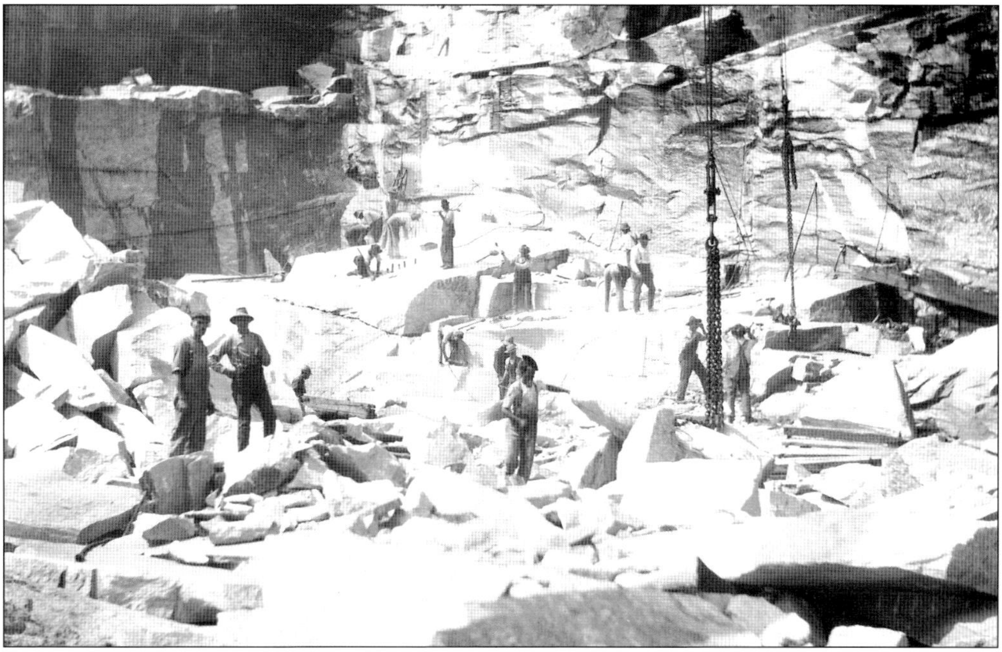

Records are lost as to when quarrying began on Mine Hill, but men toil in the quarries even today. In 1905, Joseph West photographed workers in hats, caps, overalls, and suspenders hauling the heavy rock from Mine Hill. The fine granite is prized for building hearths, chimneys, terraces, walkways, and other stone structures. (Cameron Gardella.)

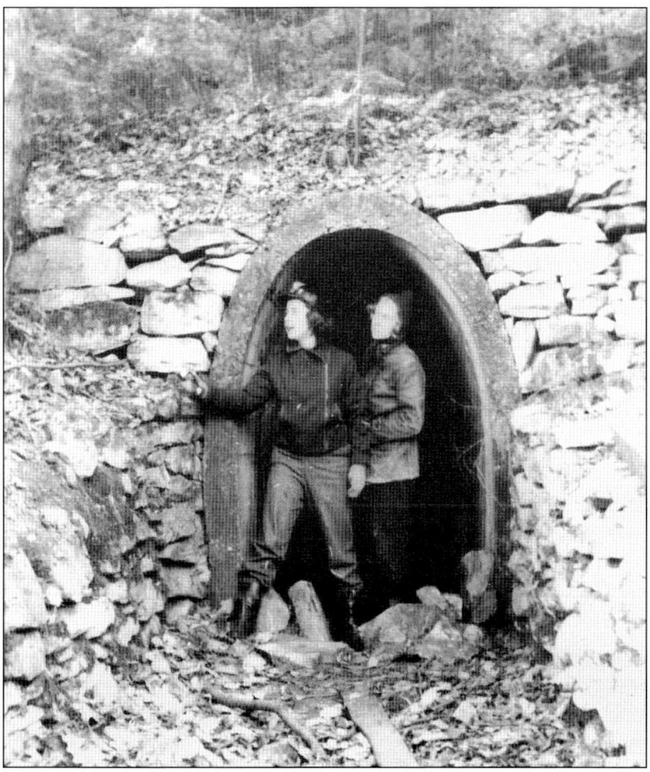

On December 21, 1956, Charles Mohr, naturalist at the Greenwich Audubon Society, photographed Mrs. Arthur Johnson of Waterbury (left) and Mrs. LeRoy Foote of Middlebury (right) peering into a cave for hibernating bats at the main entrance to the Roxbury Iron Mine. Four rare species of bats have been known to winter in the tunnels—the pippistrel, the little brown bat, the big brown bat, and the Keen's bat. (RLT.)

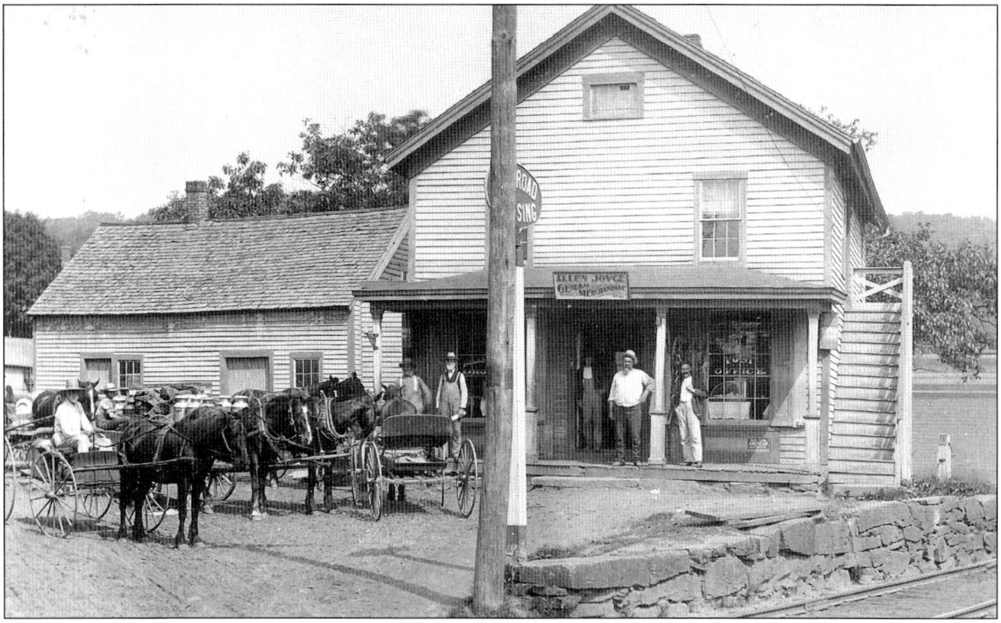

The Allen Joyce General Merchandise store was buzzing with activity in 1907 when Joseph West photographed farmers waiting at Roxbury Station in horse-drawn wagons and carriages to deliver their milk to the nearby creamery for processing. The heavy milk cans were then loaded onto the Shepaug Valley Railroad cars and shipped to larger towns. (Cameron Gardella.)

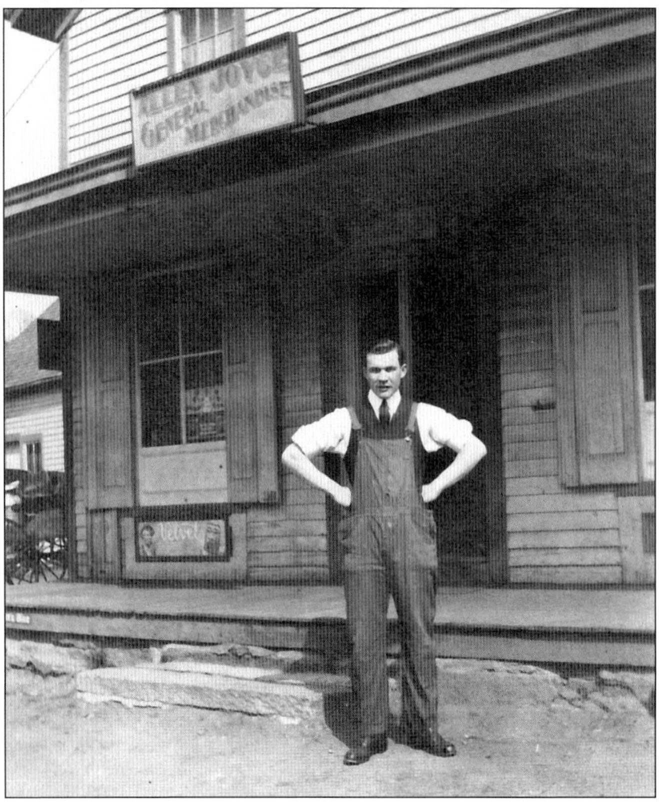

William Whalen worked as a clerk in the Allen Joyce store at Roxbury Station. Apparently, bib overalls with large pockets over a white-collared dress shirt with vest and tie were the uniform of the day. The fabric of his overalls has a pinstripe, which was also typical of a railroad worker's uniform. (RM.)

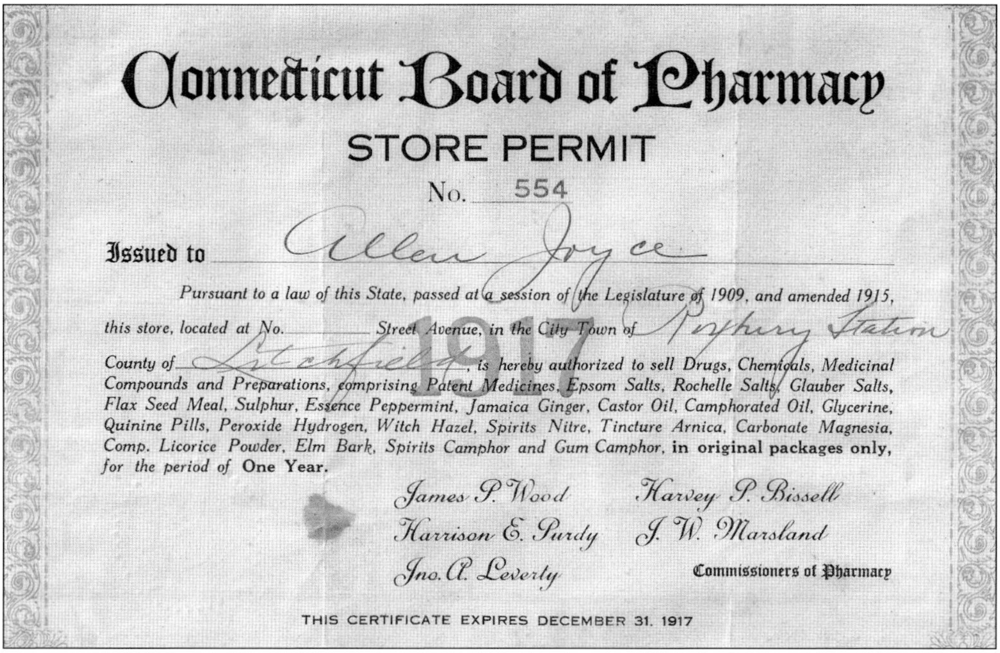

Connecticut Board of Pharmacy

STORE PERMIT

No. 554

Issued to Allen Joyce

Pursuant to a law of this State, passed at a session of the Legislature of 1909, and amended 1915, this store, located at No. ______ Street Avenue, in the City Town of Roxbury Station County of Litchfield, is hereby authorized to sell Drugs, Chemicals, Medicinal Compounds and Preparations, comprising Patent Medicines, Epsom Salts, Rochelle Salts, Glauber Salts, Flax Seed Meal, Sulphur, Essence Peppermint, Jamaica Ginger, Castor Oil, Camphorated Oil, Glycerine, Quinine Pills, Peroxide Hydrogen, Witch Hazel, Spirits Nitre, Tincture Arnica, Carbonate Magnesia, Comp. Licorice Powder, Elm Bark, Spirits Camphor and Gum Camphor, in original packages only, for the period of One Year.

1917

James P. Wood
Harvey P. Bissell
Harrison E. Purdy
J. W. Marsland
Jno. A. Leverty

Commissioners of Pharmacy

THIS CERTIFICATE EXPIRES DECEMBER 31, 1917

Owners of general stores often provided products beyond groceries and other household items. Allen Joyce, manager of a general merchandise store at Roxbury Station, apparently also sold medicines. This "Connecticut Board of Pharmacy Store permit" with an expiration date of December 31, 1917, was probably posted in his store. (RM.)

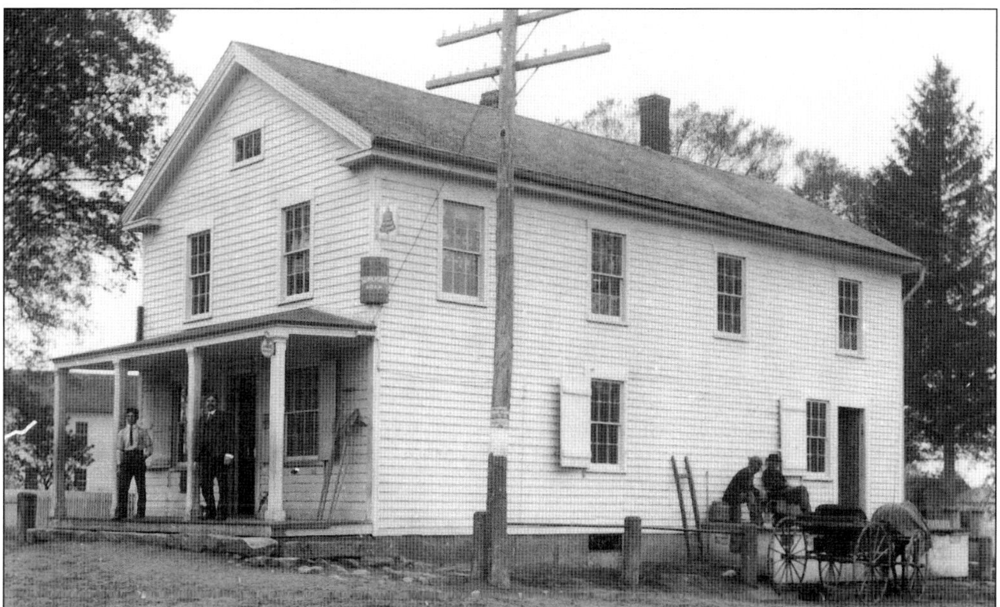

George Hurlburt (1809–1904) was a prominent merchant, farmer, hatter, and postmaster in Roxbury. His home and general store were on the corner of Wellers Bridge Road and South Street. In this undated image, two men stand on the porch, and two men and two dogs relax beside a four-wheeled one-horse carriage at the side of the store. Hurlburt's house is to the left of the store. (Cameron Gardella.)

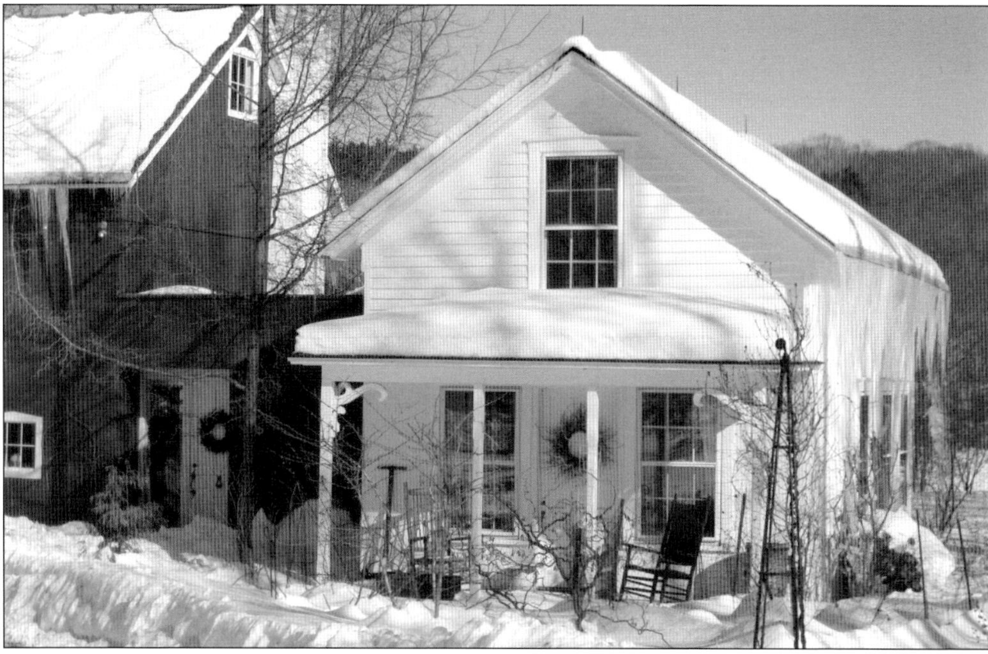

The store and shoe shop was owned by Hamlin and Beach in the 19th century and is one of the few remaining commercial buildings in Roxbury Center. The shop was once moved to a different location, then moved back and attached to a barn. Today, the barn and shop on South Street are a private residence. (Jeannine Green.)

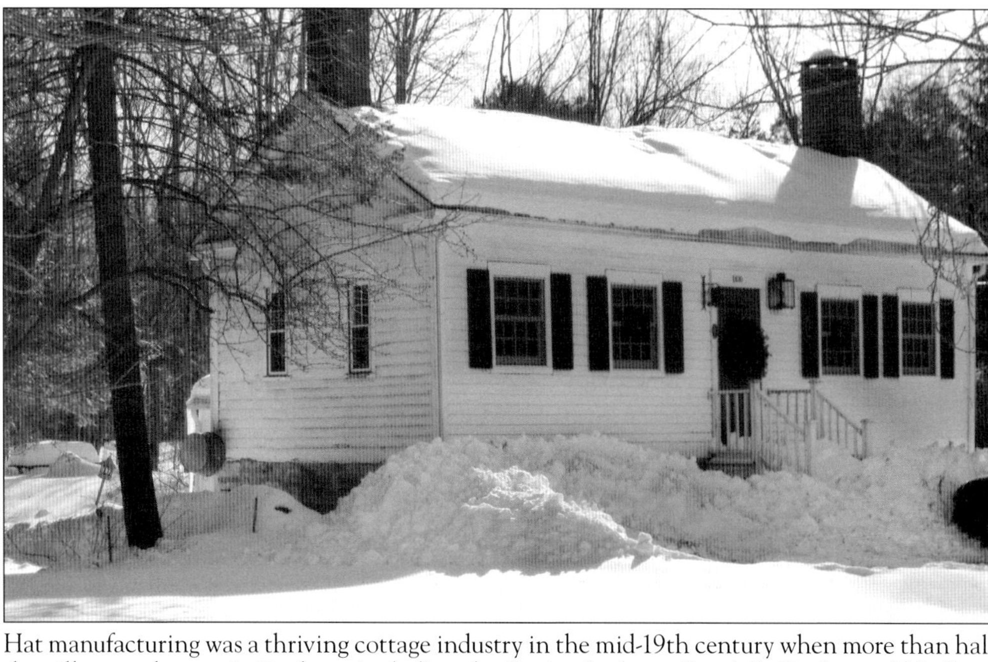

Hat manufacturing was a thriving cottage industry in the mid-19th century when more than half the village tradesmen in Roxbury, including the Squire, Lathrop, Randall, Crofut, and Hurlburt families were involved in it. Frederick W. Lathrop built this hat shop in 1840, but by the Civil War, the manufacture of rough-formed hats that supplied urban finishers and wholesalers had become mechanized and was no longer a viable industry. (Jeannine Green.)

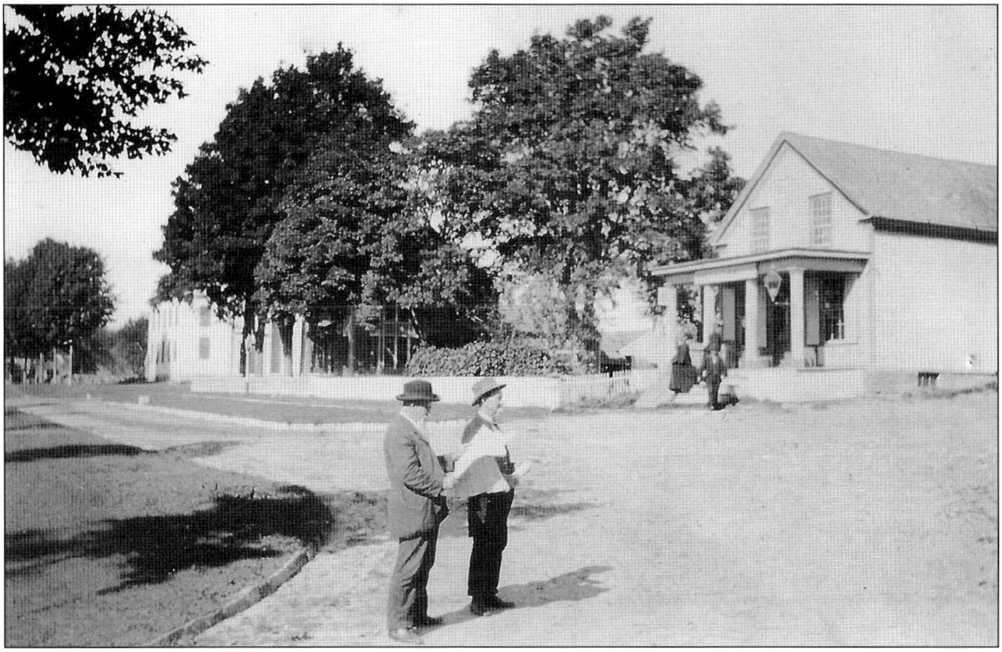

The Peck House is seen in the background in its original location, north of the Hatch Store. It was moved south to make way for a larger home on the prestigious corner location. The Peck House is now the home of the Bridgewater Historical Society. (BHS.)

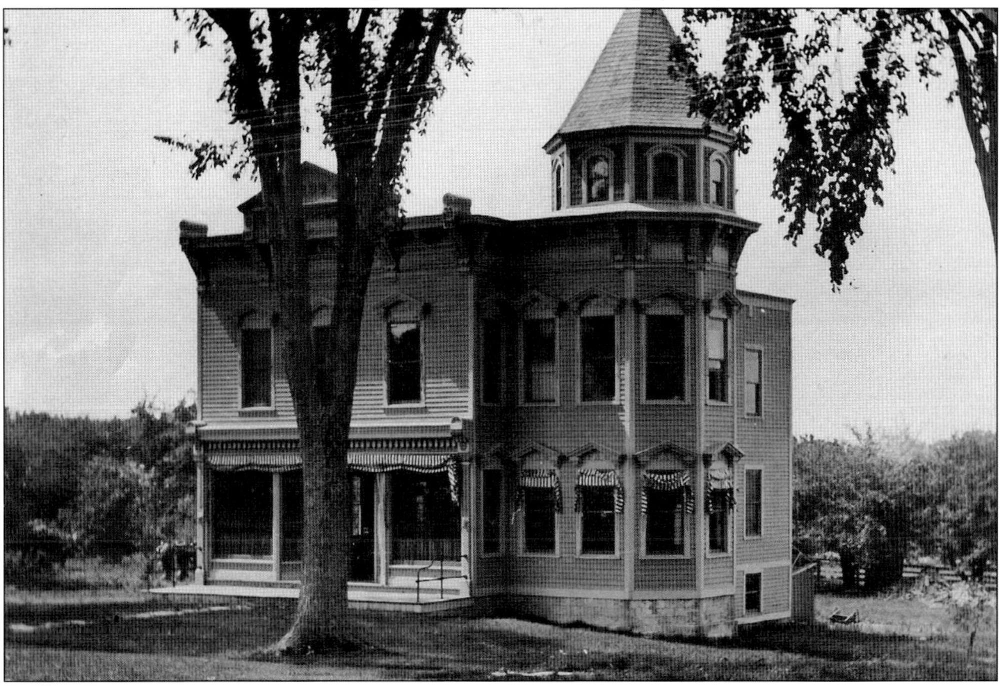

C.B. Thomson renamed himself, becoming "Charles Bridgewater Thomson." The entrepreneur was a pioneer in the mail-order business. He offered "premiums" to his sales force when they reached their goals. Everything from perfume to patterns for children's dolls was sent from the Bridgewater Post Office. The building became the general store and post office. (BHS.)

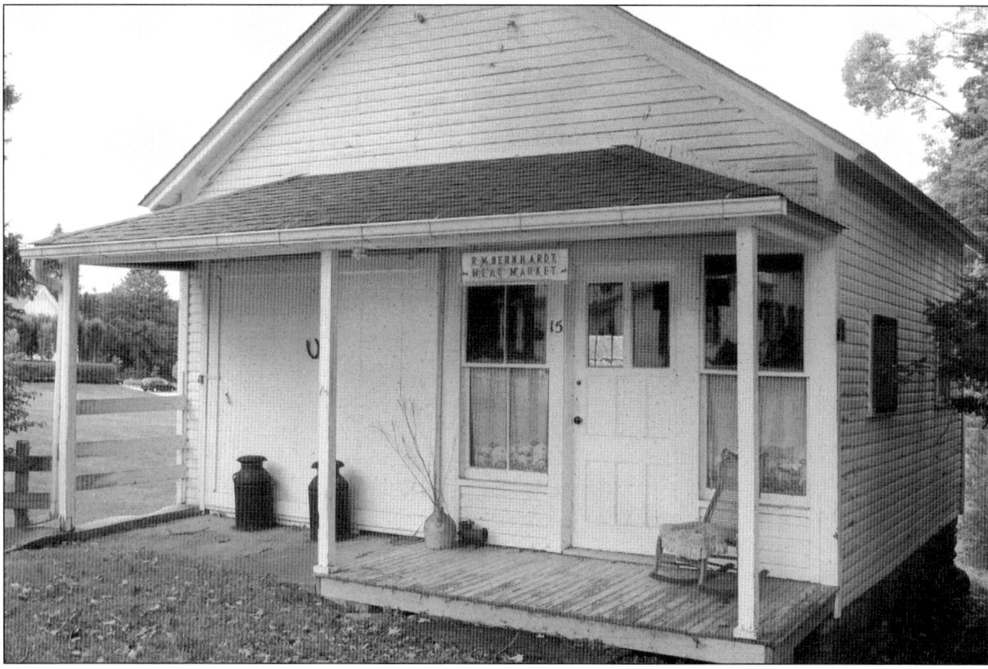

This tiny white building, built in 1921, was owned and operated by Rulley McKinstry Bernhardt (1878–1955), who raised Holstein and Guernsey cattle, operated a slaughterhouse in Roxbury Hollow, and sold his meat in this market at 15 South Street. Today, the market is a museum with sawdust on the floor, flypaper hanging from the ceiling, butcher-block tables, and vintage butcher implements. (Jeannine Green.)

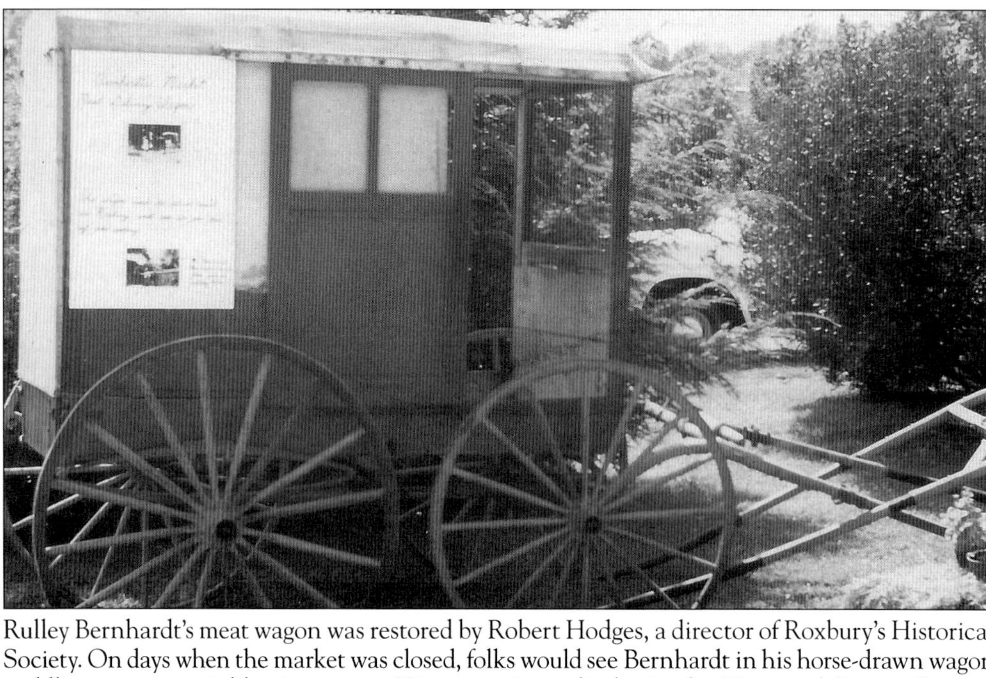

Rulley Bernhardt's meat wagon was restored by Robert Hodges, a director of Roxbury's Historical Society. On days when the market was closed, folks would see Bernhardt in his horse-drawn wagon peddling meat to neighboring towns. His wagon is on display in the Historical Society Barn at Toplands Farm. (Elinor Hurlbut.)

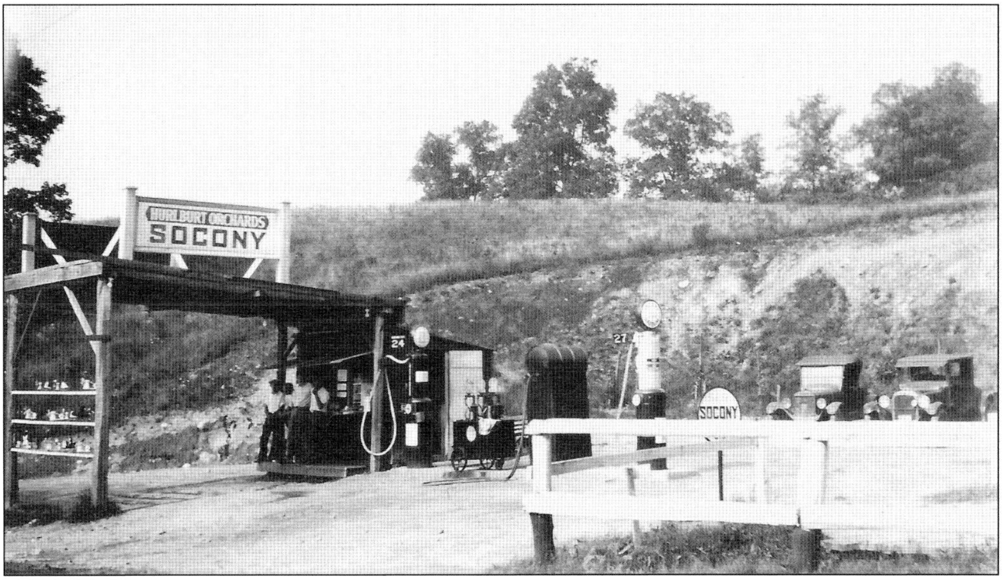

Business appears to be slow at Hurlburt Orchard's Socony filling station, where customers could buy Socony (Standard Oil of New York) fuel at the corner of Ranney Hill Road and North Street in Roxbury. (RM.)

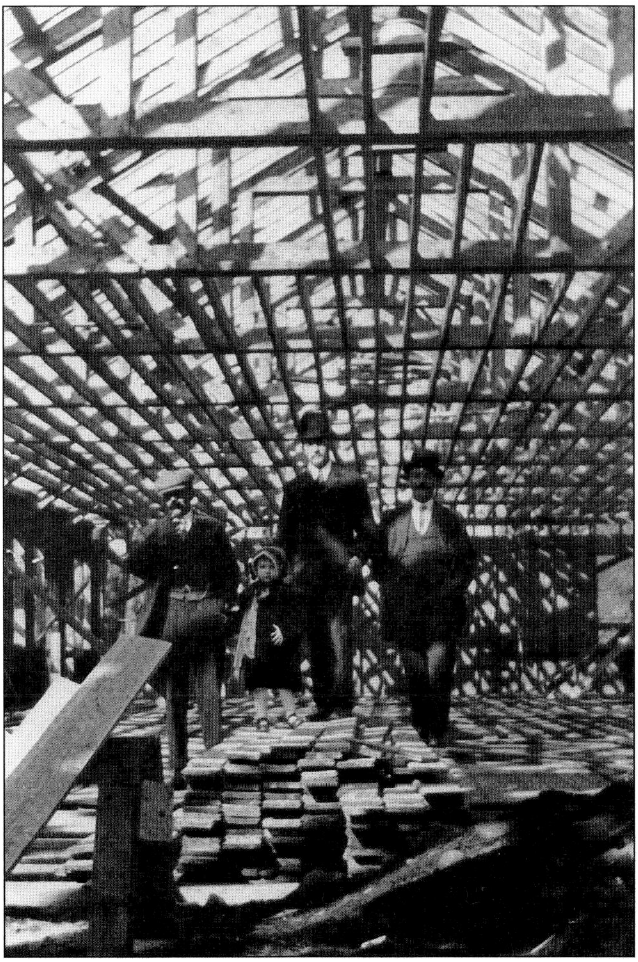

Little is known about the Murray and Sorenson Brothers factory on Baker Road near Roxbury Station. The building is gone now, and only a stone foundation remains. It is thought to have manufactured products related to the brass industry. In this undated image, three men and a young girl appear to be checking on the progress of the building. (MML.)

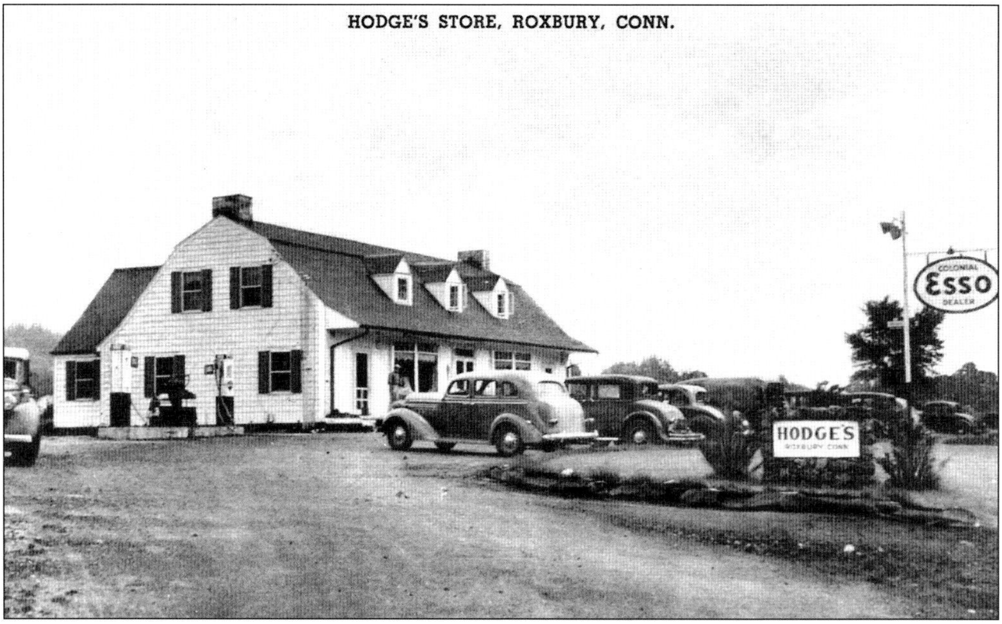

Burton Hodge and his son, Philo, owned and managed a general store in Roxbury Center during the 1920s and 1930s. They sold groceries and household goods and devoted one corner to collecting the mail, as Burton Hodge was also the postmaster during the days of rural free delivery. Merchandise came by freight to Roxbury Station and was hauled over country roads by teams of horses. (RLT.)

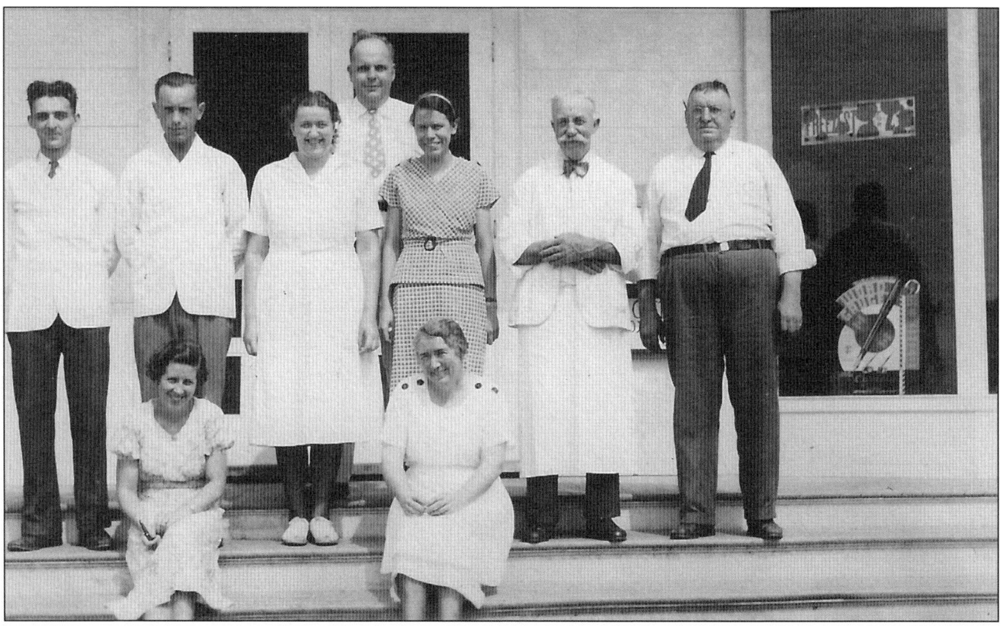

Burton Hodge purchased George W. Hurlburt's store at the corner of South Street and Wellers Bridge Road. In the late 1930s, Burton and his son, Philo, built a new store in the town center that stands today, though it has had several owners during its history. Hodge's employees gathered for this undated photograph in front of the Hodge and Son store. (Constance N. Sherman, Raymond Livingston Booth.)

Seven

Getting Together

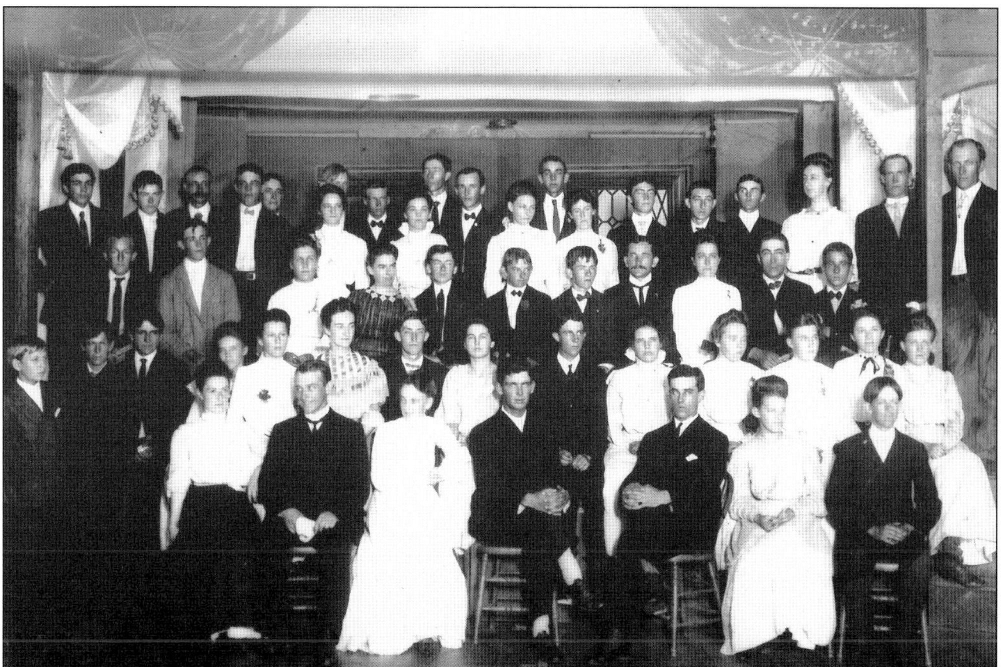

Roxbury's Old Town Hall had a stage that was a popular place for theater and dancing. All dressed up and ready to waltz, this group gathered on the stage to pose for a photograph in September 1905. In the style of the day, the women are dressed in high-necked, long gowns; some are wearing corsages or ribbons. The men and boys are in dark suits with a variety of neckties. (RM.)

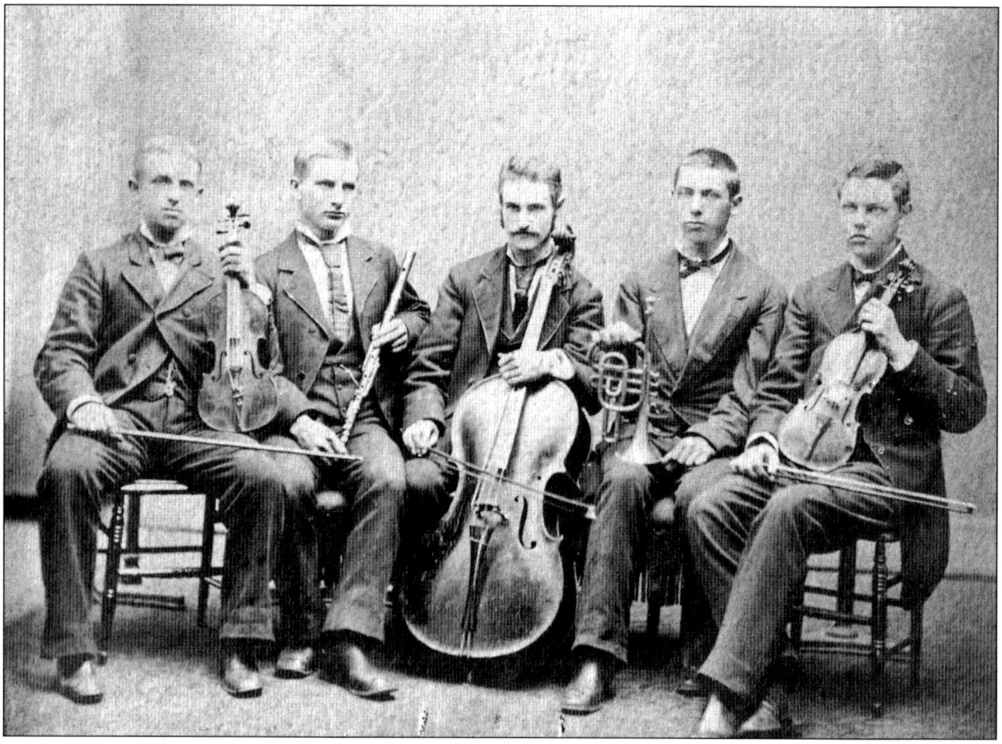

On August 31, 1878, this group of young musicians gathered together for this portrait. Bridgewater's youth enjoyed band concerts and dances, so these men were probably kept busy. (BHS.)

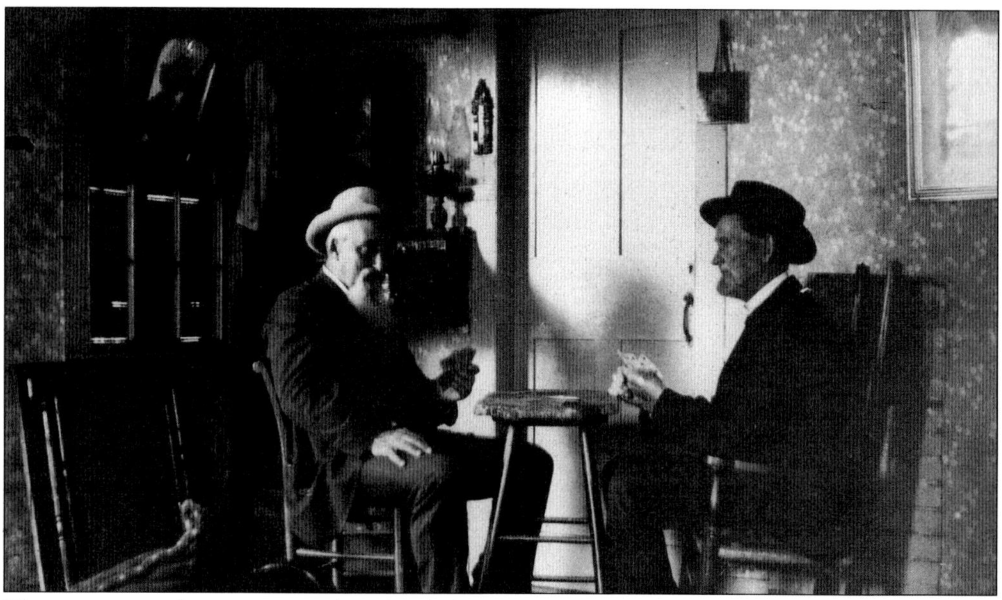

The caption on this picture reads "Old Sledge." It referred to a variation of a card game created in Great Britain in 1674 that became very popular in New England throughout the 19th century. Other names for it included "All Fours," "Seven Up," and "High-Low-Jack." Old friends Austin H. Gillette and Smith R. Weeks are pictured here playing cards in Bridgewater in 1903. (BHS.)

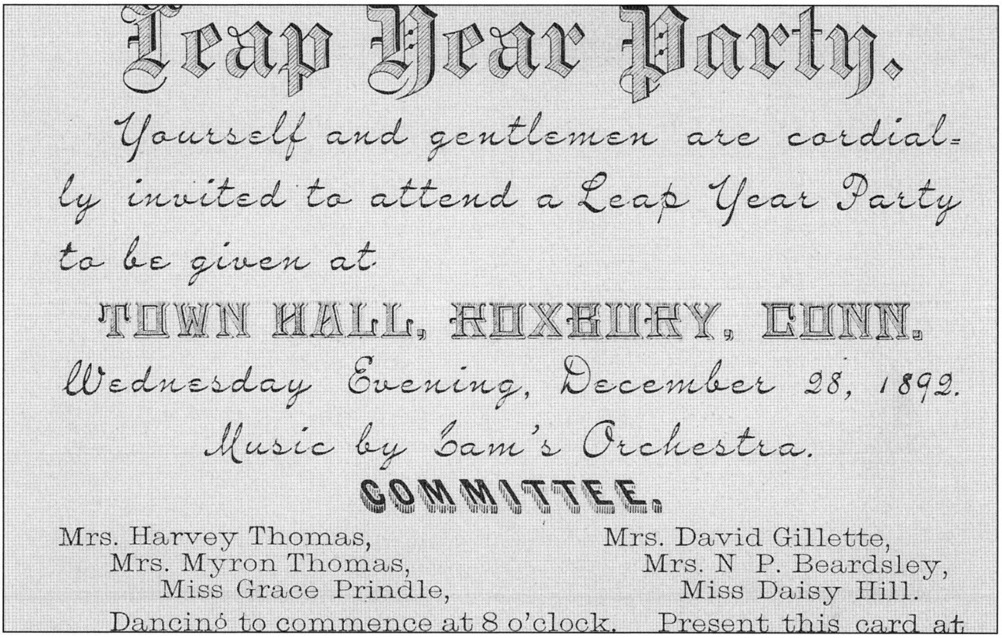

Leap Year Party.

Yourself and gentlemen are cordially invited to attend a Leap Year Party to be given at

TOWN HALL, ROXBURY, CONN.

Wednesday Evening, December 28, 1892.

Music by Cam's Orchestra.

COMMITTEE.

Mrs. Harvey Thomas,	Mrs. David Gillette,
Mrs. Myron Thomas,	Mrs. N P. Beardsley,
Miss Grace Prindle,	Miss Daisy Hill.

Dancing to commence at 8 o'clock. Present this card at

This decorative card invited locals to celebrate Leap Year. Women probably made sandwiches, men brought wood for heat, and people lugged cans of water since the town hall had no water. Folks danced until the old floors shook and, when the dancing stopped, everyone went home on foot or by horse and buggy. When Leap Year came around again four years later, gentlemen were invited to bring refreshments. (RM.)

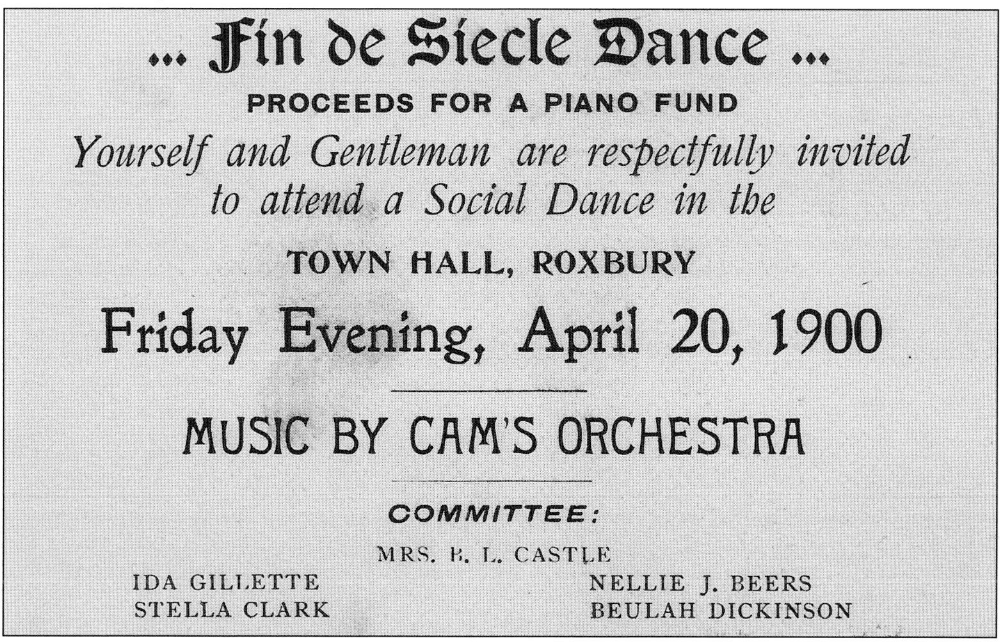

... Fin de Siecle Dance ...

PROCEEDS FOR A PIANO FUND

Yourself and Gentleman are respectfully invited to attend a Social Dance in the

TOWN HALL, ROXBURY

Friday Evening, April 20, 1900

MUSIC BY CAM'S ORCHESTRA

COMMITTEE:

MRS. B. L. CASTLE

IDA GILLETTE	NELLIE J. BEERS
STELLA CLARK	BEULAH DICKINSON

What better time to celebrate the end of a century than in April? The setting was perfect—a raised stage for an orchestra and a large ballroom on the second floor. In the late 1880s, members of Crescent Lodge No. 243—Hodge, Castle, Squire, Minor, Leavenworth, Sanford, Pons, Bradley, and others—met in this same place every Friday night to preach the gospel of temperance. (RM.)

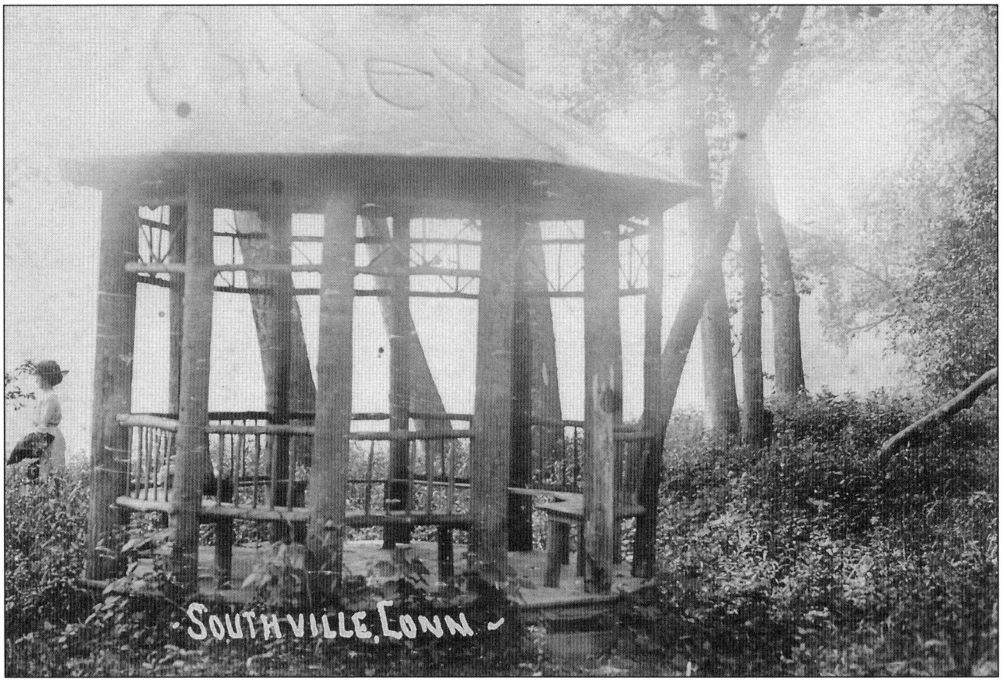

An elegant lady is shown here leaving the Southville Bandstand. Musical entertainments were very popular in the late 19th and early 20th century, and most communities had groups who played—both for fun and for profit. (BHS.)

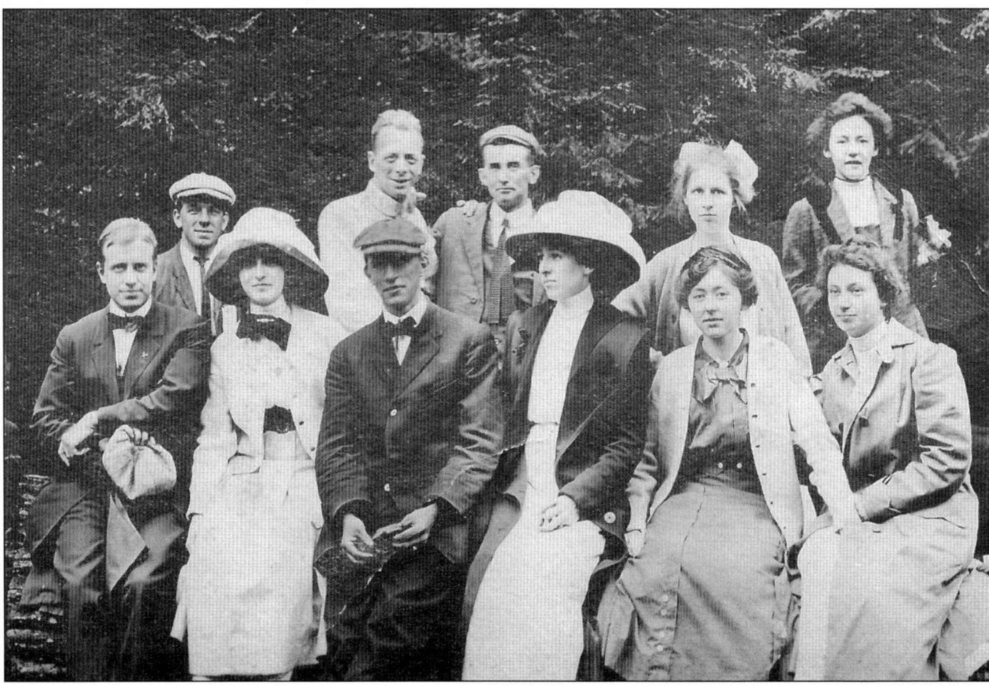

This image was labeled "Youth of the Town—c. 1915." The young Bridgewater people were identified as "unknown boy, Robert Treat, Helen Keeler, Amos Treat, Mabel Keeler, Me, Katherine. Back row- Pitcher Boys, Henry Sanford, Grace Treat, Ruth Marsh." (BHS.)

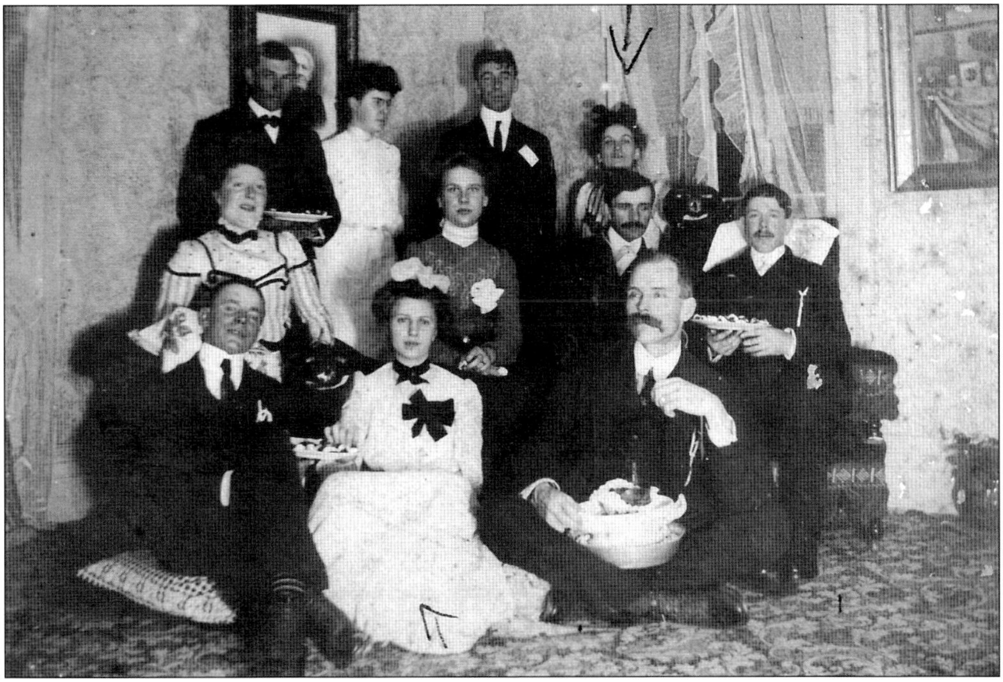

This group of Bridgewater partygoers gathered in the corner of the sitting room for a photograph. The gentleman in the front row (left) was identified as Levi Warner. The lady in the back row on the right was Ella Beardsley. (BHS.)

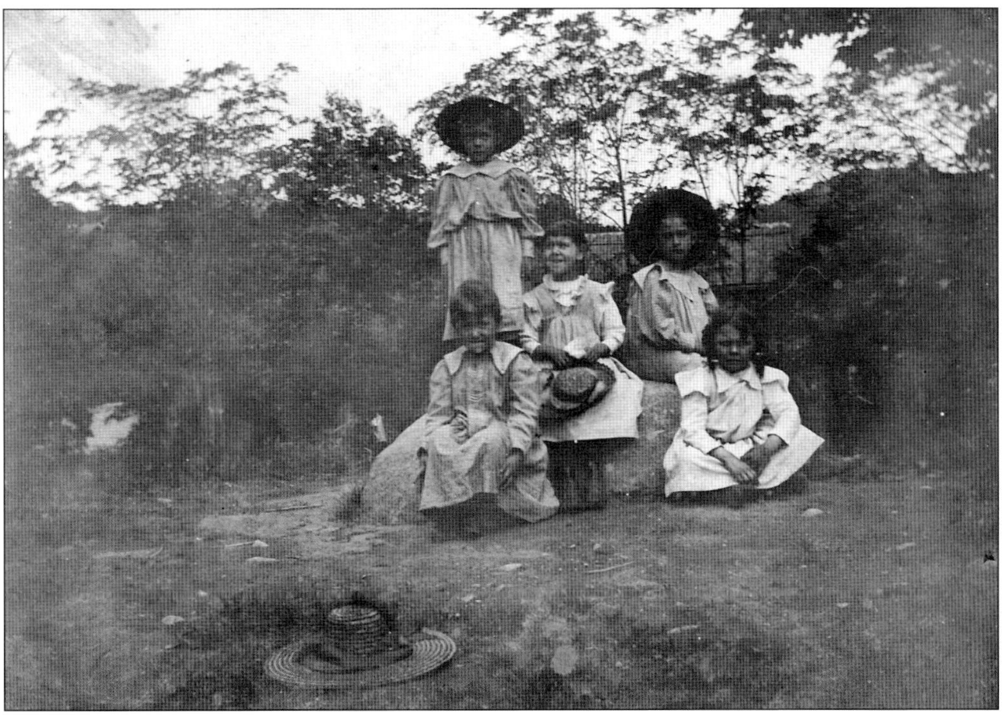

Five young Bridgewater ladies sporting summer hats pose for this picture. They were Phebe Marsh (Sheridan), Ruth Marsh (Frost), Mattie Taylor (middle), Eva Pulver, and Sadie Allen. (BHS.)

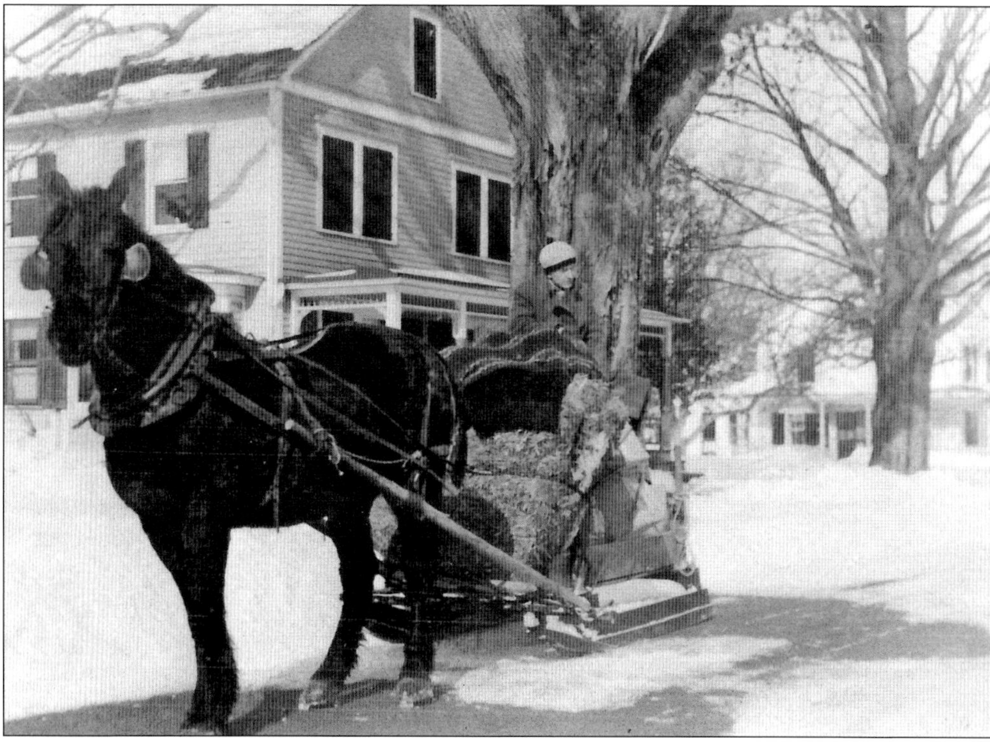

The unidentified man in this photograph appears bundled up with lap robes, hat, gloves, and warm clothing for his sleigh ride. He may even have tucked a foot-warmer with hot coals underneath the blankets. Whether off to the local general store or on his way to visit a neighbor, he will enjoy a cold ride along snow-covered roads in his one-horse open sleigh. (MML.)

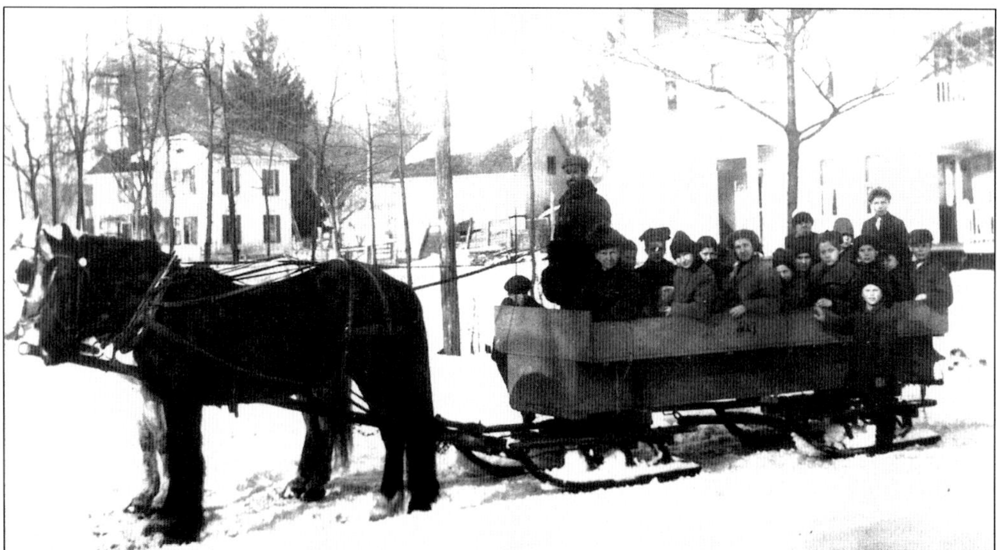

Nearly 20 people have piled into a sleigh wagon pulled by two horses. The wagon has "No 3" written on the side; it looks like it might be a railcar with runners or a homemade vehicle of some kind. Most occupants appear to be men and boys, perhaps on their way to work at Mine Hill, cut lumber in the woods, or work on the roads. (RM.)

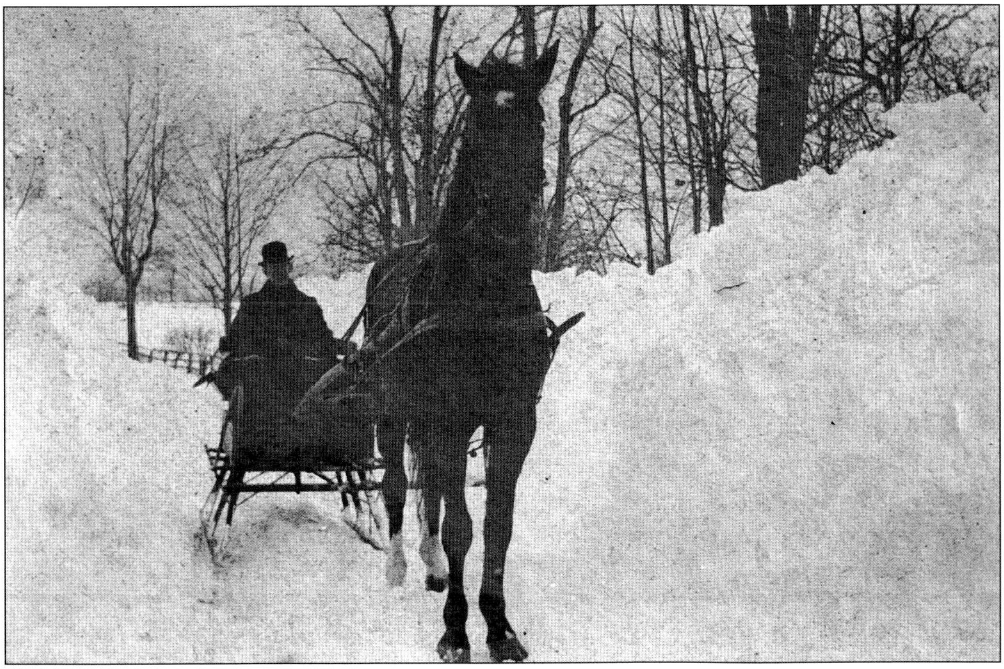

On the Sunday after Thanksgiving, Charles A. Northrop hitched up his horse and headed out in his sleigh. Sleigh riding was popular with the young people, but it was also a much-needed form of transportation in winter. This picture was taken by Mark Hatch. (BHS.)

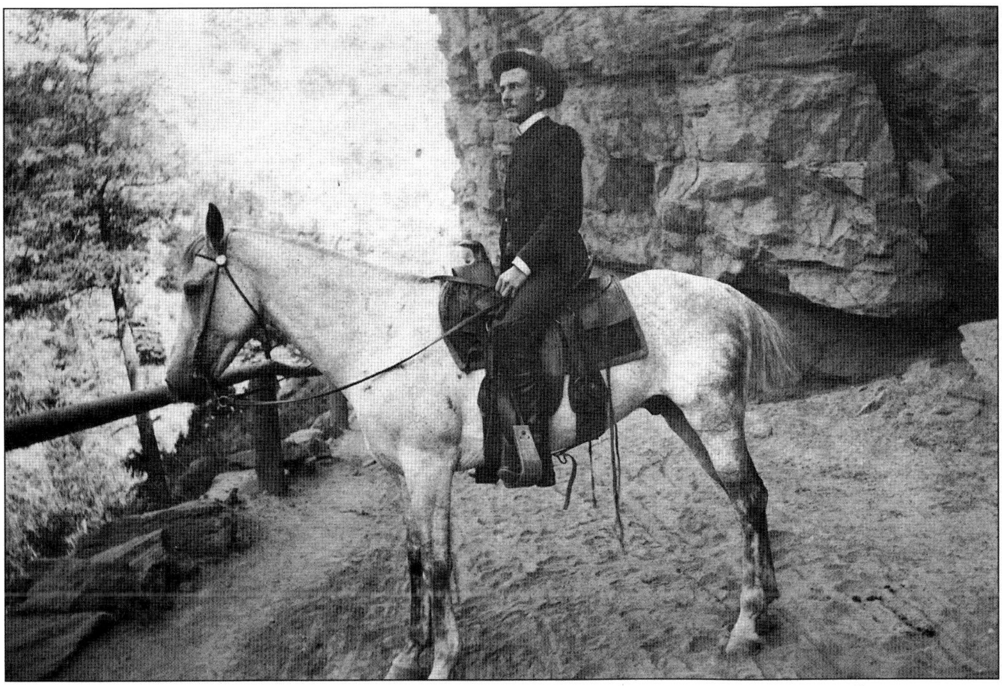

Joseph H. Nettleton had his picture taken on September 6, 1887, to commemorate his trip to Ute Pass, near Rainbow Falls, in Manitou Springs, Colorado. Members of the Nettleton family were farmers and had lived in Bridgewater for many years. (BHS.)

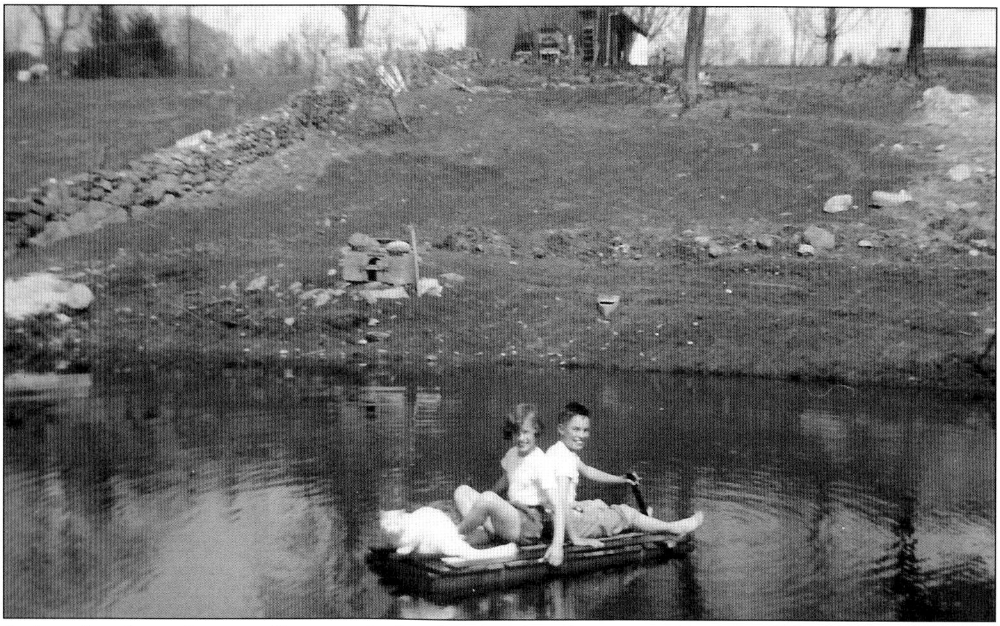

Before the days when small towns had volunteer fire departments, many homes and farms had a fire pond nearby. However, when a major fire raged, not enough hands could haul water fast enough, and many of the towns' older homes burned to the ground. This 1995 photograph shows Dale (left) and John Coleman (right) enjoying the fire pond behind their home on South Street in Roxbury. (John Botsford Coleman.)

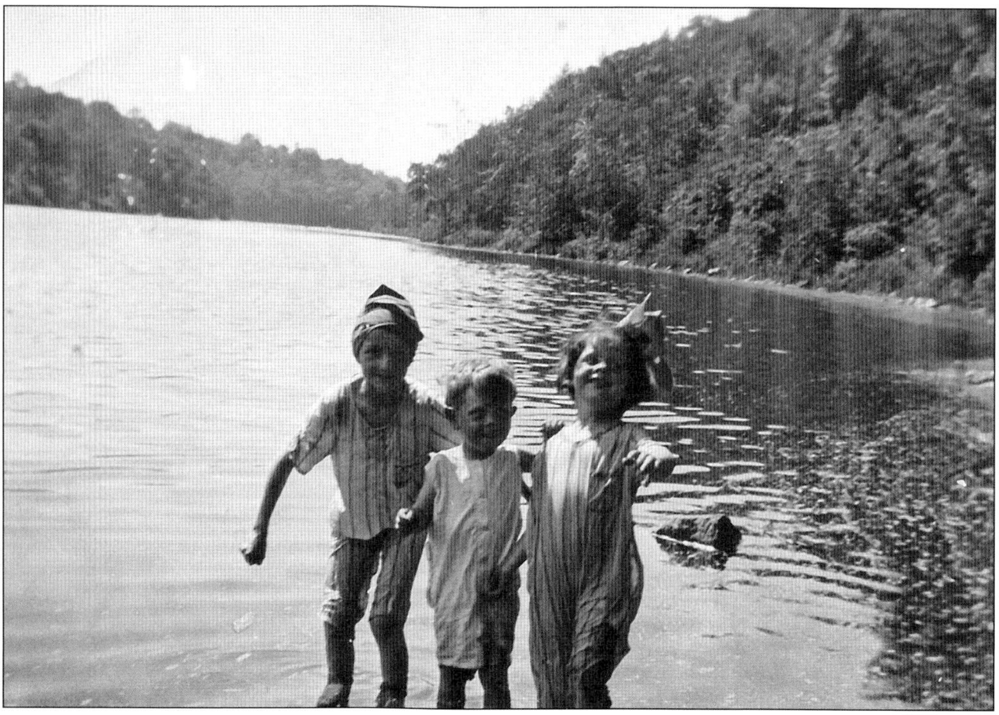

Three children enjoy a swim in 1927 at "The Point" in Southville. Once called "The Neck" or "Shepaug Neck," this was a popular recreational area. (BHS.)

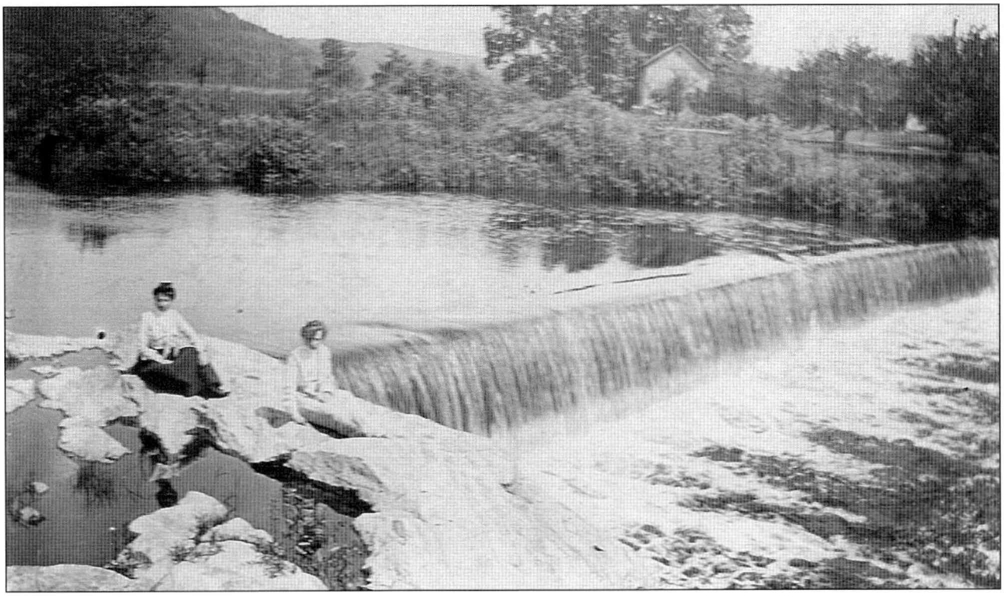

In this undated photograph, Emily Joyce (left) and Alice Bixley (right), enjoy a leisurely afternoon sitting on the boulders, watching the water flow over the rocks, and looking for tiny fish in the pools formed between the stones in the Shepaug River. (RM.)

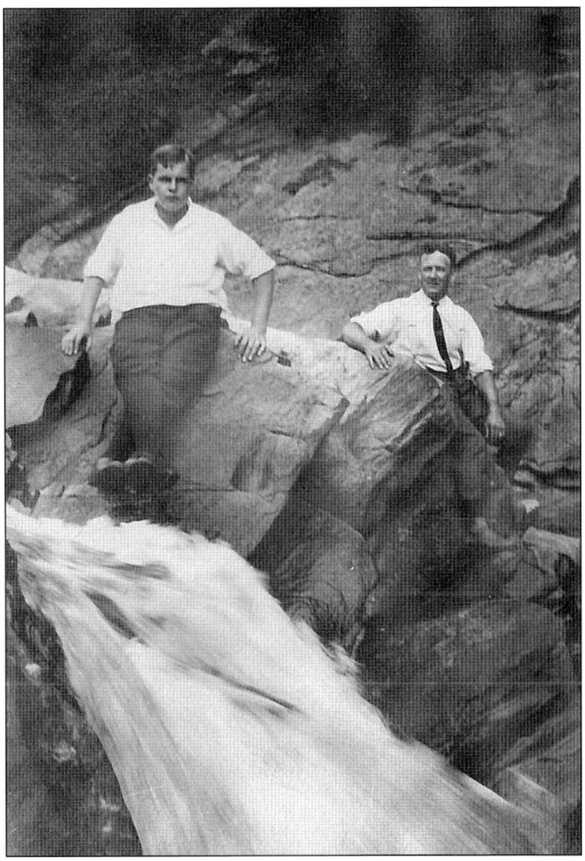

On Sunday, August 24, 1919, these men relaxed and enjoyed the cool spray from falls that tumbled over massive gray boulders along the banks of the Shepaug River off Minor Bridge Road in Roxbury. The falls were a favorite gathering place in the days before builders blasted the boulders, cut down trees, and diminished the roar and drama of these falls to build the Shepaug Railroad. (RM.)

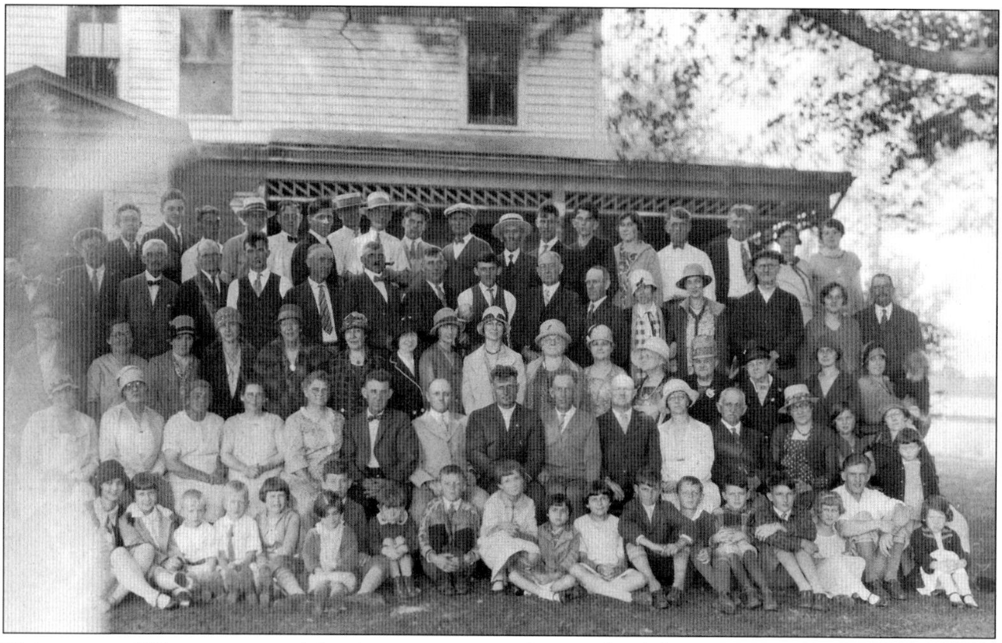

This group of Grangers posed for their picture on the porch of the Curtis Farm. Annual outings were an important part of this organization's social outreach. (BHS.)

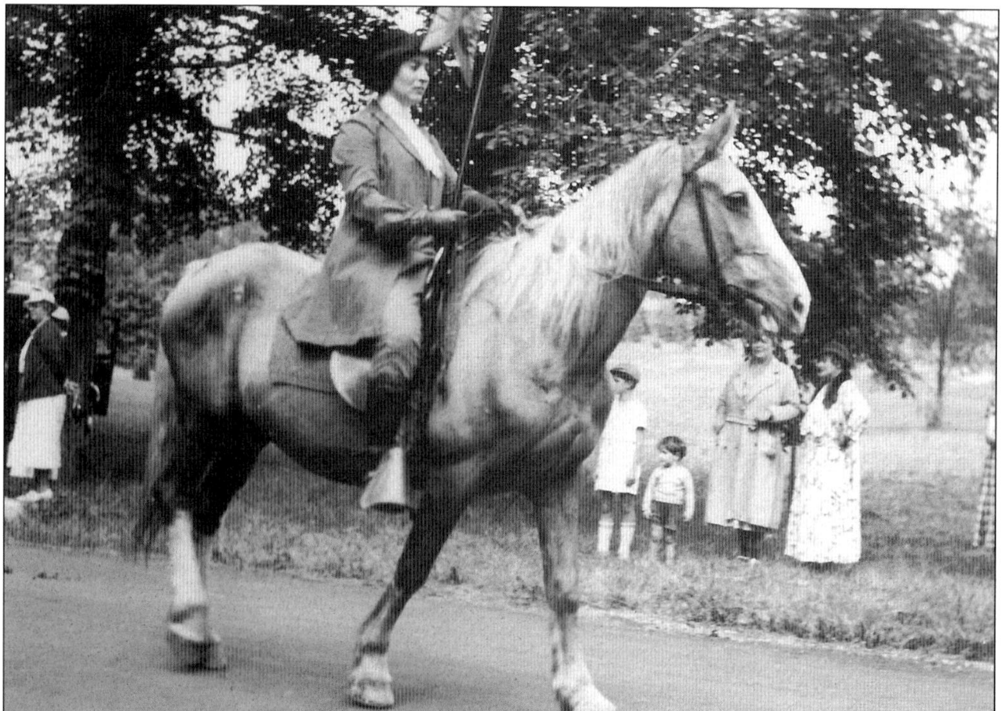

"The Tercentenary Parade" in 1935 was a widely attended event. Emma Randall is seen on horseback carrying a banner. Horses have always played an important part in life in Bridgewater. The Fairfield County Hounds, founded in 1924, moved from Westport to Bridgewater in 1987 and is located on Botsford Hill Road, on the Roxbury-Bridgewater line. (BHS.)

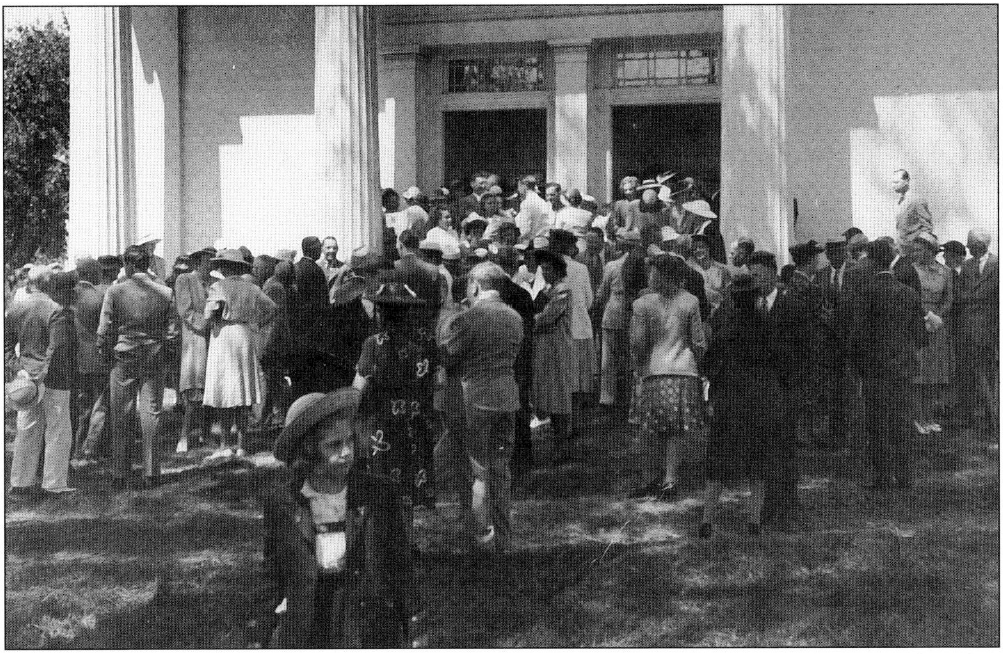

Church has long been a gathering place where people get together, not only to worship, but also to meet their neighbors and catch up on news of the town. When a crowd gathered at the Congregational Church in this undated photograph, the young girl in the foreground was more interested in the cameraman. (RCC.)

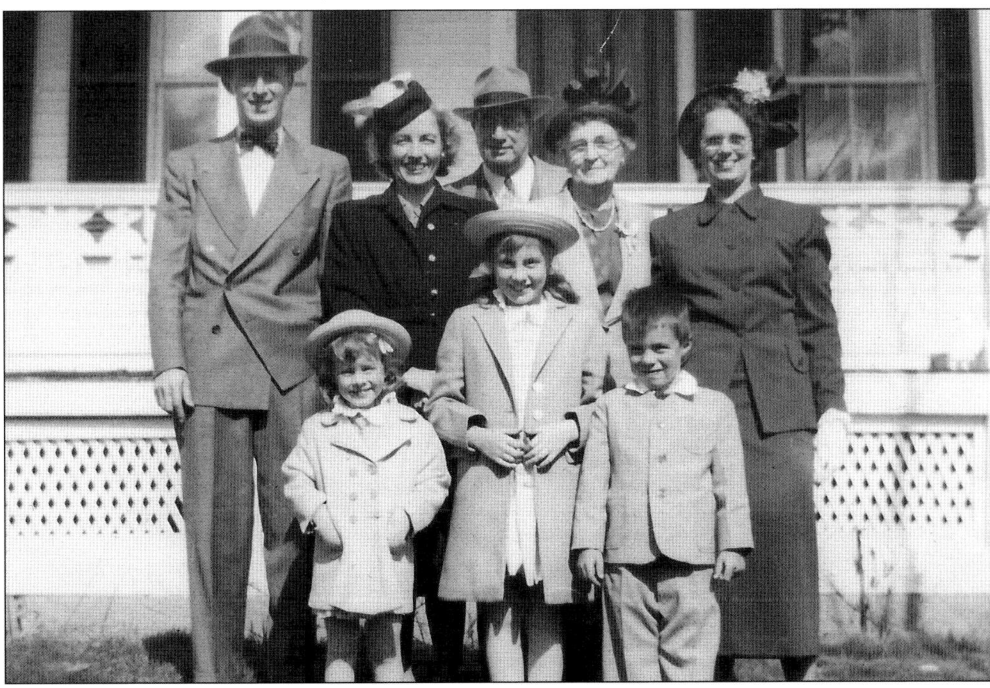

The Coleman family gathered at Hannie Dickenson's home on Painter Hill Road in Roxbury on Easter Sunday, April 17, 1949. From left to right are (first row) Dale, Ann, and John; (second row) Lester, Marjorie, Willis, Alice, and Barbara. (John Botsford Coleman.)

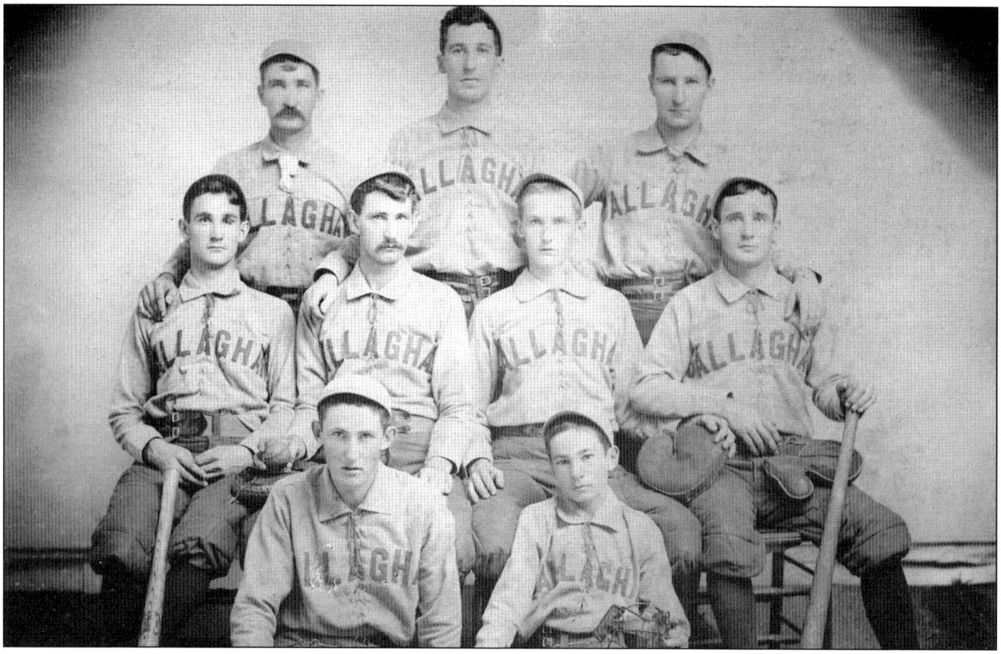

Nine brothers and their only sister made up the Callahan baseball team. Mary was the umpire. Jack, known as a great pitcher, became a railroad conductor. Michael became the "dean of the stonecutters" in Roxbury and worked in quarries throughout the United States. Joseph was said to have hollered so loud celebrating Glover Cleveland's election that he was hoarse for a week. (RM.)

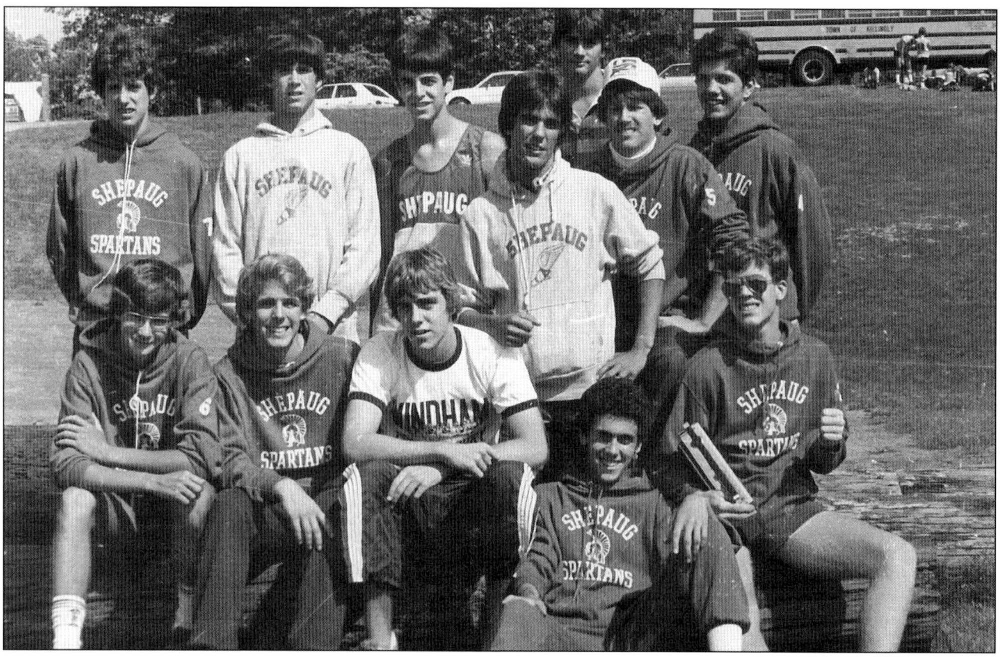

A group of Shepaug's Spartans posed for this picture in the 1980s on the school's playing field. That was a time of many winning teams, including the Connecticut state baseball champions. (Woolwich Family.)

Eight

Community Spirit and Traditions

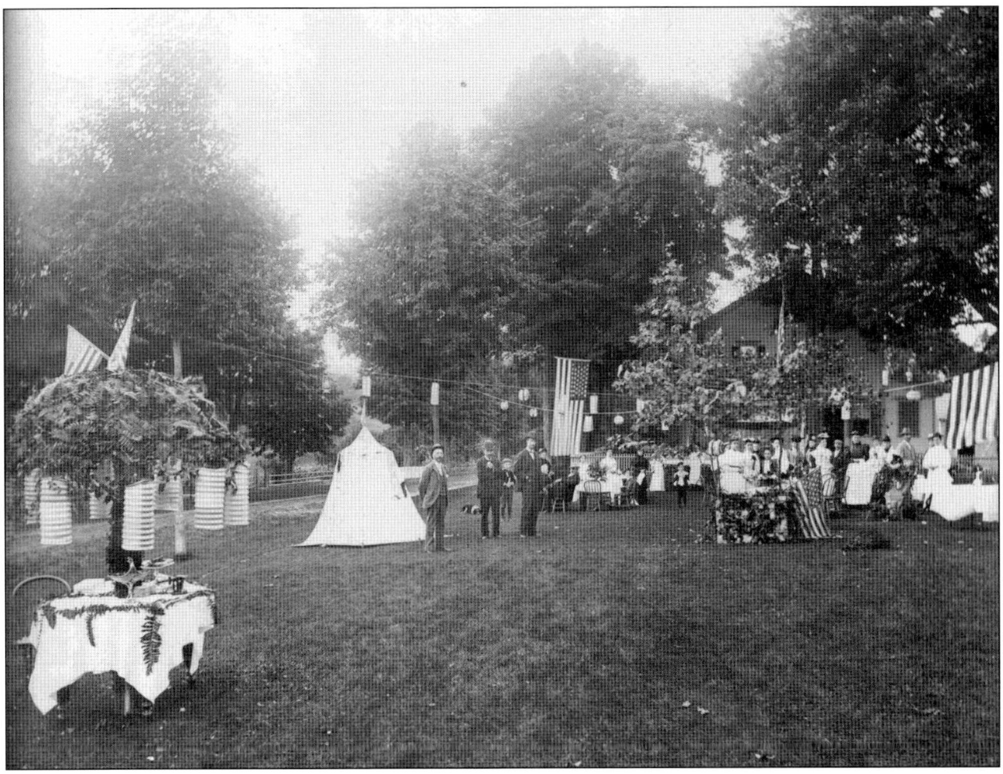

In 1896, Mrs. C.N. Hatch invited members of the Bridgewater Village Improvement Society to an entertainment on the lawns of her home. This society, founded to enrich the town culturally and add to its scenic quality, had as one of its initiatives the planting of trees along Main Street. The decorations for this event included "artificial trees" made from ferns, Chinese lanterns, and American flags. (BHS.)

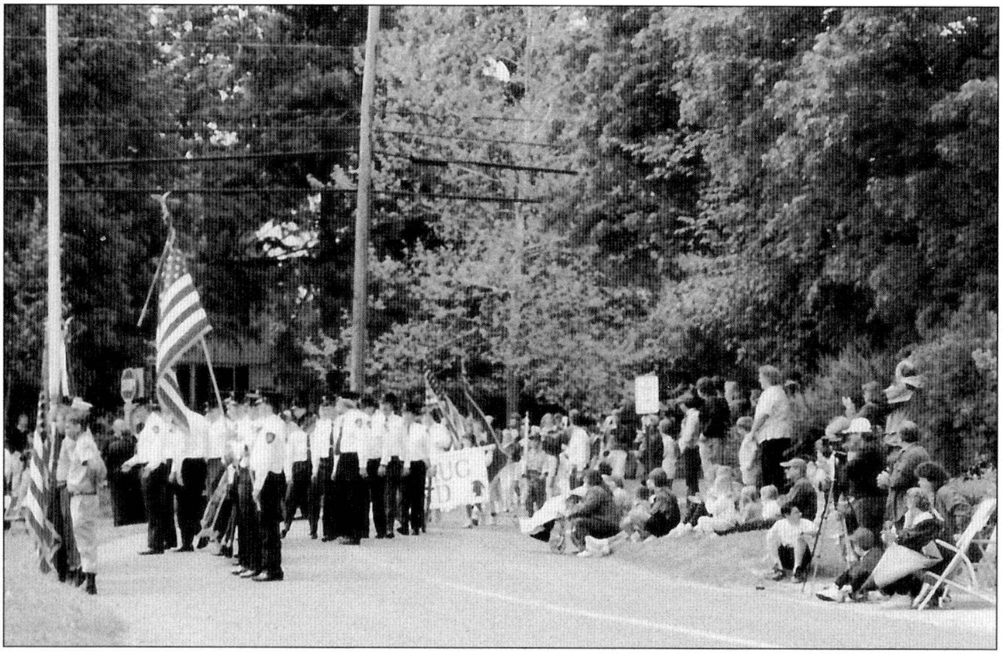

Everybody loves a parade. Crowds gathered on Roxbury's town green to meet and greet their neighbors, listen to speeches, and join firemen, soldiers, Scouts, and students to march through town with bands playing and flags waving. In this image, pets and babies in strollers join in as onlookers watch the passing parade. (Marie Swanson.)

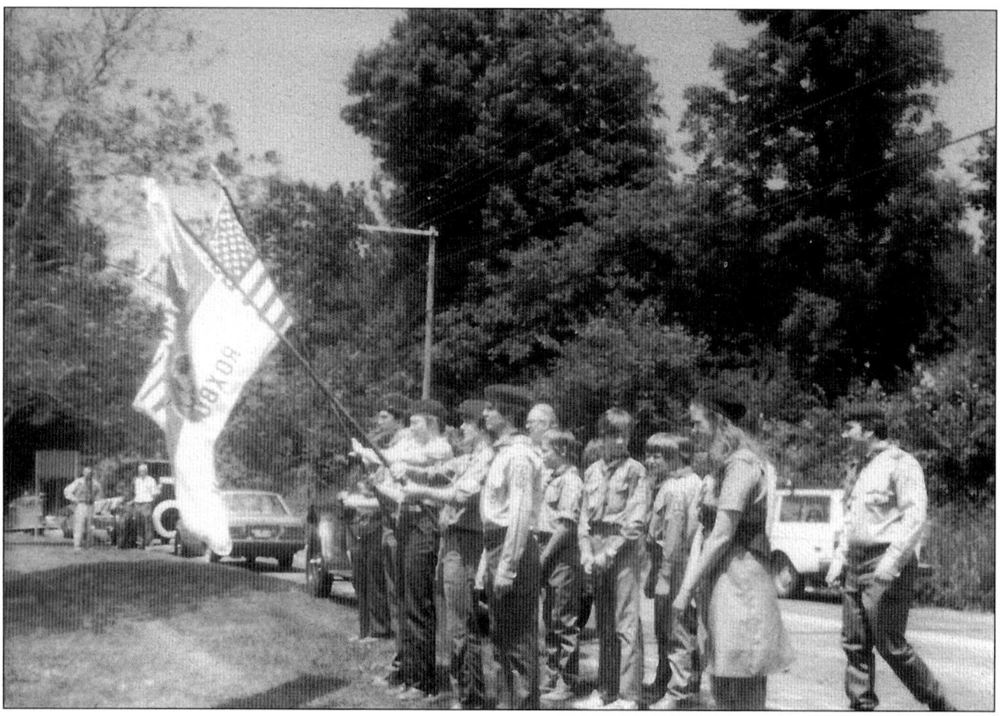

Scouts have a long tradition in Roxbury of participating in parades. They are shown here before marching through the town center as honor guards. (Marie Swanson.)

To the delight of audiences, Bridgewater and Roxbury firemen and Scouts joined Roxbury's award-winning drum and bugle corps, known as the Roxbury Strutters, as they paraded through the annual August Bridgewater Country Fair, a benefit for the Bridgewater Volunteer Fire Department. Though undated, this photograph was probably taken in 1962 or 1963. (Constance N. Sherman, Raymond Livingston Booth.)

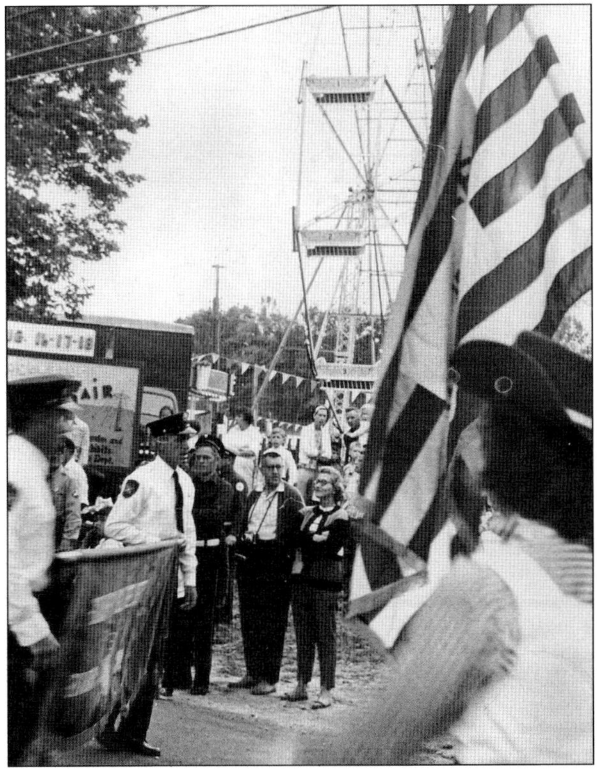

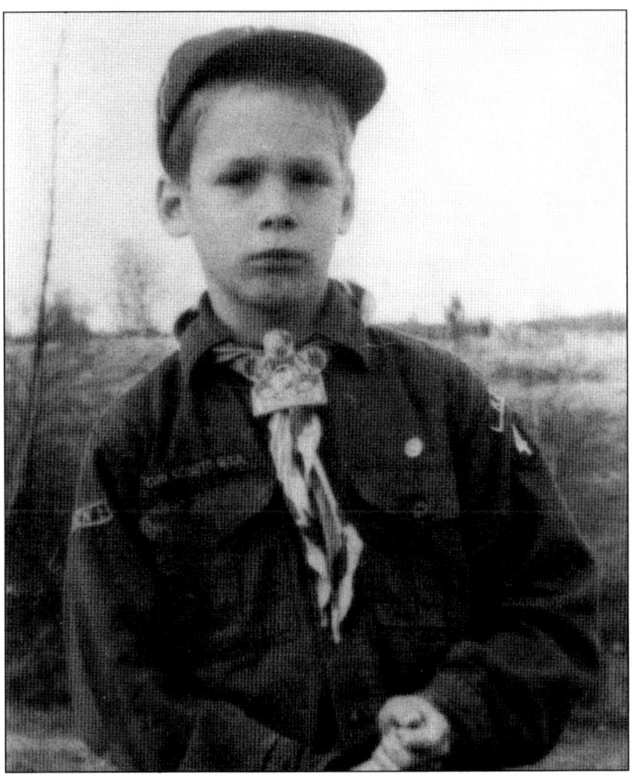

Scouts have long been active in Roxbury community service projects. This undated photograph shows Jonathan Hurlbut as a Cub Scout of eight or nine years old, seemingly poised to take on a serious project. (Elinor Hurlbut.)

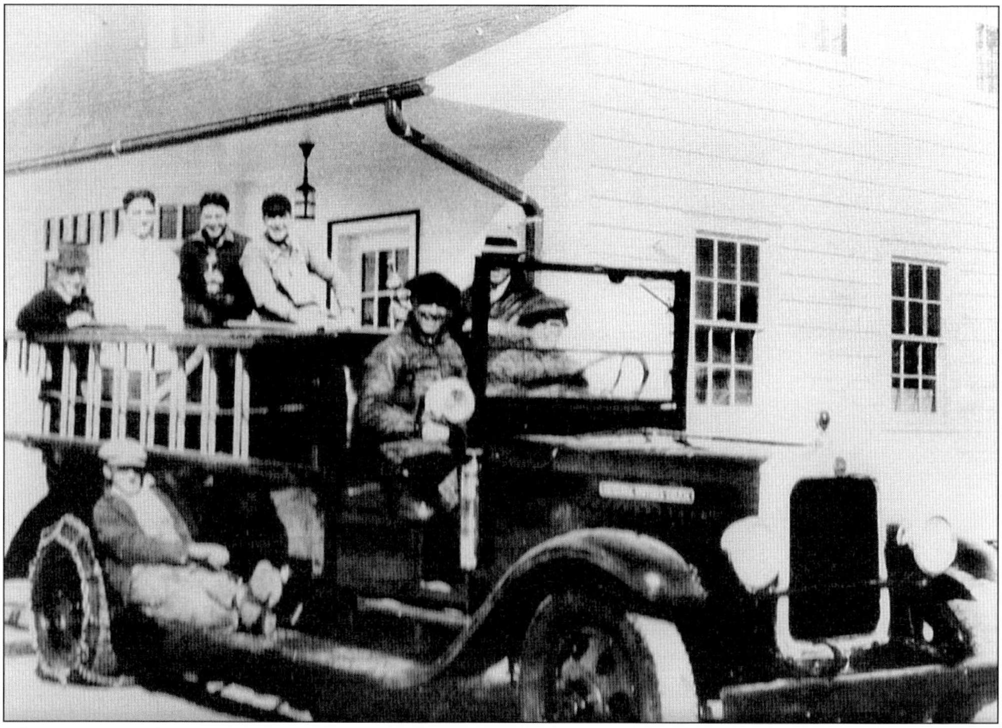

This converted 1926 GMC 1.5-ton truck was Roxbury's fire engine until 1948. In the spring of 1935, George Booth was in the driver's seat with Joseph Hartwell on his right and John Matula to his left. Charles Frizzel is on the running board. From left to right in the rear are Kenneth Conklin, Edward Felix, Frank Smith, and Bill Mathews. (RM.)

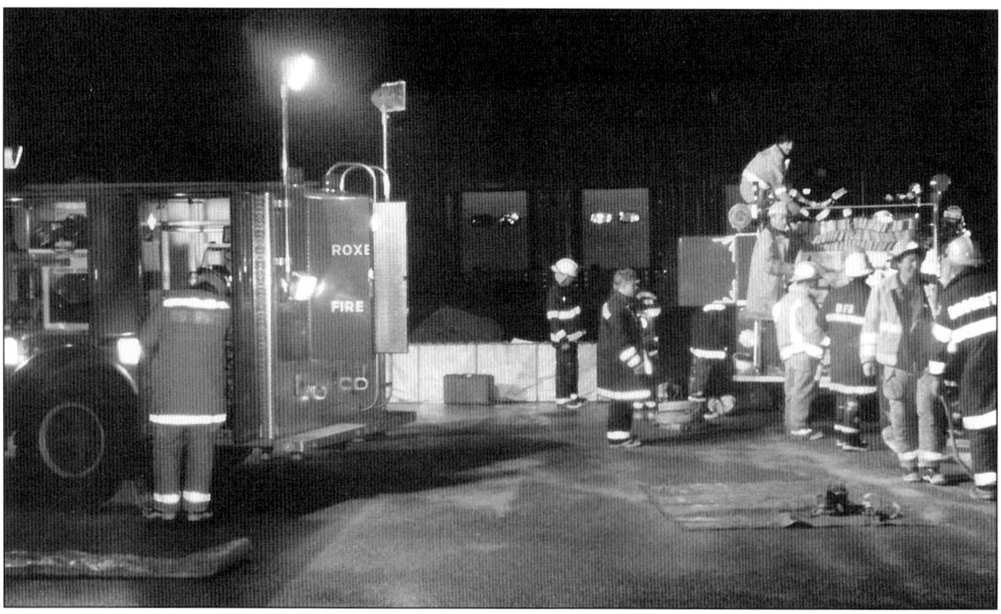

Volunteer firemen and emergency personnel train and work to deal with emergencies in all kinds of conditions. Here, in the dark of night, the Roxbury Volunteer Fire Department does their job in their small town that has no lights and no fire hydrants. (RVFD.)

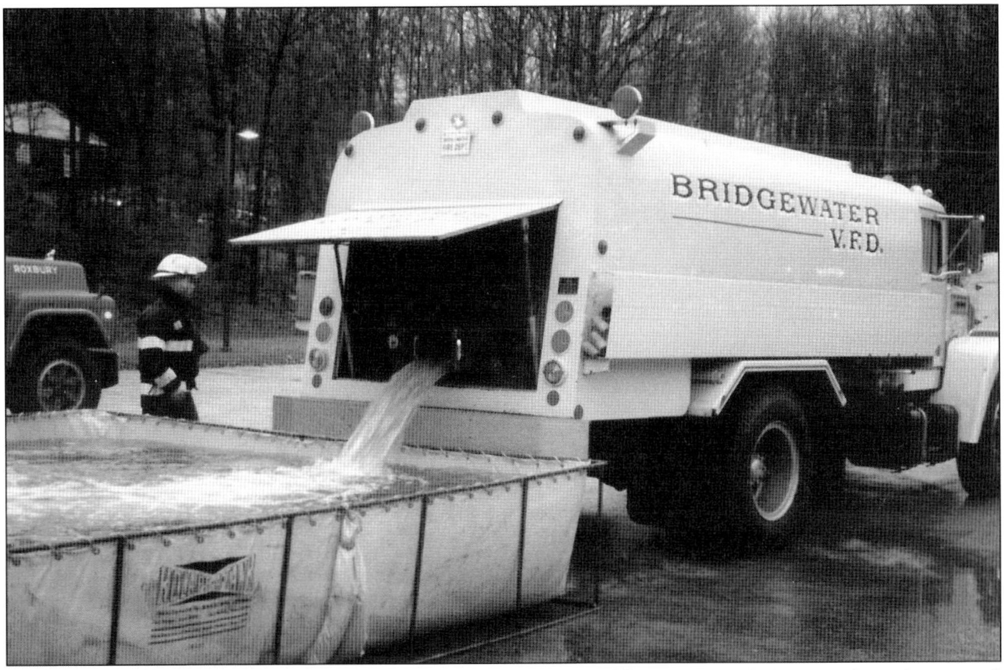

Neither town has hydrants from which firefighters can readily get water. Most residents have well water, and the firemen need to fill trucks mostly from rivers and streams. In this undated image, a Bridgewater fire truck dumps water into a pool. (RVFD.)

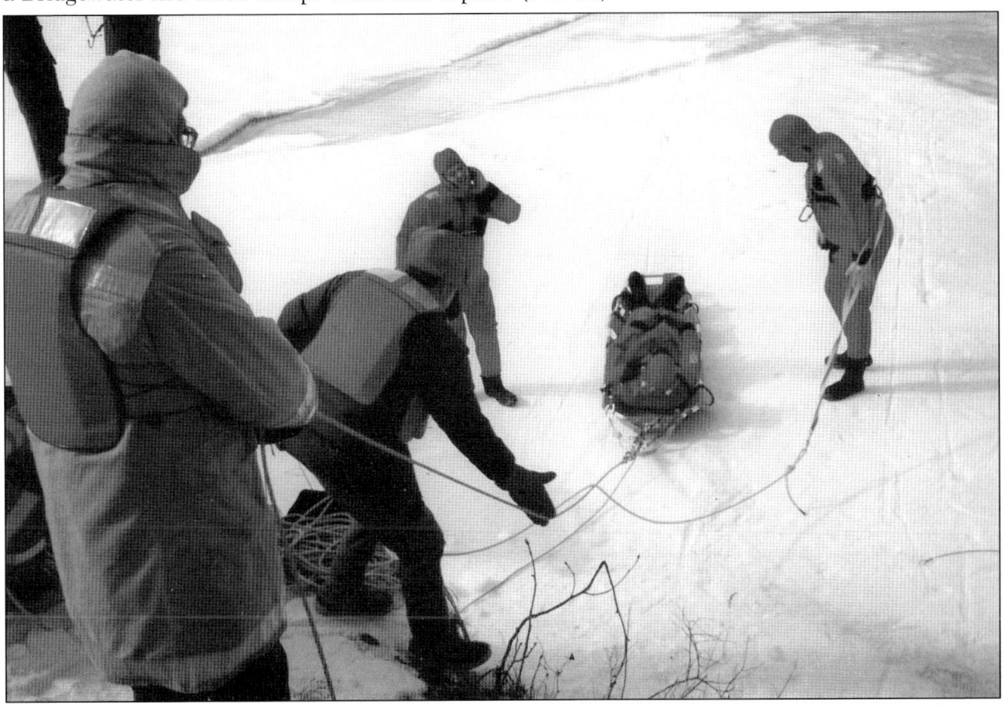

Winter emergencies are inevitable when ice skaters and ice fishermen find themselves in danger or animals wander onto a pond with thin ice. Volunteer firemen and emergency workers are trained to come to the rescue in ice and snow conditions. (RVFD.)

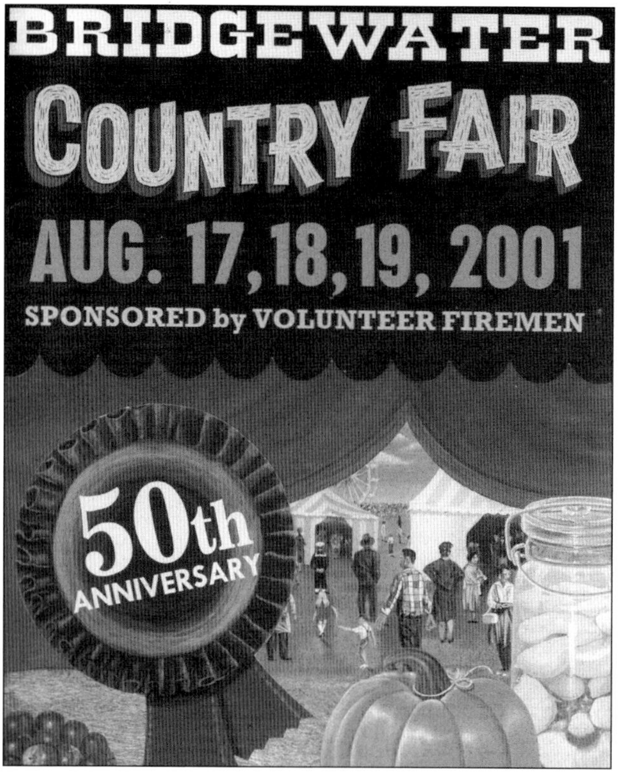

This Bridgewater Country Fair Booklet marked the fair's 50th anniversary in 2001. Proceeds from this annual event pay for the expenses of the Volunteer Fire Department, including equipment and training. No state money is used to fund the department. (BVFD.)

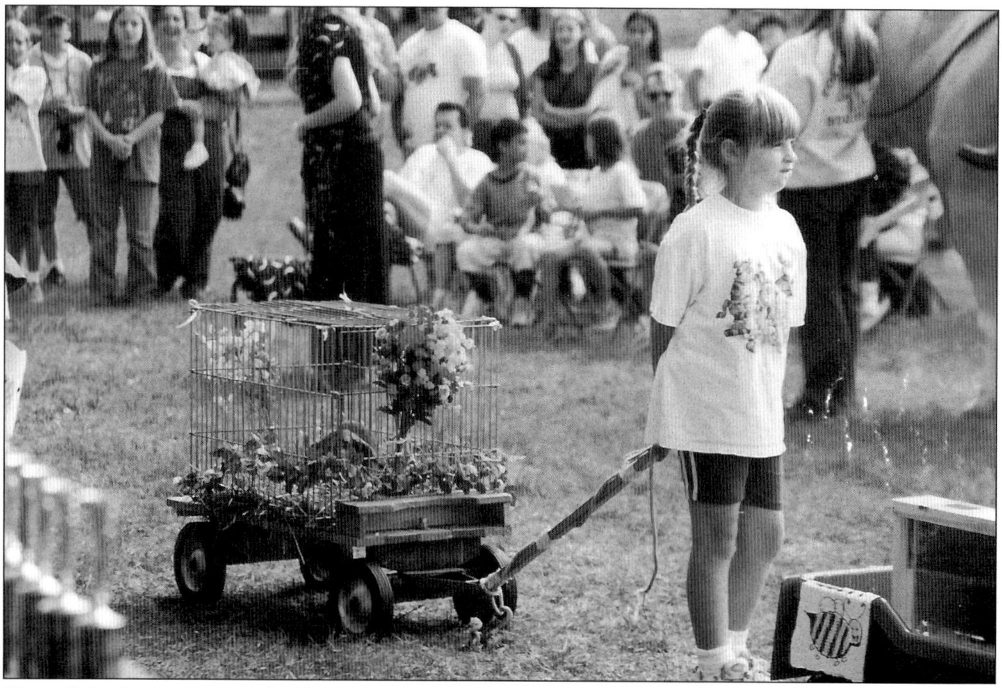

One of the first events at the Bridgewater Country Fair is the Pet Parade. All children are invited to march with their animals, some of which are dressed up in costumes, while others prefer to go au naturel. (BWA.)

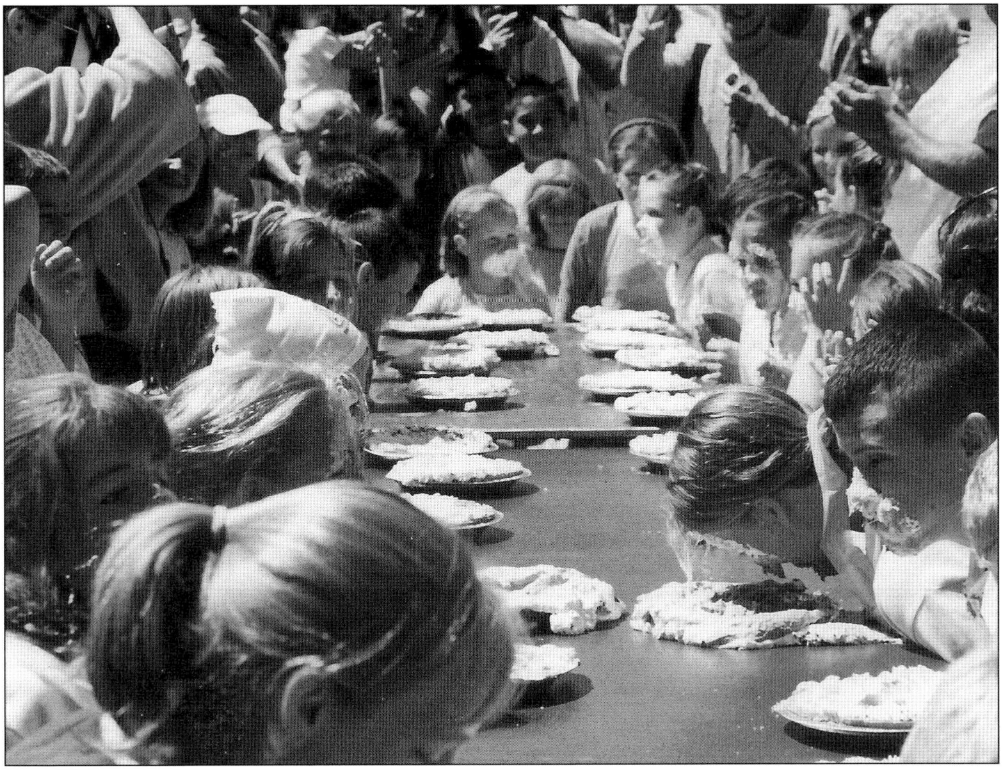

These pies do not stand a chance when they are faced by Bridgewater's children in the Pie Eating Contest. (BWA.)

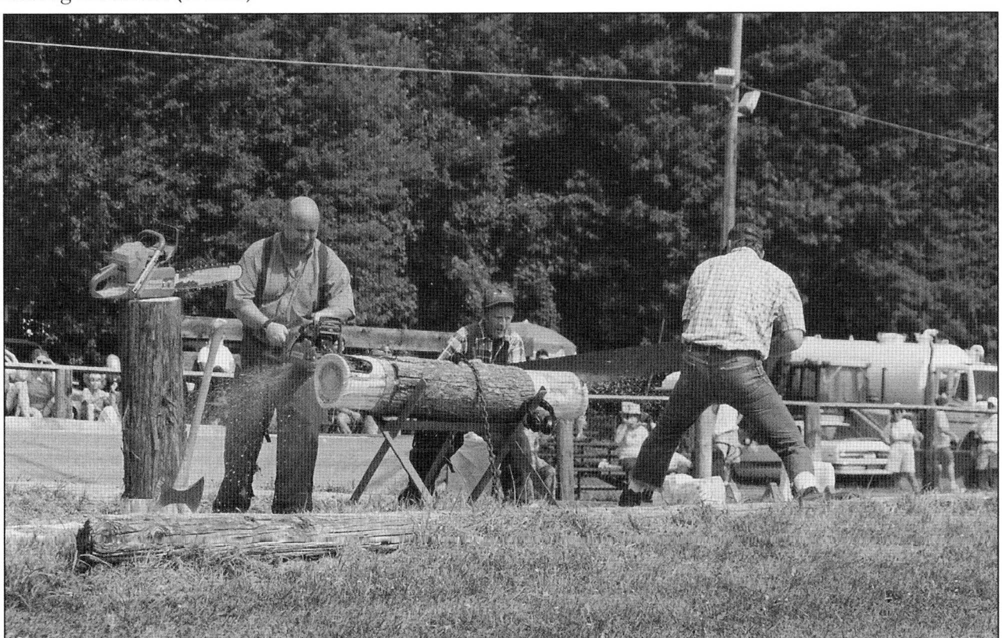

One of the more popular events of the Bridgewater Country Fair is shown here. Lumberjacks race the clock to cut through logs in record time. (BWA.)

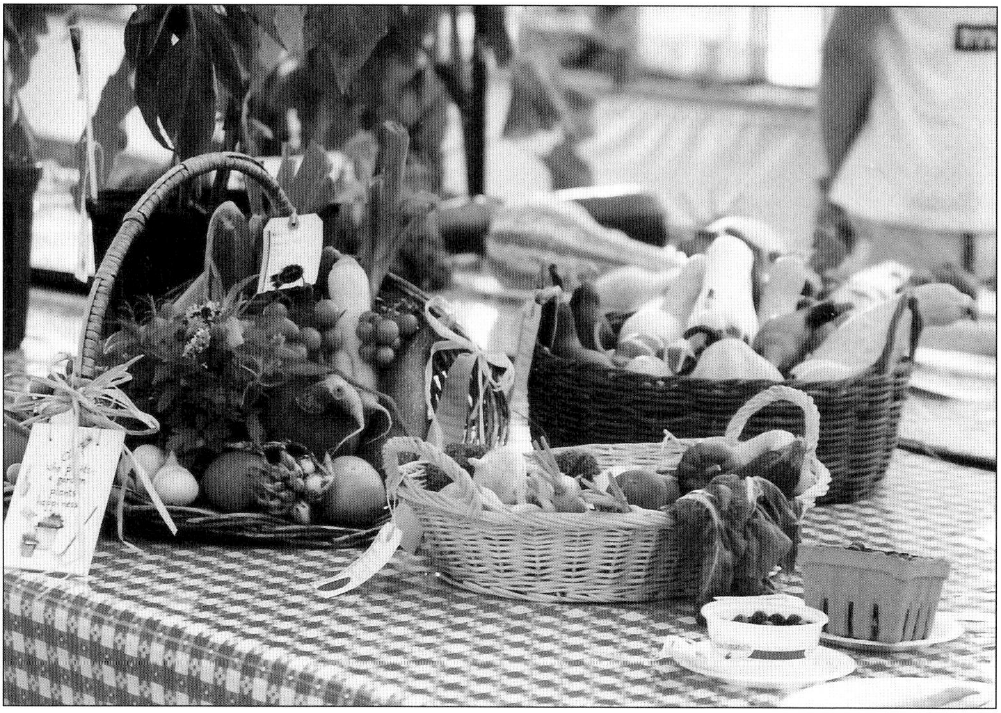

Beautiful flowers, delicious fruit and vegetables, cakes, pies, jams, and jellies are all judged to determine the winners of each category at the Bridgewater Country Fair. (BWA.)

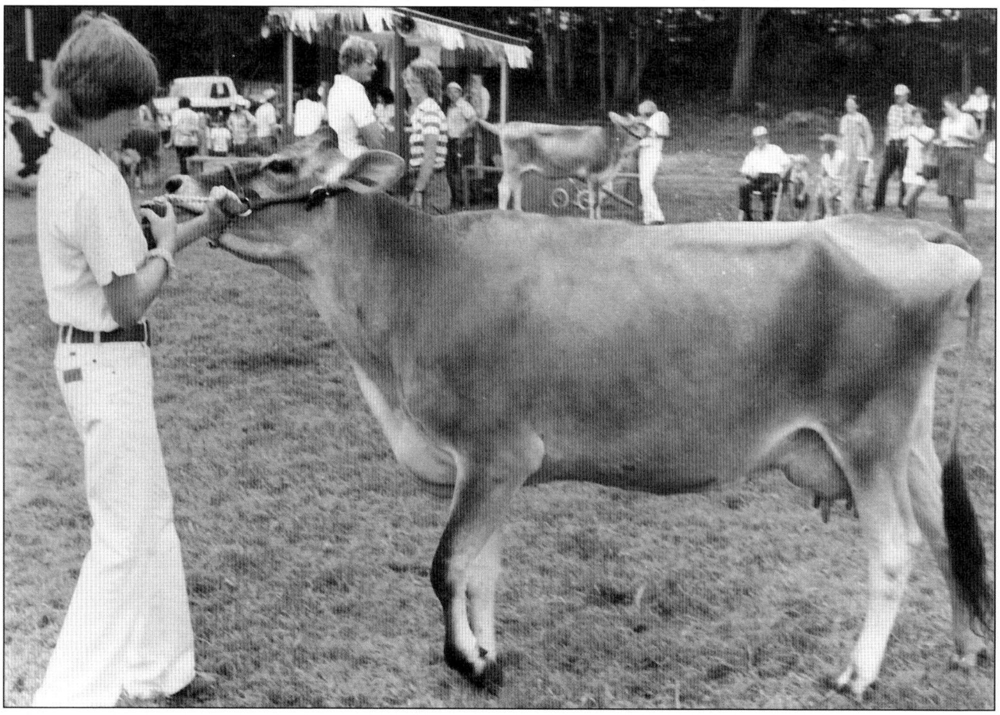

Alan Woolwich enters the fairgrounds with his cow, Jill, in the late 1970s. He went on to win Best of Show and Best of Breed at the Bridgewater Country Fair. (Woolwich Family.)

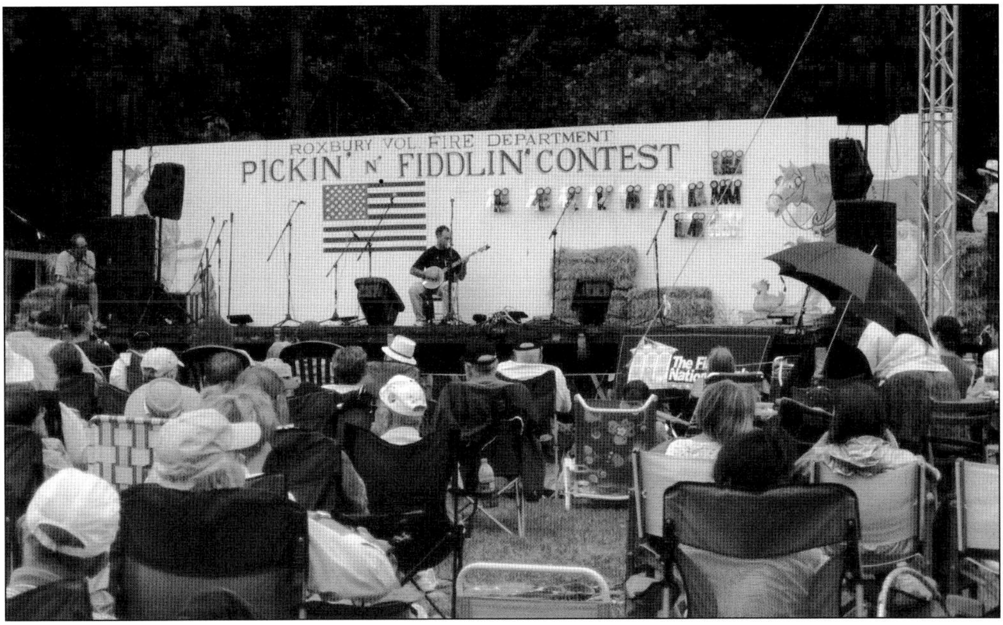

Thousands of folks gather each year to enjoy the annual Pickin' 'n Fiddlin' contest, with cash prizes for the best players on the old-time fiddle, banjo, mandolin, finger- and flat-pick guitar, and bluegrass banjo. Individuals and bands—juniors and seniors—entertain the crowds with their musical talents. In 2010, Roxbury celebrated its 36th Pickin' 'n Fiddlin' contest, a Roxbury Volunteer Fire Department benefit event. (Jeannine Green.)

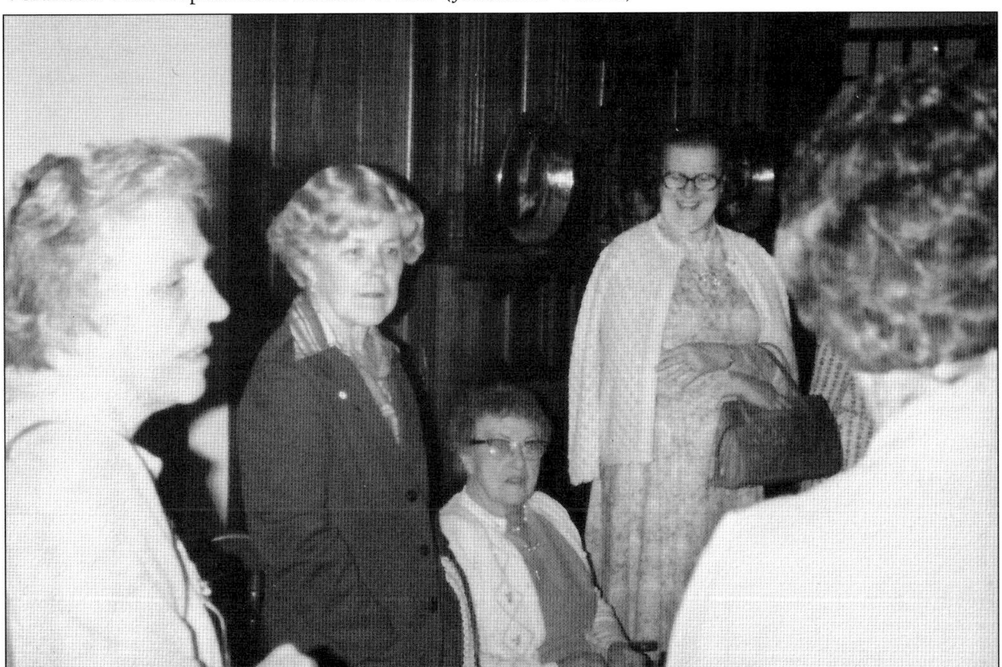

A social service organization, the Shepaug Club celebrated its 105th anniversary in 2010. In this photograph, members discussed the next event at its 75th anniversary party held May 17, 1979, at the Mayflower Inn in Washington, Connecticut. (Elinor Hurlbut.)

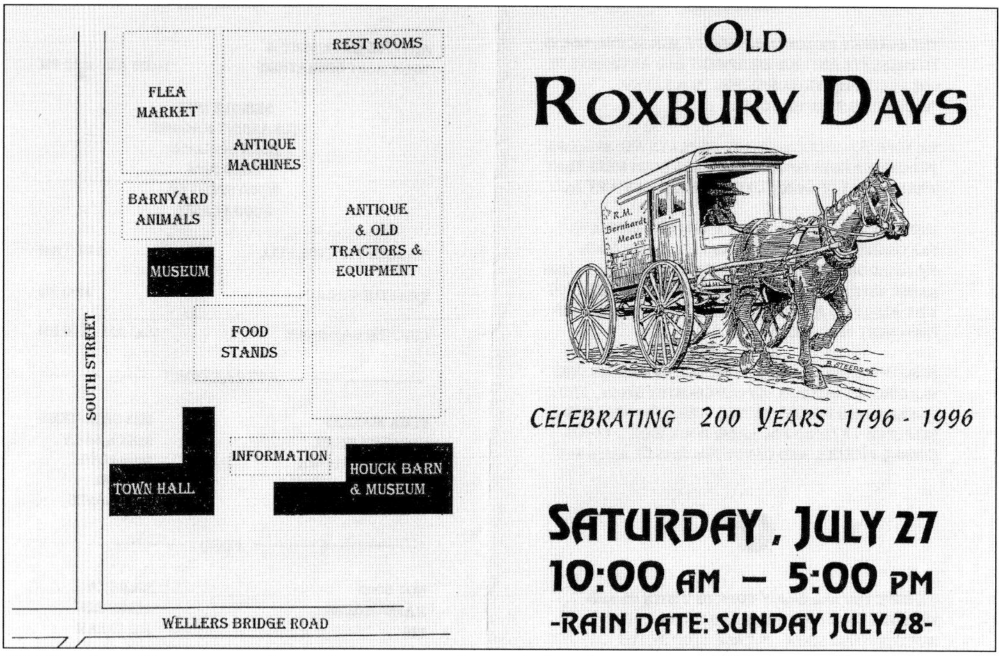

Old Roxbury Days was a three-day country festival that began in 1972 to raise money for a new firehouse. The last festival, July 25, 1998, was held by the Roxbury Historical Society. Crowds enjoyed crafts exhibits, a country store that sold ice cream and penny candy, antique car displays, and field events with horses and carriages. (RM.)

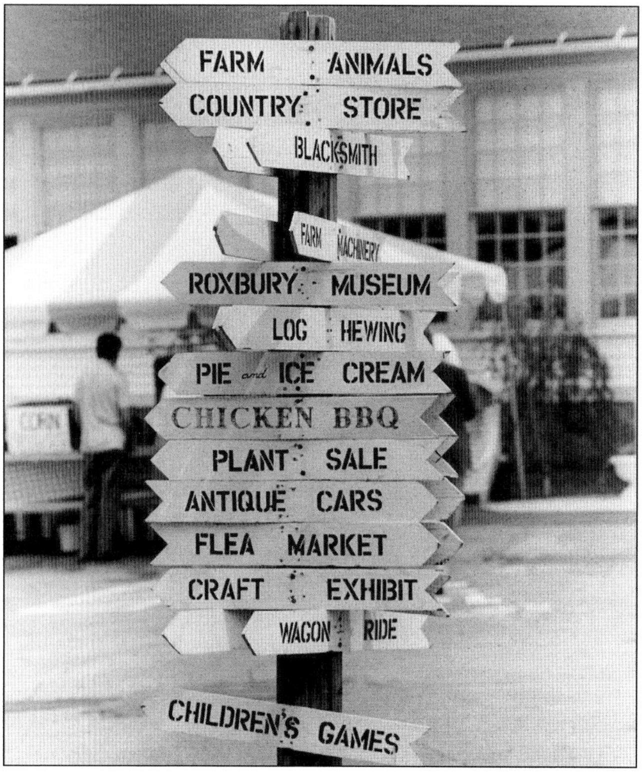

Old Roxbury Days signs pointed in all directions on South Street and invited crowds to the variety of events taking place: a flea market, crafts, wagon rides, and demonstrations by a blacksmith. There was seemingly no end to the activities, all of them relating to country life. (RM.)

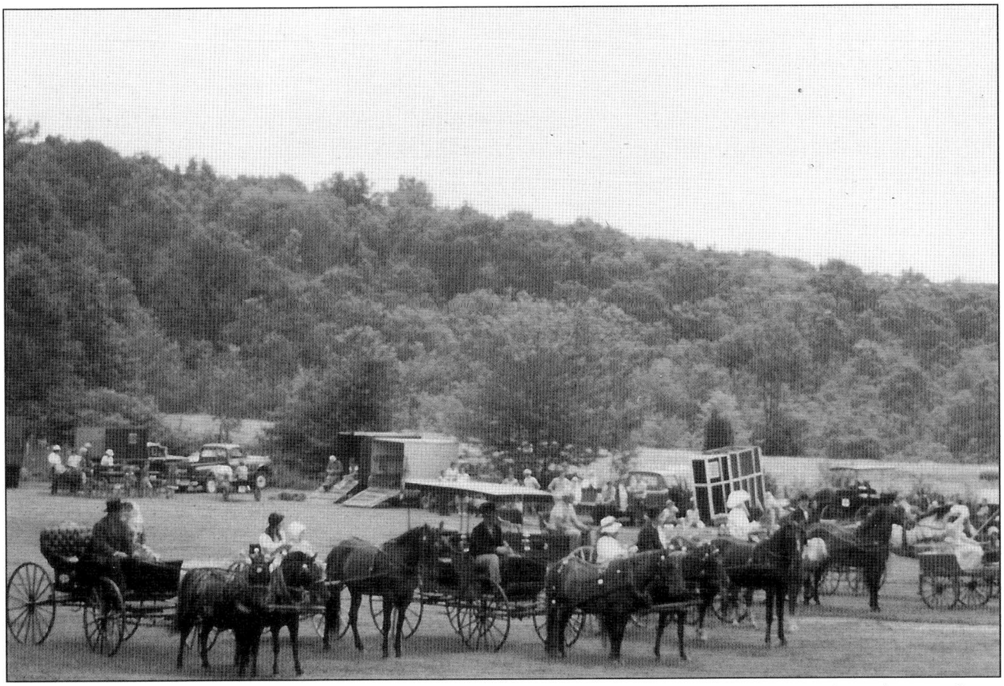

A popular Old Roxbury Days event was the field of horses and carriages that gathered to perform and compete behind the Booth Free School on South Street. In this undated image, horses, drivers, and carriages are ready to show off their skills. (Elinor Hurlbut.)

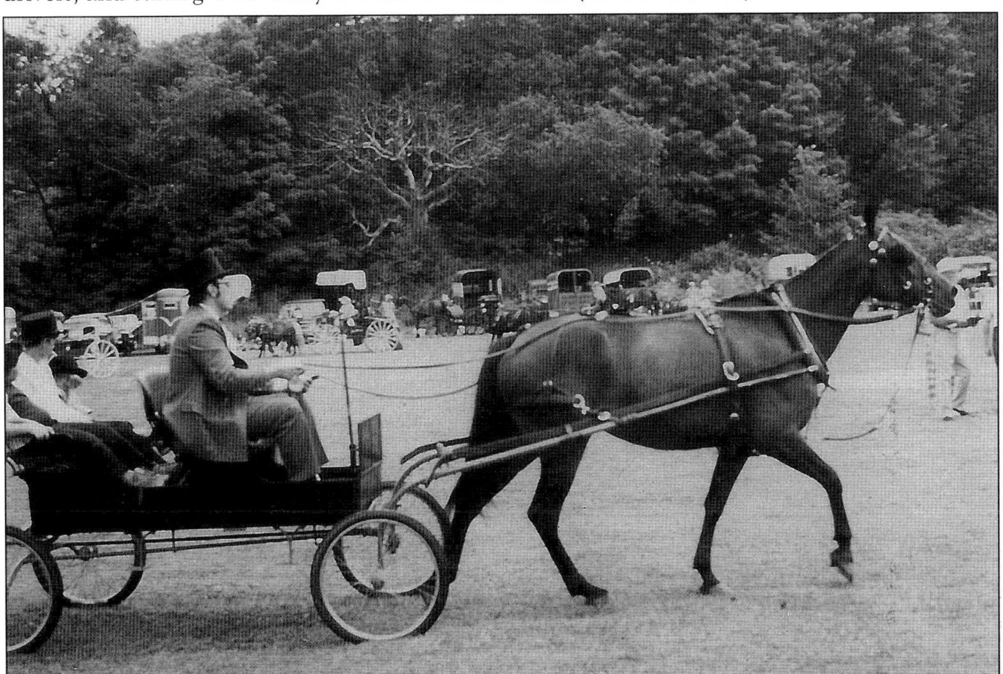

A driver in top hat with young passengers drives his horse-drawn four-wheeled carriage across the field. In this Old Roxbury Days field event, drivers would display their carriages and wagons for the crowds to view. Carriage races were sometimes the main event. (Elinor Hurlbut.)

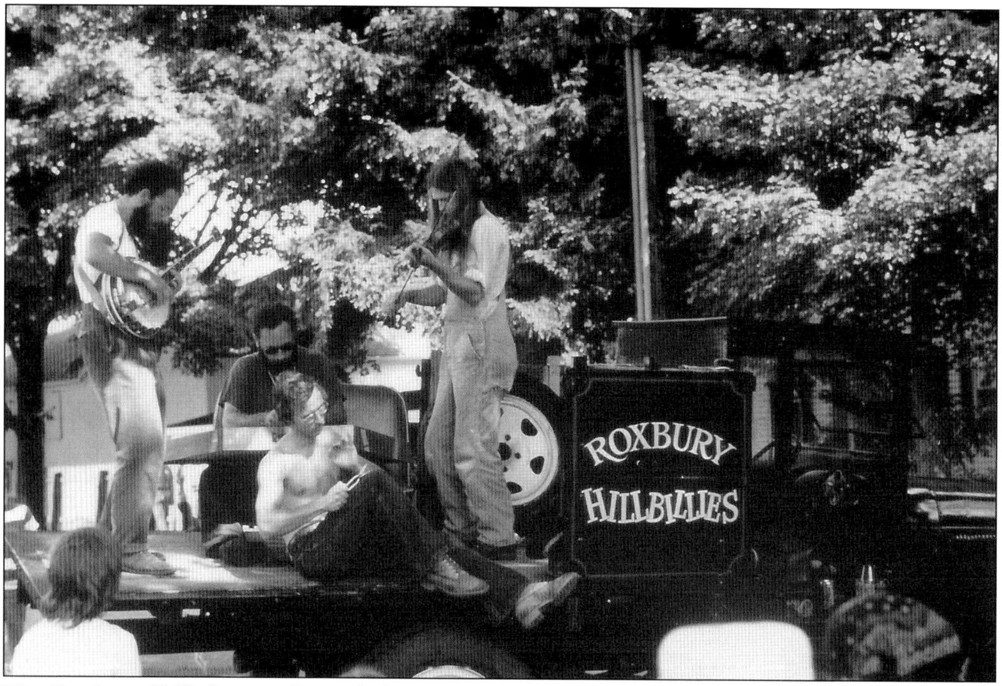

The Roxbury Hillbillies performed almost continuously for three days at the Old Roxbury Days country festival. The fair was sponsored by the Roxbury Volunteer Fire Department, and, in later years, by the Roxbury Historical Society. (Elinor Hurlbut.)

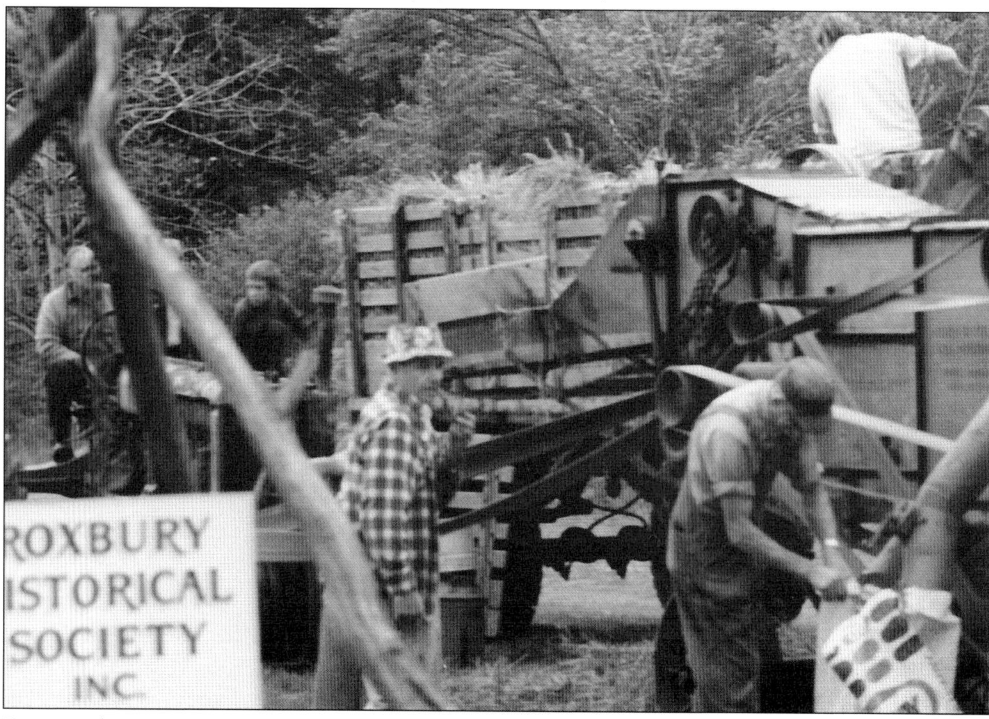

Farmers demonstrate the fine workings of the threshing machine at this First Threshing Bee sponsored by the Roxbury Historical Society in September 1976. (Elinor Hurlbut.)

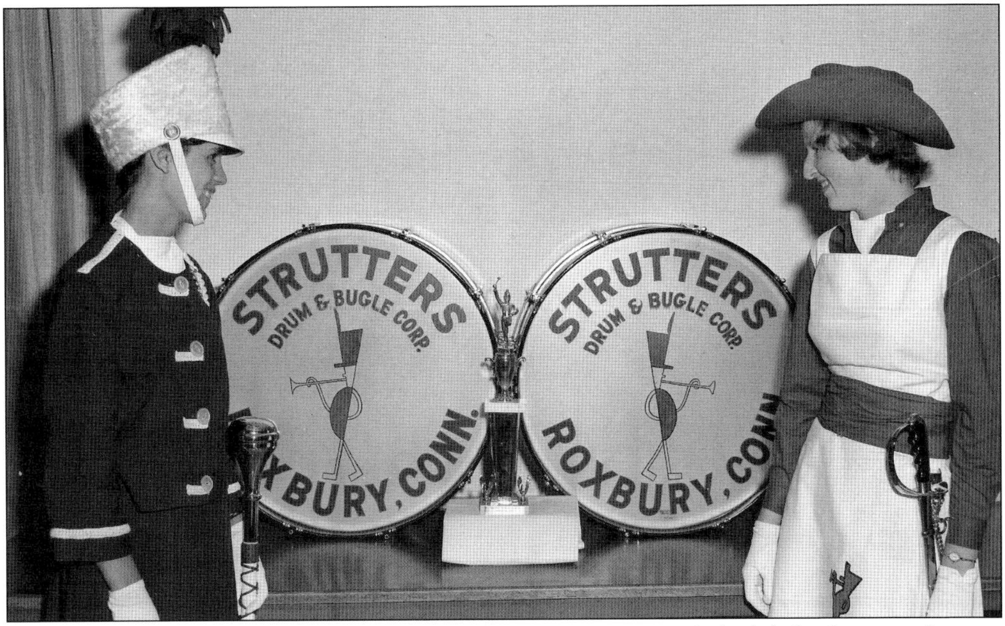

Roxbury Strutters Betty Jane Booth (left) and Patricia McCormick (right) display a trophy won by the popular drum-and-bugle corps. Though this photograph is undated, it may be an image of the trophy for the best Drilled Junior Corps, which the Roxbury Strutters won at the State Firemen's Convention in Naugatuck, Connecticut, in 1963. (Constance N. Sherman, Raymond Livingston Booth.)

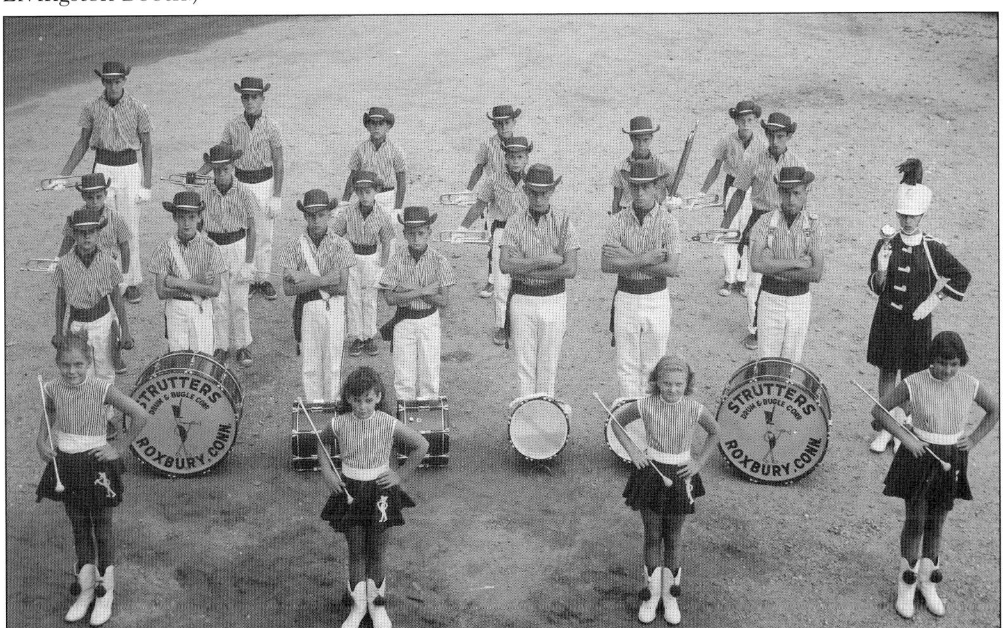

Henry "Chip" Booth organized the Roxbury Strutters, which became an award-winning corps of young men and women who, during the 1960s, often performed at firemen's conventions, parades, and competitions throughout the state. In this undated image, the corps poses in their dashing red-and-white uniforms. (Constance N. Sherman, Raymond Livingston Booth.)

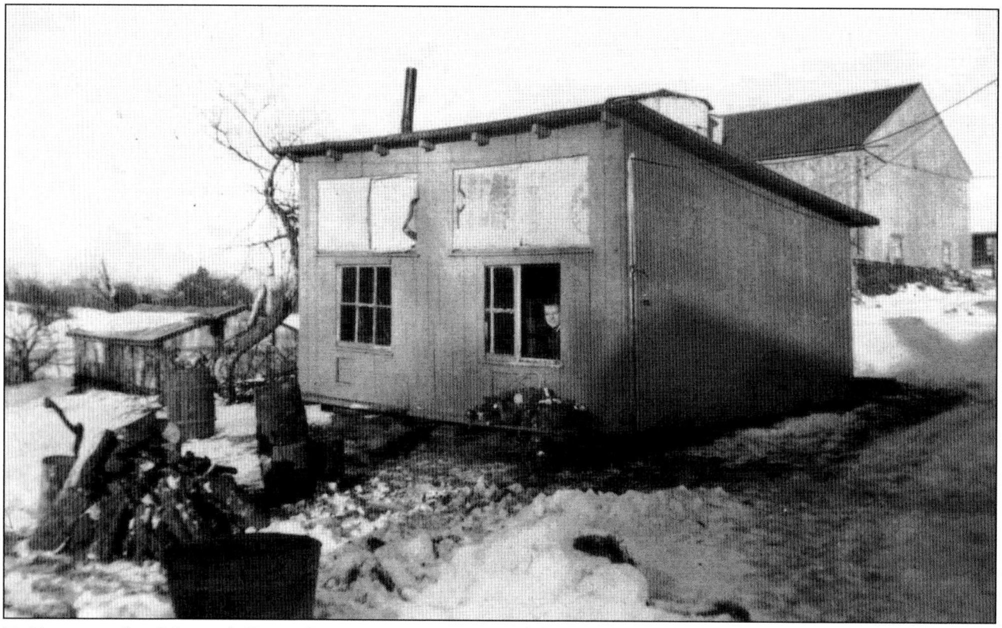

Following the United States' entrance into World War II, small towns all over the country mobilized. Many, like Bridgewater, established observation towers to scan the skies, searching for enemy planes. In December 1941, a temporary observation post was founded in Lester Randall's brooder house. The pictures show the snowy ground and wood ready for use in the potbelly stove inside. (BHS.)

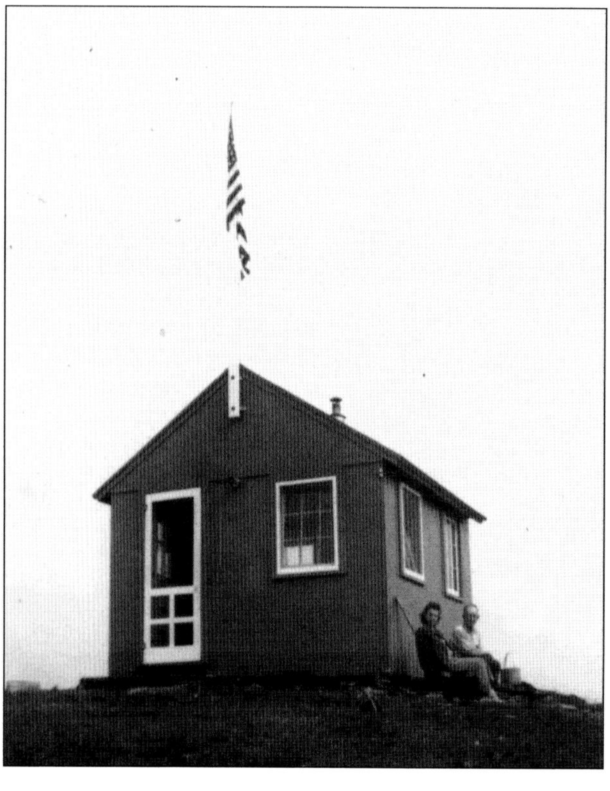

Watch periods were in four-hour shifts around the clock, rain or shine. In April 1942, the New Observation Post No. 31-E was established on a hilltop north of Lester Randall's barn. Here, watchers lean against the building on their shift. Dozens of volunteers manned the observation post year-round during the war years. (BHS.)

Following the war, the post was deactivated and moved along Route 133 to a new location. A citation was issued to the town for "faithful and continuous service as the eyes and ears for the U.S. Army." Two water towers were also used as observation posts. The last was demolished in the late 1990s. (BHS.)

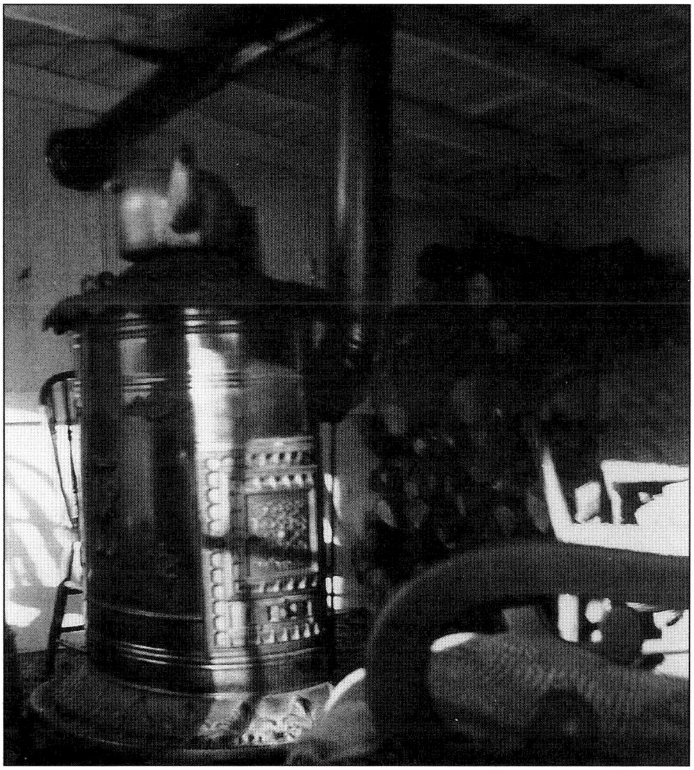

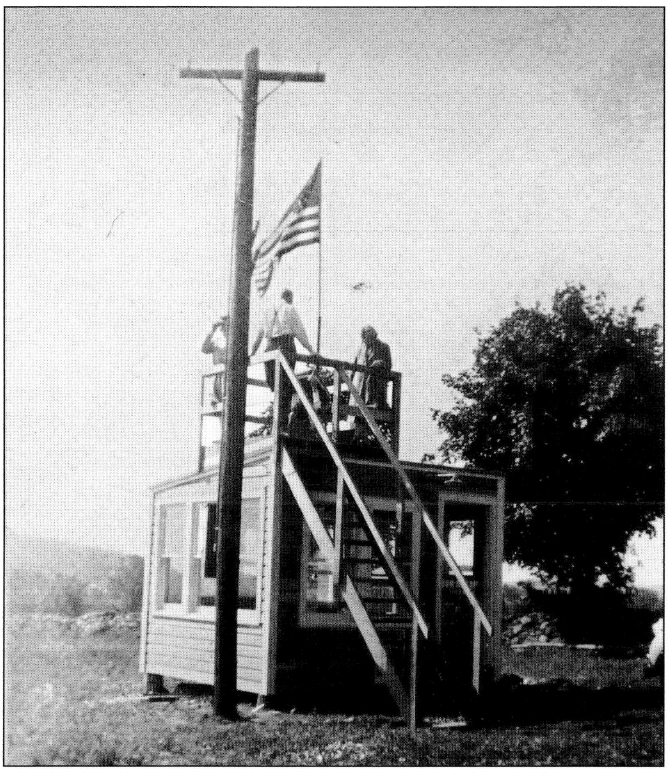

Spotters watched for enemy planes from this Roxbury Observation Post on Kenneth B. Reis's property on Wellers Bridge Road, dedicated in September 1942. In the background, newspapers headlined blackouts, rations, and encouraged readers to "buy war bonds." Citizens salvaged everything for the war effort—scrap metal, newspapers, and tin cans. Louis Pokrywka resigned as head of the local salvage committee when he was inducted into the US Army. (Albert Pokrywka.)

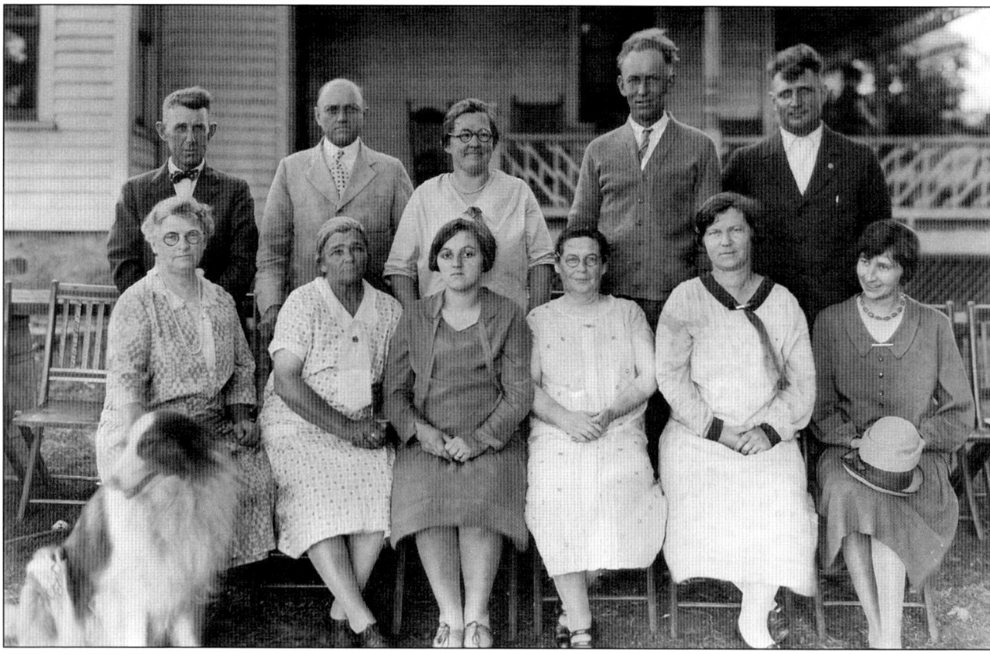

The Bridgewater Grange was Chapter 153, founded on March 17, 1900. Later, Roxbury Grangers joined this chapter. The Home Economics Committee of the Grange is shown in this photograph taken at their annual Clam Bake and Picnic at the Bridgewater farm of William B. Curtis on August 30, 1927. (BG.)

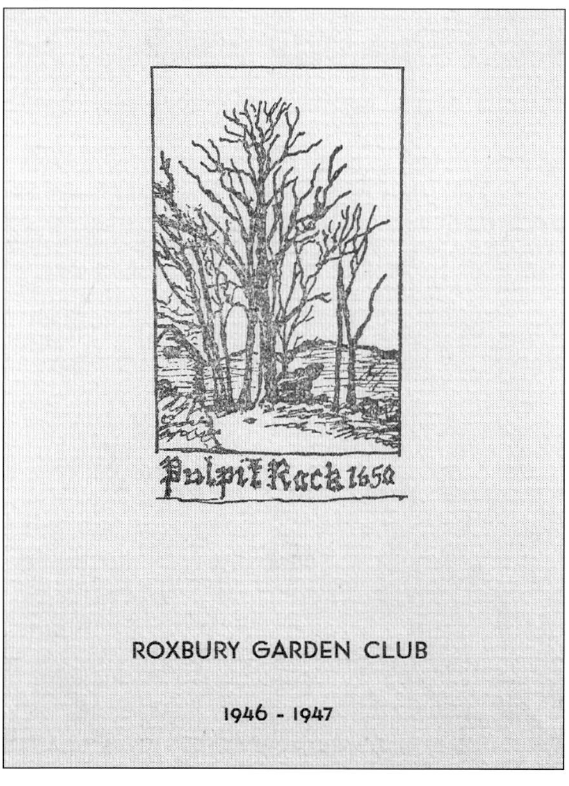

Pulpit Rock dates to a time when Algonquin Indians lived in the Shepaug Valley. Legend has it that John Eliot (1604–1690), apostle to the Indians, preached from this pulpit. In August 1942, the Roxbury-Bridgewater Garden Club held a fundraising event near Pulpit Rock to raise emergency war funds and, in 1946–1947, selected a "Pulpit Rock 1650" motif for its annual flower show program design. (RBGC.)

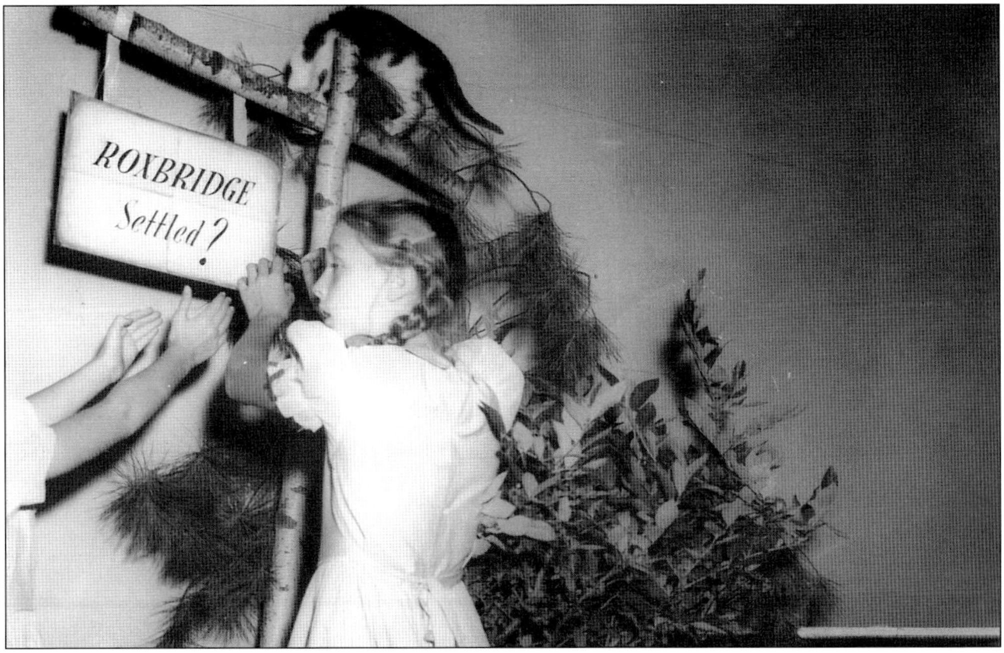

While judges of the Roxbury-Bridgewater Garden Club were presenting a Special Award of Merit for the "Roxbridge" display, a little grey kitten made its way into the auditorium of the Booth Free School where the flower show was being held and made himself part of the award-winning display. (RBGC.)

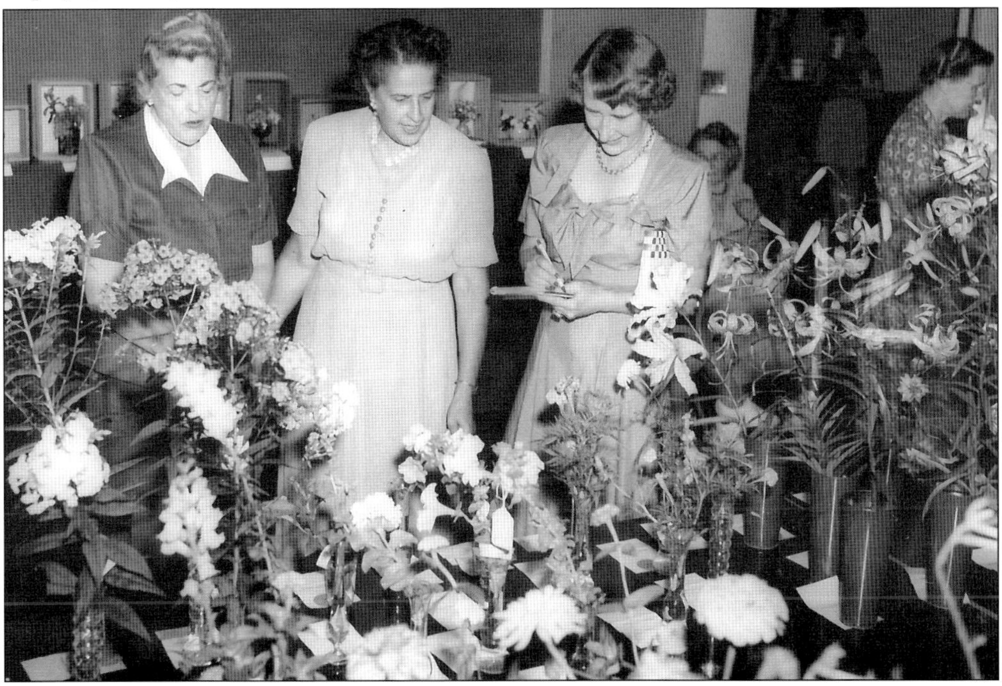

Judges of the Roxbury-Bridgewater Garden Club look over awards presented in the horticultural class at an annual flower show. Seen here from left to right are co-chairman Mabel Bogardus, chairman Margaret Todd, and Mrs. H.K. Miller, program chairman. (RBGC.)

www.arcadiapublishing.com

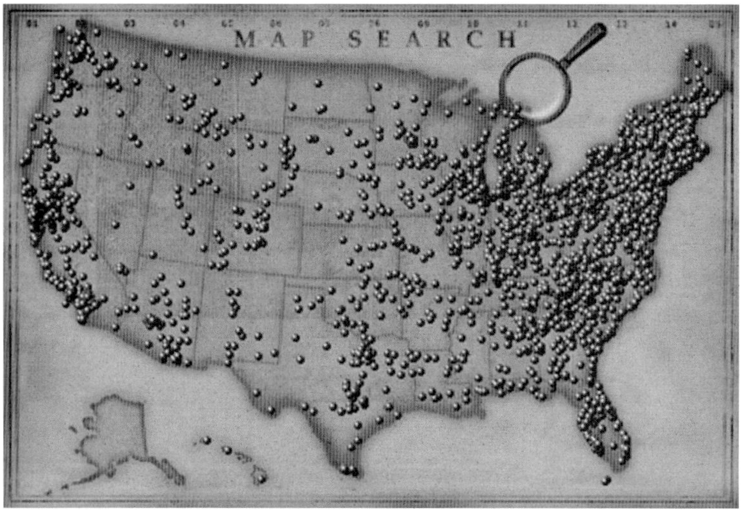

Discover books about the town where you grew up, the cities where your friends and families live, the town where your parents met, or even that retirement spot you've been dreaming about. Our Web site provides history lovers with exclusive deals, advanced notification about new titles, e-mail alerts of author events, and much more.

MADE IN THE USA

Arcadia Publishing, the leading local history publisher in the United States, is committed to making history accessible and meaningful through publishing books that celebrate and preserve the heritage of America's people and places. Consistent with our mission to preserve history on a local level, this book was printed in South Carolina on American-made paper and manufactured entirely in the United States.

This book carries the accredited Forest Stewardship Council (FSC) label and is printed on 100 percent FSC-certified paper. Products carrying the FSC label are independently certified to assure consumers that they come from forests that are managed to meet the social, economic, and ecological needs of present and future generations.

FSC
Mixed Sources
Product group from well-managed forests and other controlled sources

Cert no. SW-COC-001530
www.fsc.org

Find *Your* Place in History.